QA76.87 .G35 1993
Gallant, Stephen I.
Neural network learning and expert syst

P9-CMY-889

3 4369 00068402 3

ephen I.

Neural network learning and
expert systems

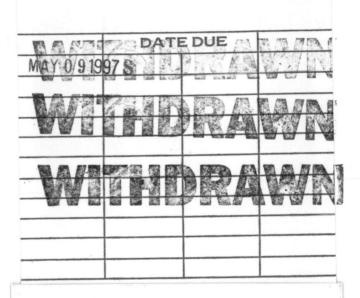

DATE DUE

MAY 0 9 1997

WITHDRAWN

WITHDRAWN

WITHDRAWN

Neural Network Learning and Expert Systems

Neural Network Learning and Expert Systems

Stephen I. Gallant

A Bradford Book

The MIT Press
Cambridge, Massachusetts
London, England

Second printing, 1994

© 1993 Massachusetts Institute of Technology
All rights reserved. No part of this book may be reproduced in any form by any electronic
or mechanical means (including photocopying, recording, or information storage and
retrieval) without permission in writing from the publisher.

This book was set in Times by Asco Trade Typesetting Ltd., Hong Kong, and was printed
and bound in the United States of America.

Library of Congress Cataloging-in-Publication Data

Gallant, Stephen I.
  Neural network learning and expert systems / Stephen I. Gallant.
    p. cm.
  Includes bibliographical references (p.   ) and index.
  ISBN 0-262-07145-2
  1. Neural networks (Computer science) 2. Expert systems (Computer science) I. Title.
  QA76.87.G35   1993
  006.3—dc20   92-20864
                                                                          CIP

To Julia, Benji, Leah, and Fran

307124

Contents

Foreword

I have several goals for this book. First, I want to provide a systematic development of neural network learning algorithms that is suitable for researchers and students in computer science, engineering, psychology, or physics. The book is also designed to help computer professionals who want to learn about this exciting field, and to serve as a basic reference. Parts I through III give a thorough, step-by-step exposition of the main algorithms in current use.

My second goal is to present neural network expert systems. Part IV shows how a neural network can serve as the knowledge base for an expert system that does classification tasks. The big advantage of this approach is that the learning algorithms can take training examples and generate expert systems *automatically*. Typical applications are credit and loan decisions, process control, medical diagnosis, and stock forecasting and trading. Virtually any decision becomes a strong candidate for a neural network expert system if training data is available. Moreover the use of automated methods to produce expert systems makes them so cheap that qualitatively new classes of expert systems become practical. I can envision the day when we will use "throwaway," short-lived expert systems for temporary tasks, and call upon a host of "personalized" expert systems for individual use. My hope is that this book will bring that day closer by helping to demystify and popularize neural network expert systems.

The main focus of this book will be *performance* rather than *psychological modeling*. We will examine networks that accomplish particular tasks under various constraints, and leave to others the important study of how closely these networks model human cognition. Thus the approach is an artificial intelligence or engineering approach, rather than a cognitive science or philosophy approach. Nevertheless, psychologists should find the techniques presented here to be useful for constructing their simulation models of human information processing.

The book has four parts and an appendix. Part I gives basic definitions and concepts that almost everyone interested in neural networks should be aware of. The second chapter in part I focuses on representation, a vital issue for neural networks and for artificial intelligence in general. Part II covers learning in single-cell and single-layer models, including perceptron-based algorithms, the Widrow-Hoff rule, autoassociators, and unsupervised learning. These algorithms are capable of modeling data for a wide range of practical problems, and in many cases single-cell algo-

*

rithms are preferable to more complex multilayer models. Single-cell learning algorithms also serve as the computational heart of most multilayer algorithms.

Part III is devoted to learning in multilayer models. One way to assure reasonable speed when training multilayer models is to extend single-cell learning algorithms to multilayer models, and chapter 8 and chapter 10 give ways of doing this. The latter chapter is concerned with constructive algorithms that *grow* networks in the course of learning. Chapter 9 gives an introduction to computational learning theory with examples of how single-layer algorithms can be analyzed under this framework. Chapters 11 and 12 are devoted to backpropagation, currently the most popular neural network learning algorithm. Chapter 11 gives a detailed exposition of backpropagation, including a numerical example, some practical considerations, and a proof that the algorithm accomplishes gradient descent. Chapter 12 demonstrates how this important algorithm can be creatively applied to many diverse problems. The final chapter in Part III discusses simulated annealing and Boltzmann Machines.

Part IV covers neural network expert systems. We can directly employ the learning techniques from earlier parts to construct neural network–based decision systems, and several examples show how to do it. Chapter 15 focuses upon the MACIE neural network expert system, which possesses features that are usually associated with conventional expert systems. These capabilities include inferencing from partial information, justifications by If-Then rules (even though If-Then rules are not explicitly in the knowledge base), and applicability to noisy and redundant domains. Chapter 17 takes up the question of extracting If-Then rules from neural network expert system knowledge bases. Finally, the appendix gives additional theory concerning representations.

I have tried to accommodate various levels of interest in different topics by marking *optional* sections with a star (*). But trying to appeal to everybody is also the textbook author's classic mistake. This puts the additional responsibility on you, Dear Reader, of having to skip chapters, without skipping the remainder of the book! My hope is that you will skip with a clear conscience, knowing that remaining chapters are still there if you need to look something up or if your interests expand.

Here are some possible programs of study:

Goal	Chapters
• Introduction to neural networks and back-propagation	1, 2 (parts), 11
• Graduate or upper-level undergraduate course in neural networks	1–3, 5–8, 11, 12, 14, 15
• Full-year course in neural networks and neural network expert systems	1–8, 10–17
• Basic introduction to neural network expert systems	1, 2, 14, 15
• Thorough introduction to neural network expert systems	1–4, 6, 11, 12, 14–17
• Research	1–18 (by interest)

Many exercises are included, and they are graded by difficulty with hard exercises marked by stars. For researchers I also list a number of research topics. Many of these would make excellent Ph.D. theses (if they can be solved!). One of the joys of a rapidly developing field is the abundance of interesting, yet solvable, open questions.

All of the neural network models we will examine can be implemented using standard programming languages on microcomputers. Of course if special parallel hardware is available, then the models can be made to run much faster. This could be useful for the slowest of the learning algorithms, but once connection weights have been found, any standard microcomputer can easily simulate very large models.

Part of the fun of this field comes from doing simulations to test out new ideas. In this respect neural network research is very much a laboratory science. There is a certain thrill and sense of wonderment when these simple models discover something surprising that gives insight into a particular problem. Therefore I have included a set of programming projects that gradually lead to the construction of powerful neural network learning and expert system software. These projects should be especially useful for students.

It was difficult deciding what to include and what to emphasize. A number of factors entered into my choices, such as the focus on performance over modeling, emphasis on algorithms suitable for generating networks for expert systems, personal predispositions, etc. The hardest omission was reinforcement learning (Barto, Sutton, and Anderson [18];

Williams [199]; Sutton [185]), but I thought that this was a somewhat advanced topic whose story could better be told by others. I apologize to researchers whose work has been underemphasized or has not been included, but it seemed like a good idea to actually finish this book.

I would like to thank the National Science Foundation, NTT (Yokosuka, Japan), the Institute for Scientific Interchange (Turin, Italy), Northeastern University, the Vienna Institute for Advanced Study, and HNC Inc. for support during my work on this book. Also thanks to the referees, Matthew Abbate, Gail Carpenter, Mark Frydenberg, Yoichi Hayashi, David Hinkle, Donna King, Mario Marchand, Teri Mendelsohn, Ryohei Nakano, Jeff Peng, Wyn Snow, Sangeeta Sreenivas, Betty Stanton, and Ron Williams for suggestions, encouragement, and other help. Any mistakes, however, remain at my doorstep.

It is difficult to express my enthusiasm for neural network research without overselling its accomplishments and possibilities, and without indulging in "neurohype." I hope the book makes clear that neural network models have certain advantages over standard AI techniques, and that they give hope for great advances in AI (and cognitive science). Nevertheless the difficult fundamental problems—such as commonsense reasoning, general-purpose machine vision, and robust language understanding—are not about to roll over and play dead for the new kid on the block. And so my advice, Dear Reader, is to be cautiously excited.

Steve Gallant

Cambridge, Massachusetts
May 1, 1992

I BASICS

1 Introduction and Important Definitions

What are neural networks, and why are they so appealing?

Briefly stated, a *neural network model* (also called a *connectionist network*) consists of a set of computational *units* (also called *cells*) and a set of one-way data connections joining units as pictured in figure 1.1. At certain times a unit examines its inputs and computes a signed number called an *activation* as its output. The new activation is then passed along those connections leading to other units. Each connection has a signed number called a *weight* that determines whether an activation that travels along it influences the receiving cell to produce a similar or a different activation according to the sign (+ or −) of the weight. The size of the weight determines the magnitude of the influence of a sending cell's activation upon the receiving cell; thus a large positive or negative weight gives the sender's activation more of an effect on the receiving cell than a smaller weight. Section 1.2 gives a more detailed definition of these terms.

The connections and their weights are the important parameters in any model. They determine the behavior of a model, and can be compared to instructions in a conventional computer program.

The motivation for connectionist models comes from the neuroanatomy of living animals, with cells corresponding to neurons, activations corresponding to neuronal firing rates, connections corresponding to synapses, and connection weights corresponding to synaptic strengths. This analogy should not be taken too literally. Connectionist models are far too simple to serve as realistic brain models on the cell level, but they might serve as very good models for the essential information processing tasks that organisms perform. This remains an open question because we have so little understanding of how the brain actually works.

This chapter gives a brief overview of the appeal of connectionist models and presents basic definitions and notation to be used throughout the book.

1.1 Why Connectionist Models?

Why study connectionist models? Why has this field virtually exploded over the last few years, with the number of researchers and commercial ventures increasing by an estimated factor of 100? There are a number of reasons.

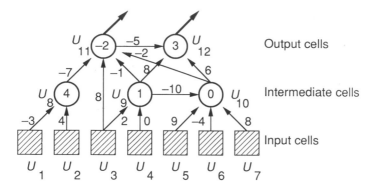

Figure 1.1
Connectionist model showing weights for connections. The numbers inside cells are biases
(section 1.2.2).

1.1.1   The Grand Goals of AI and Its Current Impasse

Ultimately artificial intelligence aims to make computers perform as well
as humans in such tasks as learning, vision, language, and robotic motion.
Fully achieving this goal is extremely difficult, and perhaps even impossible. When some researchers suggested these difficulties as early as 20 years
ago they were severely maligned by the AI community, but now there is a
much better appreciation of just how hard the most ambitious AI tasks
really are. Currently there is no promising approach for achieving general-
purpose computer vision, human-level natural language understanding, or
commonsense reasoning. Even Patrick Winston, the head of MIT's AI
Laboratory, has stated that he has seen disappointingly little progress in
standard AI approaches over the last few years.

It is interesting to notice that the difficult AI tasks are easy for humans.
Sometimes they seem so trivial that someone new to the field of AI
wonders where the problem lies. Consider the task of recognizing a person, something we do every day. Somehow we must correct for all of
the different lighting conditions, different views and orientations, clothes,
makeup, partial views, noisy images, unreliable light receptors, and on and
on. These are all difficult problems for computers.

Or consider driving in the rain, an extreme example of something that
people do without noticing how really difficult it is. Here we must contend
with a road image we have never seen before. We peer out through a rainy
windshield that distorts the road image, and both the road image and the

distortion change with time. To make matters even harder, the principal activity in our field of vision is the sweep of the windshield wipers, something we totally and automatically ignore.

How could a computer program ever accomplish such difficult AI tasks? One conventional AI/computer vision approach would be to first perform low-level image processing to extract line segments, regions, etc. Then we would have to deduce shading and other information, eventually leading to segmented, three-dimensional objects and the construction of a semantic network. Finally automated reasoning and inference would take place in the semantic network representation. This approach is a general one, but it has no chance of working for the above two tasks. Once we get past low-level image processing, building general-purpose systems becomes much too difficult. The problem is that humans cannot foresee and explicitly program responses for enough of the cases that commonly occur.

Another conventional AI approach would be to find a special-case "trick" to solve the problem. For driving in the rain we might concentrate on finding the center line of the road and then use it to compute a steering-wheel position. Such tricks sometimes work, but they tend to be "brittle" and to fail miserably if conditions are not exactly right. In particular, the center line trick would be useless if the center line were obliterated by road construction or if the road had no center line.

Upon reflection, the difficult AI tasks seem so hard that we would be tempted to throw up our hands and declare these feats impossible, except for the fact that billions of living creatures perform these functions with the utmost of ease—without even consciously thinking about them!

There is a growing awareness that a fresh approach is needed in artificial intelligence. Here connectionist models are attractive because they are computational models with similarities to human information processing. It is only natural to look at models that possess qualitative similarities with the only information processing devices known to be able to perform difficult AI tasks. Since it is possible that some form of connectionist structures may be *necessary* for performing these functions, we should seriously consider working with them if we aim to eventually achieve the difficult AI goals.

Of course other computational methods might also work. Moreover we should be wary of restricting ourselves to overprecise models of biological systems. The easiest way to build airplanes uses wings based upon Bernoulli's principle, but the wings do not flap up and down. Another reason to avoid overprecise biological models is that our knowledge of how biological systems process information is rapidly developing and changing over time. By using information processing models that are at a higher level than the individual cell, we minimize the risk that new developments will contradict an overly specific, fine-grained model.

Ultimately we must acknowledge that connectionist models are not guaranteed to be able to overcome the current hurdles for AI; we must always be on the lookout for more promising approaches (and for proofs that current approaches cannot work). However, the following points give us hope that we will eventually be able to perform the difficult AI tasks. They also give us optimism that, at the very least, connectionist models will be able to do a number of tasks much better than is currently possible using standard approaches.

1.1.2   The Computational Appeal of Neural Networks

From a computational viewpoint neural networks offer two primary attractions, learning and representation, that are qualitatively different from standard AI approaches. Other important features include robust behavior with noisy data, inherent parallelism, and suitability for automatically generated expert systems.

Learning

Many researchers believe that machine learning techniques give the best hope for eventually being able to perform difficult AI tasks. Certainly a program that learns from training and experience might be able to perform more difficult tasks than could a program based solely upon a list of eventualities that had to be explicitly foreseen and analyzed by human programmers. This makes machine learning approaches very appealing for AI.

Machine learning refers to computer models that improve their performance in significant ways based upon their input data. Machine learning techniques are usually divided into supervised and unsupervised models, as illustrated in figure 1.2. In *supervised learning* a *teacher* or *critic* supplies additional input data that gives a measure of how well a program is performing during a training phase. The most common form of supervised learning is trying to duplicate behavior specified by a set of *training examples*, where each example consists of input data and the corresponding correct output.

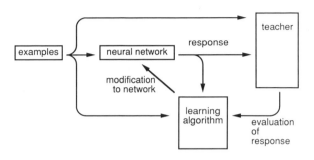

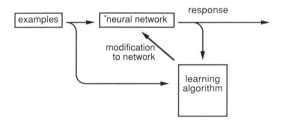

Figure 1.2
Supervised learning (top) and unsupervised learning (bottom).

In *unsupervised learning* there is no performance evaluation available. Without any specific knowledge of what constitutes a correct answer and what constitutes an incorrect answer, the most that can be expected of these models is to construct groups of similar input patterns. In the pattern recognition literature this is known as *clustering*.

Perhaps the strongest appeal of connectionist models is their suitability for machine learning. Machine learning in connectionist models consists of adjusting connection weights to improve performance of a network. This is a very simple and pleasing formulation of the learning problem. It abstracts out essentials of learning and invites the construction of general algorithms. We will see many of these algorithms in following chapters.

Knowledge Representation
A fundamental prerequisite for machine learning is a method for recording whatever has been learned. Connectionist models represent information in

a powerful way that may seem very strange at first. For connectionist models, knowledge representation consists of a network, connection weights, and semantic interpretations attached to cells and activations. For example, in a medical context we might identify a particular cell with the disease of tuberculosis. Furthermore an activation of $+1$ might indicate presence of the disease, -1 absence of the disease, and 0 lack of knowledge about presence or absence of the disease. Throughout the book we will frequently make use of this convention:

$+1 \leftrightarrow$ True

$-1 \leftrightarrow$ False

$\quad 0 \leftrightarrow$ Unknown

Thus cells can correspond to Boolean variables and the behavior of a network specifies relationships among such variables. In chapter 2 we will see how a group of cells can also represent non-Boolean variables.

It is easy to express commonly used representations such as disjunctive normal form (DNF) expressions or decision trees using connectionist networks.[1] Section A.1 defines the notion of a *polynomially stronger (π-stronger) representation* and shows that connectionist networks are π-stronger representations than DNF expressions or decision trees. The practical implication of this is that there are some Boolean functions that we can easily represent as networks, but if we try to represent them by DNF expressions they would be too large to fit into any present (or future!) computer.

Another important aspect of connectionist models is that whenever cells compute their activations they can examine hundreds or even thousands of activations from other cells. By contrast DNF representations tend to involve fewer Boolean values for their computations because they are usually constructed by hand, perhaps to represent a rule used by a human expert. We will see in chapter 16 that this simplicity can be harmful in problems involving noise and redundancy. We can think of connectionist models as *wide-angle* models. Such models stand in contrast to models exhibiting *tunnel vision* that force too much simplicity, and that resist having large numbers of inputs at the basic computational level.

---

1. An example of a DNF representation of a function is $A\bar{B} \vee C \vee \bar{A}DE$. See section A.1 for a more precise definition.

Original imputs:	+1	+1	+1	−1	−1	−1
Noisy inputs:	+1	+1	$\boxed{-1}$	$\boxed{+1}$	−1	−1
Noisy inputs with only partial information:	+1	+1	$\boxed{-1}$	$\boxed{+1}$	$\boxed{0}$	−1

Figure 1.3
Noisy and partial information.

It is important that connectionist models give a natural way of integrating inputs from diverse sources such as visual, auditory, and tactile systems. This is because all data is represented uniformly by activation levels of cells. Therefore for higher-level processing it is easy to take into account a variety of inputs, something encouraged by the wide-angle property of the model.

Automatic Inferencing from Noisy and Partial Information
Noise refers to the probabilistic introduction of errors into data. This is an important aspect of real-world applications, and connectionist models can be especially good at handling noise.

Noisy or partially absent data creates a problem for any system. Suppose, for example, there are p relevant binary input variables. Then each input might be true, false, or absent, as illustrated in figure 1.3.

The presence of noise guarantees that every conceivable pattern of p input variables might actually occur, even for simple problems where only a few basic patterns would ever appear if there were no noise. Therefore every system that allows noise is always faced with 2^p possible input patterns. Similarly if partial information is possible but no noise is present, then there are at least 2^p possible input patterns that a system must deal with. Allowing both noise and partial information raises the number of patterns to 3^p. It does not take many input variables before there are too many possible patterns to verify by hand (≈ 6) or by computer (≈ 20). Therefore for medium-sized problems *it is not possible* to handle partial or noisy data by considering all the cases. Instead, *the computational model itself must have some general rule that handles partial or erroneous data in a reasonable manner.*

Most connectionist models naturally extend to cases where some inputs are unknown. We saw an example of this in the last section where an activation of 0 represented the fact that we did not know whether tuberculosis was present or absent. Because cells can easily examine large numbers of inputs, they naturally tend to be less sensitive to noise; the greater number of correct input variables can outvote the fewer number of incorrect input values. This is a benefit of naturally wide-angled computational models.

In addition to handling probabilistic errors in the input data, connectionist models are also resistant to hardware errors present in the implementations of the models themselves. Once again, the wide-angle principle allows a majority of data from good cells to outvote a minority of data from bad cells. Hardware errors were fairly frequent in the early days when researchers such as Bernard Widrow of Stanford were soldering together hardware implementations by hand. New technologies such as wafer scale integration might make such fault tolerance an important consideration once again.

Naturally Parallel Models of Computation

Connectionist models are well suited to parallel hardware, because algorithms expressed at the cell level almost automatically become parallel algorithms for a collection of cells.

Some tasks, such as vision processing in real time, are inconceivable unless a highly parallel system is used. If we consider a 500 by 500 pixel retina, is obvious that we want to do as much processing as possible locally and in parallel. This speeds the computation and avoids sequential passes over the retina. Connectionist models can easily compute low-level vision features, for example line segments, in parallel. The extent to which they will be able to perform high-level vision tasks (with the help of learning) is a key open question.

It is clear that the increasing availability of parallel hardware should enhance the attractiveness of connectionist and other basically parallel models.

Neural Network Expert Systems

A major attraction of connectionist models is that they can serve as knowledge bases for classification expert systems.

Many of the previously mentioned features of these models come into play here. Most importantly, learning algorithms allow us to generate knowledge bases automatically from training examples. The ability to handle partial and noisy data is also important for these systems.

Part IV will present neural network expert systems in detail.

1.2 The Structure of Connectionist Models

It is time for a more careful and detailed description of connectionist models. Connectionist models can be described according to their *network, cell, dynamic*, and *learning properties* as follows:

1.2.1 Network Properties

As we saw in figure 1.1, a connectionist model consists of a network of (more or less) autonomous processing units called cells that are joined by directed arcs. (The cells and arcs comprise the network *topology*.) Each arc ("connection") has a numerical weight, $w_{i,j}$, that specifies the influence of cell u_j on cell u_i. Positive weights indicate reinforcement; negative weights represent inhibition. The weights determine the behavior of the network, playing somewhat the same role as a conventional program. We shall see in chapter 2 that any computer program can be simulated by an appropriate network.

In some models a subset of cells, $\{u_1, \ldots, u_p\}$, are considered *network inputs* that are set externally and that do not recompute their outputs. These cells have no entering arcs and are represented by squares in figure 1.1.

Other *output cells* have outputs that are taken to be the outputs of the network as a whole. In figure 1.1 the output cells are u_{11} and u_{12}, and they are pictured with heavier exit connections.

Cells that are neither input cells nor output cells are called *intermediate cells*. Intermediate cells are necessary for a network to compute difficult functions known as *nonseparable* functions; more on these functions later.

We sometimes consider a network $\mathcal{N}$ as a black box function as shown in figure 1.4. Here the external world presents inputs to the input cells and receives network outputs from output cells. Intermediate cells are not seen externally, and for this reason they are often called *hidden units*. If x is a vector of inputs to network $\mathcal{N}$ we can represent the vector of outputs of the network by $\mathcal{N}(x)$ to emphasize this functional emphasis.

We classify networks as either *feedforward networks* if they do not contain directed cycles or *recurrent networks* if they do contain such cycles. For example, the network in figure 1.1 is a feedforward network, while figure 1.5a depicts a recurrent network.

It is often convenient to organize the cells of a network into layers. We define a *k-layer network* as a network where cells are grouped into $k + 1$

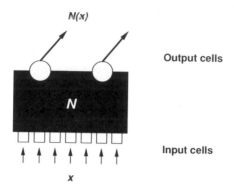

Figure 1.4
View of figure 1.1 as a black box function.

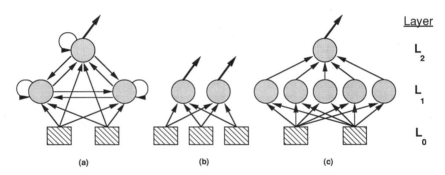

Figure 1.5
Totally connected network (a), single-layer network (b), flat network (c).

subsets (layers) L_0, L_1, ..., L_k such that if cell u_j in layer L_a is connected to cell u_i in layer L_b then $a < b$. For a *strictly k-layer network* we require in addition that cells be connected only to cells in the next layer, i.e., $b = a + 1$. One of the exercises at the end of the chapter is to prove that a k-layer network is a feedforward network such that all cells in layer L_0 are input cells, all trainable cells are in layers L, ..., L_k, and all (nonsuperfluous) cells in layer L_k are output cells.[2]

2. Some authors count the number of layers differently; for example they consider figure 1.5c to be a 3-layer network. This seems more appropriate for figure 1.5c, but then a single trainable cell would be considered a 2-layer network, and a 1-layer network would consist only of input values. Therefore the current terminology was adopted. It is a good idea to remove any doubt by simply mentioning the number of intermediate (i.e., hidden) layers.

Two important classes of networks are *single-layer* networks and *flat networks*, as pictured in figure 1.5. Single-layer networks are strictly l-layer networks where every input cell is connected to every output cell. Flat networks are strictly 2-layer networks where all input cells are in L_0, all output cells are in L_2, and every u_j in layer L_a is connected to every u_i in layer L_{a+1} for $a = 0, 1$.

1.2.2 Cell Properties

Each cell, u_i, computes a single (numerical) cell output or *activation*. For example the output of u_{11} in figure 1.1 is both an output of the network as a whole and an input for cell u_{12} to be used in the computation of u_{12}'s activation.

Cell inputs and activations may be *discrete*, taking on values $\{0, 1\}$ or $\{-1, 0, 1\}$, or they may be *continuous*, assuming values in the interval $[0, 1]$ or $[-1, +1]$. Where there is no confusion we use u_i to refer to both the cell and the numerical activation of that cell.

By convention there is a cell u_0 whose output is always $+1$ that is connected to every other cell u_i (except for input cells). The corresponding weights $(w_{i,0})$ are called *biases*. To make figures simpler we usually do not picture cell u_0 and instead we place bias weights within each cell.

Typically every cell uses the same algorithm for computing its activation. The activation for a cell must be computed from the activations of cells directly connected to it and the corresponding weights for those connections. Thus in figure 1.1 when u_{11} is reevaluated, its activation is determined by the activations of u_3, u_8, u_9, and u_{10} and the weights $w_{11,0}$, $w_{11,3}$, $w_{11,8}$, $w_{11,9}$, and $w_{11,10}$. We refer to the weights $w_{i,*}$ as the *weights of cell u_i*. W is sometimes used for the vector $w_{i,*}$ when i is understood from the context.

Every cell u_i (except for input cells) computes its new activation u_i as a function of the weighted sum of the inputs to cell u_i from directly connected cells:

$$S_i = \sum_{j=0}^{n} w_{i,j} u_j \qquad (1.1)$$

$$u_i = f(S_i).$$

The biases are merely a constant term added to the sum in equation (1.1). Note that if u_j is not connected to u_i then $w_{i,j} = 0$.

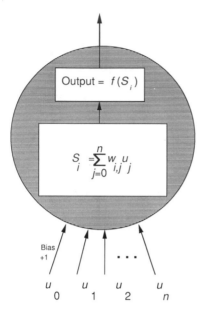

Figure 1.6
Activation (or output) computed for a single cell.

Figure 1.6 illustrates how a single cell computes its activation. This type of cell is called a *semilinear* cell because of the dependence upon the (linear) weighted sum S_i. Because of the "weighted voting" process used to compute S_i, we automatically get a degree of tolerance for noise and missing data.

The *activation function*, $f(\ )$, is usually a nonlinear, bounded, and piecewise differentiable function such as either

$$f(x) = \begin{cases} +1 & \text{for } x > 0 \\ 0 & \text{for } x = 0 \\ -1 & \text{for } x < 0 \end{cases} \quad \text{or} \quad f(x) = \frac{1}{1 + e^{-x}}.$$

Sometimes $f(x)$ is *stochastic*, so that its output is determined probabilistically by a distribution selected according to x. For example

$$f(x) = \begin{cases} 1 & \text{with probability } \dfrac{1}{1 + e^{-x}} \\ 0 & \text{otherwise.} \end{cases}$$

1.2.3 Dynamic Properties

A connectionist model must specify the timing for when each cell computes its new activation value and when the change to that cell's output actually takes place. Usually in feedforward models cells are visited in a fixed order, each cell reevaluating and changing its activation before the next one is visited. In this case the network achieves steady state after one pass through the cells, provided the cells are correctly numbered (see exercise 1).

For recurrent models there are several possibilities. One possibility is to make one ordered pass through the cells, as with feedforward models; but we are no longer guaranteed that the network will reach steady state.

Another possibility is to make repeated passes through the network. For discrete models the network will either reach a steady state or it will cycle; for continuous models the network will either reach a steady state, cycle, approach a steady state in the limit, blow up, or some combination of these things.

A third possibility is to compute new activations for all cells simultaneously and *then* make changes to the cell outputs simultaneously. This is similar to the previous case.

Still another possibility is to select a cell at random, compute its new activation, and then change its output before selecting the next cell. In this case we have no guarantee of any sort of limiting or cyclic behavior unless other constraints are placed upon the model.

1.2.4 Learning Properties

Each connectionist model we will examine is associated with one or more algorithms for machine learning.

The input to these algorithms consists of a finite[3] set of *training examples* $\{E^k\}$. E^k is a p-vector of values that gives settings for the corresponding input cells of a network model, as illustrated in figure 1.7. The jth component of an example, E_j^k, is assigned to input unit u_j.

For supervised learning problems each example E^k is associated with a correct response C^k from the network's output cells. For networks with more than one output cell, C^k is a vector with components C_i^k. For super-

---

3. In some situations a training example is generated at every time step, so that there is no bound on the number of training examples. Nevertheless a learning algorithm can access only a finite number of the training examples and must ignore the rest.

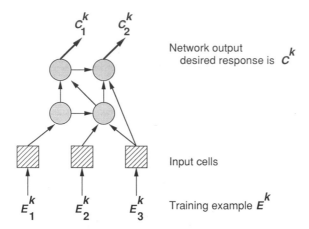

Figure 1.7
Training example inputs and outputs for a supervised learning model.

vised learning problems we consider the term *training example* to encompass both the input E^k and the desired response C^k.

For unsupervised learning problems, there are no specified correct responses for the network.

Supervised learning problems are further subdivided into *easy learning* and *hard learning* problems. An *easy learning* problem has training examples that specify input values and correct activations for all intermediate and output cells. By contrast, a *hard learning* problem involves intermediate cells, but the training examples do not specify correct activations for these cells; they only give correct activations for output cells given a set of input values. Finally we can divide hard learning problems into *free-network* problems and *fixed-network* problems. In free-network problems we are allowed to add intermediate cells and make any other change to the network topology, whereas fixed-network problems specify the cells and connections, so that the weights are the only parameters that can be adjusted. See figure 1.8 for a breakdown of learning problems.

A *one-shot learning algorithm* examines each training example only once in the course of computing a set of weights for the network. Generally these are the fastest learning algorithms.

By contrast an *iterative learning algorithm* examines each training example many times, either cycling through the set of examples or choosing one at random for each cycle. Iterative algorithms are more powerful than one-shot algorithms, but of course they are slower. Speed of learning is a

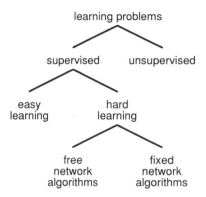

Figure 1.8
Various types of learning problems.

major consideration for connectionist models; some algorithms are too slow to be practical, even for medium-sized problems.

Network properties, cell properties, dynamic properties, and learning properties provide us with a concise framework for specifying connectionist models. Throughout the book we will use this framework to describe a variety of important models.

1.3 Two Fundamental Models: Multilayer Perceptrons (MLP's) and Backpropagation Networks (BPN's)

This section will present the two most common neural network models, multilayer perceptrons and backpropagation networks. We will be working with these models for most of the remainder of the book.

1.3.1 Multilayer Perceptrons (MLP's)

The first model we will look at is also one of the earliest connectionist models. It is perhaps the simplest connectionist model capable of representing any Boolean function and of approximating more general functions to arbitrary precision. We define the class of *multilayer perceptrons (MLP's)* as follows:

• *Network properties:* We use arbitrary feedforward networks. Cells are numbered so that the p input cells are indexed 1 through p, and so that if cell u_j is connected to cell u_i then $j < i$ (see exercise 1).

• *Cell properties:* Cell inputs and activations are discrete, assuming values of $\{+1, -1, 0\}$. We usually associate $+1$ with *true*, -1 with *false*, and 0 with *unknown*. Every cell computes its activation as a *linear discriminant* (or *threshold logic function*) as follows:

$$S_i = \sum_{j=0}^{i-1} w_{i,j} u_j$$

$$u_i = \begin{cases} +1 & (true) & \text{if } S_i > 0 \\ -1 & (false) & \text{if } S_i < 0 \\ 0 & (unknown) & \text{if } S_i = 0. \end{cases}$$

(1.2)

• *Dynamic properties:* Evaluation of the network proceeds according to the cell ordering, with each cell computing and posting its new activation value before the next cell is examined. One pass through the network brings it to steady state, and the output cell activations are interpreted as the outputs for the entire network.

• *Learning properties:* Various learning algorithms will be discussed starting with chapter 3.

Figure 1.9 shows an example of an MLP that computes the Boolean function

A *AND* (B *OR* (*NOT* C) *OR* D).

In part IV we will see how to use MLP's for expert system knowledge bases.

1.3.2 Backpropagation Networks (BPN's)

The second fundamental model we will define is the class of *backpropagation networks (BPN's)*. Currently these networks are very popular because there is an interesting algorithm for doing hard learning with them. Strictly speaking backpropagation is a learning algorithm, not a type of network. However, backpropagation is used primarily with one type of network, so it is convenient to refer to this type of network as a backpropagation network.

BPN's are defined as follows:

• *Network properties:* Same as for MLP's.

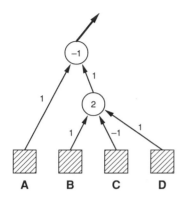

Figure 1.9
A multilayer perceptron (MLP) that computes A *AND* (B *OR* (*NOT* C) *OR* D).

- *Cell properties:* Inputs and activations are continuous, assuming values on $[0, 1]$ or $[-1, +1]$. Activations are computed as follows:

$$S_i = \sum_{j=0}^{i-1} w_{i,j} u_j$$

$$u_i = \begin{cases} \dfrac{1}{1 + e^{-S_i}} & \text{if activations in } [0,1] \text{ are used, or} \\[3ex] -1 + \dfrac{2}{1 + e^{-S_i}} & \text{if activations in } [-1, +1] \text{ are used.} \end{cases} \quad (1.3)$$

Thus u_i approaches $+1$ for large positive S_i and u_i approaches 0 for large negative S_i (or -1 if $[-1, +1]$ activation values are used). Figure 1.10 compares the outputs of a single backpropagation cell with a linear discriminant cell. The backpropagation cell can be thought of as a continuous approximation of the linear discriminant.

- *Dynamic properties:* Same as for MLP's.
- *Learning properties:* Algorithms will be presented in chapter 11.

1.4 Gradient Descent

Gradient descent is a basic technique that plays an important part in most connectionist learning algorithms, especially mean squared error (chapter

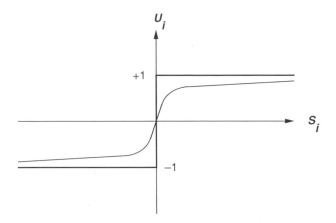

Figure 1.10
Backpropagation cell on $[-1, +1]$ and linear discriminant cell on $\{-1, +1\}$.

6) and backpropagation (chapter 11). It is so fundamental to learning algorithms that it is included in this introductory chapter.

1.4.1 The Algorithm

Suppose we have a differentiable function $\mathscr{E}$ that takes a set of network weights $W = \langle w_{p+1,0} \ldots w_{p+1,p} \rangle$ and the training examples for a single-cell problem, and produces a measure of the error, $\mathscr{E}(W)$, for those weights. Figure 1.11 illustrates the idea. The error surface gives the error for every set of weight values, W. Because the error function $\mathscr{E}(\ )$ is differentiable, we can compute its multidimensional derivative (or gradient) vector

$$\nabla \mathscr{E} = \left\langle \frac{\partial \mathscr{E}}{\partial w_{p+1,0}} \cdots \frac{\partial \mathscr{E}}{\partial w_{p+1,p}} \right\rangle$$

at any point in weight space. (This will require that the activation function, $f(\ )$, also be differentiable.)

The gradient gives the direction in weight space that would result in maximum increase of the error when an infinitesimally small weight change is made in that direction. Letting ρ be a small positive number, we can compute the revised weight vector W^* by

$$W^* = W + \rho \nabla \mathscr{E}(W).$$

Of course we are more interested in the vector $-\nabla \mathscr{E}(W)$, the vector in the

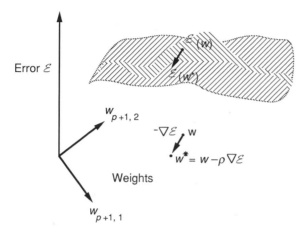

Figure 1.11
Error surface produced by an error function $\mathscr{E}(\ )$. ρ is a small constant that measures the step size.

opposite direction, that minimizes error for a small step

$$W^* = W - \rho\nabla\mathscr{E}(W).$$

This immediately suggests a learning algorithm: start at some arbitrary set of weights, W, and continue to evaluate $-\nabla\mathscr{E}(W)$ while taking small steps in that direction until some stopping criterion has been reached. We call such an algorithm *gradient descent*. An example of using gradient descent for learning in single-cell models will be given in chapter 6. Of course gradient descent is used for much more than generating weights in connectionist models; there is a long history for such algorithms that dates back to the early days of calculus.

1.4.2 Practical Problems

There are several problems with gradient descent that crop up in most of its applications.

Differentiable Error Function
To use gradient descent it is necessary that the error function be differentiable with respect to the individual weights. For neural networks this

can be a problem, because the natural measure of error—the percentage of training examples misclassified—either has derivative 0 or has undefined derivative, depending upon where the derivative is evaluated. A way around this problem is to find a closely related error function that *is* differentiable everywhere, and we will take this approach for the mean squared error algorithm (chapter 6) and for backpropagation (chapter 11). However, we must still check that the new differentiable error function is sufficiently close to the original error function.

Where to Stop

Another problem with gradient descent algorithms is deciding when to stop the algorithm, because it is often the case that the error function asymptotically approaches a lower bound. If the lower bound is known, then a way around this problem is to stop iterating when the error is within some prespecified range of its lower bound.

Step Size

The gradient descent algorithm contains a constant, $\rho > 0$, that governs how big a step is made at each iteration. Unfortunately the choice of ρ is problem-specific and can greatly affect the workings of the algorithm. A ρ that is too small will drastically slow down the algorithm, yet a ρ that is too large can cause the algorithm to oscillate and be unstable and never to converge to a minimum.

Local Minima

Gradient descent algorithms are not guaranteed to find a global minimum, even if they converge. Figure 1.12 shows the situation for the error function of a problem with only one weight. Following the (negative of the) derivative will lead to a local minimum, but not the global minimum.

For some types of problems we can prove that there are no local minima, so convergence to a global minimum is assured (provided the step size ρ is not too large). For other problems we might not know whether local minima exist or whether a minimum found by gradient descent is a local or a global minimum.

When to Update

Another practical question is whether to estimate $\nabla\mathscr{E}(\ )$ from a single training example (called *stochastic* or *on-line updating*) or compute $\nabla\mathscr{E}(\ )$ for all training examples before updating the weights. Although the latter

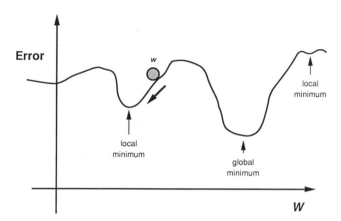

Figure 1.12
Local and global minima.

is the definition of the gradient, both practice and theory indicate that on-line updating is more efficient. See, for example, LeCun et al. [128].

1.4.3   Comments

Most, if not all, connectionist learning algorithms can be viewed as search through weight space with the aid of some estimate for the gradient. Different algorithms use gradient (and other) information in a variety of ways; perhaps the biggest advantage of gradient descent methods is this versatility.

The speed of pure gradient descent methods ranges from very fast for single-cell models to slow for fixed-network algorithms such as back-propagation. Speed and the need for setting parameters (*"handholding"*) are the biggest practical problems with gradient descent, while the biggest theoretical problem is local minima.

1.5   Historic and Bibliographic Notes

This section highlights some of the neural network research that has been most influential. It will not attempt, however, to list all of the important contributions to connectionist research; such a task is beyond this author's capabilities. The best approximation to such a list would be to combine the papers in *Neurocomputing* by Anderson and Rosenfeld [8] with the historical remarks in *Parallel Distributed Processing* by Rumelhart and McClelland [177], *Parallel Models of Associative Memory* by Hinton and James A. Anderson [98], *Learning Machines* by Nilsson [149], *Pattern Recognition and Scene Analysis* by Duda and Hart [47], and *Neurocomputing* by Hecht-Nielsen [96]. These works are also highly recommended in their own right.

1.5.1 Early Work

D. O. Hebb [94] published one of the first rules for learning by neurons that could be viewed as an algorithm: "When the axon of cell A is near enough to excite a cell B ... A's efficacy, as one of the cells firing B is increased." In other words, if cells u_i and u_j are simultaneously active then increase the weight of any connection between them. In this form Hebb's procedure needs a bit of tuning up to actually work, but it contains the seed for almost all future algorithms.

Fisher [55] developed the linear discriminant, and McCulloch and Pitts [139] are usually credited with developing the threshold logic unit. We will see more of these models in future chapters.

The person most responsible for machine learning in connectionist models was Frank Rosenblatt. He is credited with the perceptron learning algorithm (Rosenblatt [172]) and with the idea of using random cells, both of which are discussed in later chapters. Rosenblatt also did much to popularize the field and helped generate a tremendous amount of excitement in the early 1960s. His *Principles of Neurodynamics* [173] is the primary reference to his work, but it is difficult to read for modern audiences and uses awkward notation.

At about the same time as Rosenblatt was working on perceptrons, Samuel [183] was developing his famous checker-playing program. Samuel's program was a true learning program that improved its behavior with play. While usually considered as the forerunner of symbolic machine learning, Samuel's program had a distinctly connectionist flavor; the most interesting learning aspects involved changing weights associated with various features. The program also remembered past board positions and their evaluations to allow more efficient search, something Samuel regarded as a type of learning.

Also around this time Widrow and Hoff [202] developed an important variation of perceptron learning, now referred to as the Widrow-Hoff or delta rule. We will see this in chapter 6.

1.5.2 The Decline of the Perceptron

With the excitement came the hype.

Perceptron researchers grew somewhat overenthusiastic in their claims and predictions. In 1969 Minsky and Papert pointed out theoretical limitations of single-cell models in their landmark book *Perceptrons* (Minsky and Papert [145]) and in an influential paper by Minsky [144].

The publication of *Perceptrons* marked a dramatic shift away from work in connectionist models; symbolic models became the dominant paradigm in artificial intelligence. A major early work in symbolic learning was Winston's [210] program that learned a description of an arch. This was followed by important contributions by many researchers. Perhaps the best historical source for references to symbolic learning is the extensive bibliography in *Machine Learning*, volume 1 by Michalski, Carbonell, and Mitchell [142]. (Also see further volumes in this series.)

It is hard to overemphasize (and somewhat hard to believe) just how out of favor neural network research became in the 1970s and early 1980s. Perhaps the sense of anathema is best captured by an anonymous referee's comment seen on a paper as late as March 1985: "Perceptron learning has quite correctly been discarded as a technique worthy of study." Strong feelings indeed!

More typical reactions ran something like "This is just the old discredited perceptron ..." The general distaste for perceptrons presented a dilemma for researchers in the area: how were they to describe their models? Authors spent much energy distancing themselves from previous work, especially before the terms *connectionist* and *neural network* came into wide use and acceptance.

To their everlasting credit, a handful of connectionist researchers did meaningful work during the dark ages of the 1970s. James A. Anderson [7] and Stephen Grossberg (see numerous references in Grossberg [82]) did important work on psychological models. Kohonen [117, 116] developed associative memory models, Amari [2, 3] studied random cells, and Fukushima [60] worked on models for machine vision. We will see some of this work in later chapters.

1.5.3 The Rise of Connectionist Research

In the early 1980s there was a tremendous resurgence of activity in perceptronlike models. Barto, Sutton, and Anderson [18] developed their critic models and several psychological models. Hopfield [101] wrote an influential paper emphasizing energy models, content-addressable memory, and error resistance; his talks did much to rekindle enthusiasm.

Following upon Hopfield's work, Hinton, Sejnowski, and Ackley [99, 1, 177] developed Boltzmann models. This was something of a milestone. For the first time we had a way of generating *networks* from training examples, thereby overcoming some of the Minsky-Papert theoretical limitations on the learning power of single-cell models. Moreover Hinton's excitement and charisma helped motivate many researchers during the early 1980s. Hinton [97] also emphasized the importance of distributed representations, a key concept that was to be used later in the *distributed method* by this author (Gallant [64]; Gallant and Smith [74]).

Around 1982 Feldman and Ballard [53] popularized the term *connectionist*, and many researchers quickly adopted it to describe their work. Curiously Grossberg [81] used the term earlier, but he now apparently prefers to call his models *neural networks.*

Another Minsky-Papert problem, the perceptron learning algorithm's difficulty with nonseparable sets of training examples, was fixed up by this author (Gallant [65]).

During the early 1980s there was continued work by Anderson and Grossberg on psychological and computational models. McClelland and Rumelhart [137, 176] also proposed their important interactive activation model. Around this time Kohonen [118, 122] also did important work with topology-preserving maps.

Meanwhile there was a problem with Boltzmann learning: it was too slow. Rumelhart, Hinton, and Williams [178] rediscovered and popularized the much faster backpropagation algorithm, and it quickly became the model of choice for many researchers. For example Sejnowski and Rosenberg [186] showed how to apply backpropagation for learning how to pronounce words. Their taped demonstrations of a network learning to pronounce drew wide attention.

It is interesting to note that the basic idea for backpropagation has been rediscovered several times. Werbos [200] appears to have used the technique first in his Ph.D. thesis. He applied "working back of derivatives" to a computational model more general than connectionist networks, but did not exploit the technique's ability to generate weights for intermediate cells in connectionist models.

In 1982 Parker [151, 152] rediscovered the algorithm and even patented it through Stanford University. (The patent was allowed to lapse.)

By 1986 we reach the point where research activity had so expanded and time for retrospective analysis had become so short that it seems prudent to end our historical overview. However, it is clear already that the next period will be a very exciting time for connectionist work by a large number of talented researchers.

1.5.4 Other Bibliographic Notes

• See Geman et al. [77] for a good summary of related statistical techniques.

• For an excellent overview of the human brain's physiology, see the chapter by Crick in *Parallel Distributed Processing*, volume 2 (McClelland and Rumelhart [138]).

• For an introductory book from a theoretical physics perspective, see Amit [5].

• For an introduction to the field of artificial intelligence, see Winston [211].

• The most prominent critic of AI is Hubert Dreyfus, who wrote an important and controversial book *What Computers Can't Do* [44]. In the past he has often been the target of personal attacks, sometimes from people who made little effort to understand his arguments. Recently he and his brother Stuart have become interested in connectionist models (Dreyfus and Dreyfus [45]).

1.6   Exercises

1. Prove that a network is a feedforward network if and only if its cells can be numbered in such a way that

(a) all p input cells are numbered 1 through p and

(b) whenever cell u_j is connected to cell u_i then $j < i$.

2. Prove for a k-layer network:

(a) it is a feedforward network;

(b) all cells in layer L_0 are input cells; and

(c) all nonsuperfluous cells in layer L_k are output cells.

A cell is *superfluous* if we can eliminate it along with all of its connections to and from other cells without changing the input-output behavior of the network.

3. Give an example of a strictly 2-layer network where the middle layer of cells contains at least one input cell and at least one output cell.

4. (a) Prove that any k-layer network $\mathcal{N}_1$ can be represented as a k-layer network $\mathcal{N}_2$ where all input cells are in layer L_0.

(b) Give an example of a *strictly k-layer* network $\mathcal{N}$ for which there is no equivalent strictly k-layer network having all input cells in layer L_0.

5. Assuming discrete inputs $\{+1, -1\}$, what Boolean function is computed by the following network represented in matrix form (see also programming project 1):

2	1	1			{2 input cells, 1 intermediate cell, 1 output cell}
1	1	1	0	0	{This row is for the intermediate cell}
-1	-1	-1	2	0	{This row is for the output cell}

(Note that the weights in the first column are biases.)

6. For a $\{1,0\}$ backpropagation network using the weights given in the matrix in exercise 5, what would the output be if the two inputs were both 1.0?

7. Consider the activation function

$$f(x) = 11x^2 - 106x + 259.$$

(a) What is its gradient (derivative)?

(b) How many global and local maxima and minima does it have, and what are they?

8. Consider the function

$$f(x) = 4x^3 - 10x^2 + 3x + 15.$$

(a) Compute its gradient (derivative).

(b) How many global and local maxima and minima does it have, and what are they?

9. Discuss what it would take to construct a connectionist model that acted as a general-purpose computer. How could input and output be performed, say from a tape drive?

10. A human neuron takes roughly 10^{-3} seconds to respond to its inputs, yet we can physically react to complicated visual information in less than $1/10$ of a second. What does this imply for visual information processing by humans?

11. A *linear* cell is a cell that merely outputs its weighted sum

$$u_i = S_i = \sum_j w_{i,j} u_j.$$

Prove that a feedforward network consisting of linear cells can always be replaced by an equivalent (linear) single-layer network.

1.7 Programming Project

Note: The programming projects here and in future chapters build upon each other to develop a powerful connectionist learning package and a network simulator that can be expanded into a connectionist expert system inference engine. Therefore please keep code as flexible as possible to handle future modifications.

Write a simulator for feedforward networks in your favorite efficient and transportable programming language. Points to keep in mind:

1. *Network specification.* The network can be specified by a file with the following format:

• First line: the numbers of input, intermediate, and output cells. We let p be the number of input cells.

• Following lines: the matrix of connection weights

$$
\begin{matrix}
w_{p+1,0} & w_{p+1,1} & \cdots & w_{p+1,n} \\
\vdots & \vdots & & \vdots \\
w_{m,0} & w_{m,1} & \cdots & w_{m,n}
\end{matrix}
$$

See exercise 5 for an example.

2. *Inputs.* Prompt the user for values of input cells $u_1, \ldots, u_p$. For now assume discrete inputs in $\{+1, -1, 0\}$.

3. *Cell computations.* Implement MLP's for now, but allow enough flexibility so that any computation consistent with equation (1.1) could be implemented later. Test your simulation with some simple networks.

2 Representation Issues

In this chapter we will examine connectionist models' ability to represent Boolean and real-valued functions and concepts. Distributed representations and feature space representations will be introduced, and we will see how functions and concepts can be unified quite naturally within a feature space framework. We will also look at ISA relationships between concepts, and see how they can be generalized to contextual ISA's. The appendix will make comparisons with other approaches such as disjunctive normal form representations and decision trees.

2.1 Representing Boolean Functions

We have already seen one way to represent Boolean values using MLP's:

$u_i = +1 \leftrightarrow \text{True}$

$u_i = -1 \leftrightarrow \text{False}$

$u_i = 0 \leftrightarrow \text{Unknown}$

There is also the more standard $\{1, 0\}$ correspondence:

$u_i = 1 \leftrightarrow \text{True}$

$u_i = 0 \leftrightarrow \text{False}$

2.1.1 Equivalence of $\{+1, -1, 0\}$ and $\{1, 0\}$ Forms

We can define a $\{1, 0\}$ *MLP* model as an MLP with $\{1, 0\}$ inputs and activations. A $\{1, 0\}$ MLP uses the same activation computation given in equation (1.2), except the output is arbitrary whenever the weighted sum of inputs, S_i, equals 0. This formulation is commonly used because some problems are more naturally expressed in $\{1, 0\}$ rather than $\{+1, -1, 0\}$ form.

How do the $\{+1, -1, 0\}$ and $\{1, 0\}$ forms relate? If we ignore the cases where the weighted sum of inputs (S_i) is 0 then the forms are equivalent because we can transform cells in one form into cells in the other. For example, if we have a problem in $\{1, 0\}$ form with weights $\{w_{i,j}\}$ then we can write down corresponding weights $\{w'_{i,j}\}$ for a standard MLP so that the weighted sums, S_i and S'_i, are the same for corresponding inputs.

To see how to do this consider figure 2.1. Every time we change an input u_j from false (0) to true (1) in the $\{1, 0\}$ form we increase S_i by $w_{i,j}$. But if

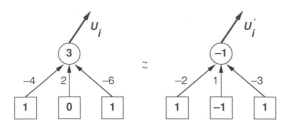

Figure 2.1
A $\{1,0\}$ MLP cell and the corresponding $\{+1, -1, 0\}$ MLP cell.

we change u_i' from false (-1) to true $(+1)$ in the $\{+1, -1, 0\}$ form, we increase S_i' by $2w_{i,j}$. Therefore if we want S_i to equal S_i' then we must set $w_{i,j}'$ equal to $(1/2)w_{i,j}$ for $j > 0$.

Next we can find the correct correspondence for the biases $w_{i,0}'$ and $w_{i,0}$ by examining the two cases where all inputs are false and all inputs are true. This leads us to the following correspondence:

$$w_{i,j}' = \frac{1}{2}w_{i,j} \qquad\qquad \text{for } j > 0 \text{ (nonbiases)}$$

$$w_{i,0}' = w_{i,0} + \sum_{j=1}^{n} w_{i,j}' \qquad\qquad\qquad (2.1)$$

$$= w_{i,0} + \frac{1}{2}\sum_{j=1}^{n} w_{i,j} \quad \text{for the bias term.}$$

For expert systems in later chapters we will be using the $\{+1, -1, 0\}$ form because it allows convenient representation of unknown quantities. However, the $\{1,0\}$ form can also be used with continuous models if we identify an activation of $1/2$ with "Unknown."

It is important to note that the choice of $\{+1, -1, 0\}$ or $\{1,0\}$ models *can* affect learning algorithms, as we shall see in section 11.3.7. $\{+1, -1, 0\}$ models usually train more quickly.

2.1.2 Single-Cell Models

Single-cell linear discriminant models can compute most of the common Boolean functions you find around the house. Consider for example the AND function defined on p inputs (using $\{+1, -1, 0\}$ values). Recall that AND produces an output of true $(+1)$ if and only if all of its inputs are true $(+1)$. Then the following weights

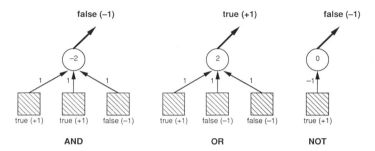

Figure 2.2
AND, OR, and NOT functions computed by single-cell linear discriminant models.

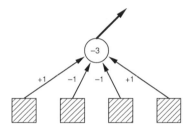

Figure 2.3
A selector cell for the inputs $\langle +1 \quad -1 \quad -1 \quad +1 \rangle$.

$$w_{p+1,0} = -(p-1)$$

$$w_{p+1,j} = 1 \qquad \text{for } j > 0$$

will compute AND for a single-cell model as illustrated in figure 2.2.

It is also easy to write down weights for the OR function (defined on p inputs) and the NOT function (defined on 1 input).

The *selector* function is an important variant of the AND function, and is illustrated in figure 2.3. A selector cell produces a true $(+1)$ output for exactly one set of inputs (where all inputs are assumed $+1$ or -1 and none are 0). For example the cell in figure 2.3 produces an output of true if and only if the inputs are $+1$, -1, -1, $+1$.

More formally, a selector cell u_i for input vector E^k is given by

$$w_{p+1,0} = -(p-1)$$

$$w_{p+1,j} = E_j^k \qquad \text{for } j > 0.$$

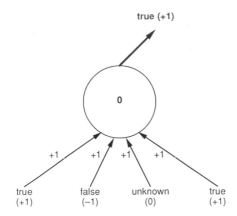

Figure 2.4
The plurality function.

Clearly selector cells are merely modified AND cells with appropriate input weights changed from $+1$ to -1.

Another important function is the *plurality* function. It is defined to be *true* if more of its inputs are true than false, *false* if more of its inputs are false than true, and *unknown* if an equal number of inputs are true and false. We can compute it with one of the simplest possible single-cell models (figure 2.4):

$$w_{p+1,0} = 0$$

$$w_{p+1,j} = 1 \quad \text{for } j > 0.$$

The plurality function provides a good illustration of how a connectionist model with $\{+1, -1, 0\}$ inputs can handle unknown inputs gracefully. For example if the first 3 inputs are unknown, the cell computes the plurality of the remaining inputs. This little function is also a veritable land mine for some representation methods, as we shall discover in the appendix.

A function that is very similar to the plurality function is the *majority* function. The majority function on p Boolean inputs is defined to be

True if more than $p/2$ inputs are true

False if less than $p/2$ inputs are true

Unknown if exactly $p/2$ inputs are true.

Notice that the majority function is exactly the same function as the plurality function if all inputs are known to be true or false. Because we normally make this assumption when considering Boolean functions, it may be a bit picky to differentiate between the plurality and majority functions. However, if we do care about behavior with unknown inputs and outputs, then it is worth noting that the majority function is slightly harder to represent than the plurality function. Problem 4 shows that a single-cell linear discriminant cannot represent the majority function on 2 inputs while exercise 5 demonstrates that a network with a total of $p + 1$ intermediate and output cells can represent the majority function on p inputs.

One last important function is a generalization of the plurality function, the *k or more out of p* function. When all p inputs are known, this function simply computes whether at least k of them are true. More precisely, we can give its definition in terms of a single-cell model:

$$w_{p+1,0} = p - 2k + 1$$

$$w_{p+1,j} = 1 \qquad \text{for } j > 0.$$

Notice that when exactly k inputs are true and $p - k$ are false then

$$S_i = (p - 2k + 1) + k - (p - k) = +1.$$

2.1.3 Nonseparable Functions

Unfortunately a single-cell linear discriminant model cannot compute every Boolean function. Consider for example the *XOR* or *Exclusive-OR* function given in figure 2.5.

If there were weights $w_{3,0}, w_{3,1}, w_{3,2}$ for a single-cell model that correctly computed the XOR function then they would have to satisfy all four training examples in the figure:

$$w_{3,0} - w_{3,1} - w_{3,2} < 0 \tag{2.2}$$

$$w_{3,0} - w_{3,1} + w_{3,2} > 0 \tag{2.3}$$

$$w_{3,0} + w_{3,1} - w_{3,2} > 0 \tag{2.4}$$

$$w_{3,0} + w_{3,1} + w_{3,2} < 0 \tag{2.5}$$

But no set of weights can simultaneously satisfy these 4 inequalities (exercise 3). Therefore no set of weights can compute XOR for a single-cell linear discriminant model.

| Training | Inputs | | Correct output |
example	u_1	u_2	u_3
#1	false (-1)	false (-1)	false (-1)
#2	false (-1)	true ($+1$)	true ($+1$)
#3	true ($+1$)	false (-1)	true ($+1$)
#4	true ($+1$)	true ($+1$)	false (-1)

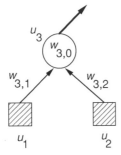

Figure 2.5
The XOR function.

We define a Boolean function to be a *separable function* if it can be computed by a single-cell linear discriminant model; otherwise it is a *nonseparable function*. XOR is the simplest nonseparable function, in the sense that no nonseparable function has fewer inputs (see exercise 10).

The *parity* function is a generalization of XOR to p inputs. It is defined to be *true* if the number of true inputs is odd and *false* otherwise. Usually we see this function represented in $\{1, 0\}$ form rather than $\{+1, -1, 0\}$ form.

It is important to note that parity is a very bizarre function; it always changes outputs whenever a single one of its inputs changes. This property makes parity a good example for exercising learning algorithms that deal with nonseparable functions, but it also makes it very unrepresentative of real-world functions. For example if we change a single pixel of an image we do not expect that our evaluation of that image will always change; to the contrary we would generally treat such a minor change as noise and simply ignore it.

We will have more to say about parity in later sections.

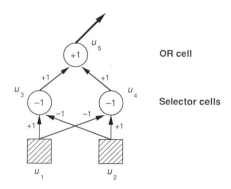

OR cell

Selector cells

Figure 2.6
Flat network for computing XOR using selector cells.

2.1.4 Representing Arbitrary Boolean Functions

A multilayer perceptron can represent any Boolean function f. One way
to do this is with a flat network using selector cells in layer L_1 and a single
OR cell in layer L_2. There is a selector cell in layer L_1 for every set of inputs
E^k that produces an output of true ($+1$) for f.

Figure 2.6 illustrates this construction for the XOR function. The network uses an intermediate cell for each of the two inputs to XOR that
produce an output of true: $\{+1, -1\}$ and $\{-1, +1\}$.

Thus we conclude:

THEOREM 2.1   *Any Boolean function of a finite number of inputs can be
represented by an MLP.*

Proof: In the flat selector network just described, every input will cause
exactly 1 or 0 selector cells to have activation $+1$, depending upon whether
the desired output is true or false respectively. This guarantees that the
output of the top OR cell will agree with the desired output.   □

COROLLARY 2.2   *Given a set of noncontradictory training examples with
Boolean features and classifications, there exists an MLP that produces the
correct output for all training examples.*   □

Being able to represent any Boolean function by a selector network is
somewhat of a Pyrrhic victory. There are many functions that have outputs of true for about half of their possible input patterns, so that the

flat selector construction would use about 2^{p-1} cells to represent these functions. This is simply too many cells.

Another drawback to the selector method for network generation is its inherent *brittleness*. A method for generating a model brittle if a model constructed on the basis of training examples is not likely to generalize to new, unseen examples. By contrast a *robust* method generates models that handle unseen examples well.

To illustrate the selector method's brittleness, suppose we have a set of training examples where each example has $p = 100$ Boolean inputs. We are not likely to have training examples for all 2^{100} possible inputs, so suppose we have only 1,000 training examples and we want to generate a network that models these training examples. We could easily generate a flat selector network using $\leq 1,000$ selector cells corresponding to those training examples that had outputs of true, and this network would indeed fit all 1,000 training examples. But the resulting network would produce true outputs *only when inputs exactly duplicated one of the true training examples*. This would give us the most brittle behavior possible.

Note that even though the selector method for producing flat networks is not very appealing, this does not mean that all procedures for producing flat networks are inherently bad. In fact we will see a much better method for producing flat networks in section 8.2.

It is worth noting that connectionist models do not automatically possess robustness as their birthright. The selector construction puts that notion to rest.

2.1.5 Representing Boolean Functions Using Continuous Connectionist Models

Connectionist models that use continuous (rather than discrete) inputs and activations are also able to represent Boolean functions. We merely apply a threshold function to the activations of their output cells, for example

$$\text{Thresholded output} = \begin{cases} \text{True} & \text{when} & activation \geq .9 \\ \text{False} & \text{when} & activation \leq .1 \\ \text{Unknown} & \text{when} & .1 < activation < .9. \end{cases}$$

It might also be helpful to threshold intermediate cell activations, but this is seldom done.

The cutoff numbers .9 and .1 were chosen somewhat arbitrarily; other cutoffs are sometimes used. Note, however, that 1.0 and 0.0 would not be suitable values for cutoffs, because these values could only arise as activations if infinitely large weights were used.

2.2 Distributed Representations

Distributed representations are an important technique for knowledge representation that are heavily used by living systems.

2.2.1 Definition

A *distributed representation* uses a collection of cells to represent a value or object, whereas a *local representation* uses one cell per value. For example suppose we wanted to learn to recognize 1,000 objects that might appear (in distorted form) on a binary 16 × 16 retina. A neural network might devote one cell to each of the 1,000 objects, thereby requiring 1,000 cells. This would be a local representation. Alternatively if we could identify 100 critical features so that no two objects had exactly the same set of critical features, then we could represent each of our 1,000 objects as a *pattern* involving 100 cells. This would be a distributed representation.

A second example, also dealing with vision, was proposed by Hinton [97] and is illustrated in figure 2.7. In the local representation a cell "sees" a small region on a retina, whereas the distributed representation assigns a much larger region to a cell so that receptive fields overlap. Even though

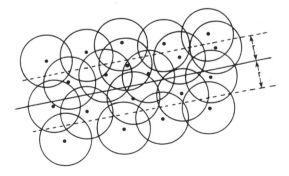

Figure 2.7
A local representation using very small receptive fields (large dots) and a distributed representation using larger receptive fields (circles).

the receptive fields arc larger in the distributed representation it is possible to locate a point by the pattern of activated cells with greater precision.

2.2.2 Storage Efficiency and Resistance to Error

The previous examples demonstrate two important properties of distributed representations: storage efficiency and resistance to error.

To store n objects using a local representation requires n cells, whereas a distributed representation requires only log n cells. In practice most distributed representations are not minimal; nevertheless their storage efficiency usually lies closer to the log n bound than to the local representation bound of n. Also notice that the increased acuity in the receptive field example (figure 2.7) can be viewed as a "dual" aspect of increased storage capacity. More capacity allows more regions to be specified, so each region can be smaller.

Turning to error resistance, let us compare 1,000 cells used to represent 1,000 concepts locally with 1,000 cells that represent these objects by random patterns, as illustrated in figure 2.8.

If we invert one feature at random in the local representation, then with probability .999 we will generate an ambiguous representation that might be either of 2 objects (because 2 values will be $+1$). Even worse, one time in a thousand we will get the useless vector of all -1's.

By contrast, suppose we change 1 bit in a distributed representation and look for the closest vector. We can compute the probability that at least one of the remaining 999 vectors will differ by at most one feature from the noisy vector by

$$1 - \left(1 - \frac{1{,}001}{2^{1{,}000}}\right)^{999} \approx \frac{2^{20}}{2^{1{,}000}} = 2^{-980}.$$

Object	Local representation	Distributed representation
1	$\langle -1, -1, -1, \ldots, -1, +1 \rangle$	$\langle +1, -1, -1, +1, +1, \ldots \rangle$
2	$\langle -1, -1, -1, \ldots, +1, -1 \rangle$	$\langle -1, -1, +1, +1, -1, \ldots \rangle$
3	$\langle -1, -1, \ldots, +1, -1, -1 \rangle$	$\langle \qquad random \qquad \rangle$
$\vdots$		$\vdots$
1,000	$\langle +1, -1, \ldots, -1, -1, -1 \rangle$	$\langle \qquad random \qquad \rangle$

Figure 2.8
Local and distributed representations for 1,000 objects using 1,000 cells.

Therefore it is virtually certain that the original concept will be closest to its noisy offspring. This example nicely shows off the error resistance properties of distributed representations. In section 5.6 we will see how Kanerva uses this property for his *sparse distributed memory* model. For more on storage efficiency, see also work by Bloom [23] and Rosenfeld and Touretzky [174].

2.2.3 Superposition

Another very important property of distributed representations is that *superposition preserves identification*. This means that if we add together several high-dimensional, uncorrelated, equal-length vectors (i.e., superimpose them), then the vector sum will preserve some of the properties of the individual vectors. In particular, the sum will give a relatively strong dot product with any of the vectors that comprise it, thereby allowing identification of those vectors.

To see this, suppose we have a collection $\{V^i\}$ of p-dimensional $\{+1, -1\}$ vectors that are roughly uncorrelated, so that

$$V^i \cdot V^j \approx 0 \quad \text{for } i \neq j. \tag{2.6}$$

Suppose V is the sum of the first 5 vectors

$$V = \sum_{k=1}^{5} V^k.$$

Now consider $V^i \cdot V$, the dot product of one of the vectors with V.

$$V^i \cdot V = \sum_j V_j^i V_j$$

$$= \sum_j V_j^i \left(\sum_{k=1}^{5} V_j^k \right)$$

$$= \sum_{k=1}^{5} \sum_j V_j^i V_j^k$$

$$= \sum_{k=1}^{5} V^i \cdot V^k.$$

If V^i is not among the 5 vectors that were added to form V, then each of the 5 terms above will be approximately 0 by equation (2.6), making

$$V^i \cdot V \approx 0.$$

On the other hand if $V^i \in \{V^1, \ldots, V^5\}$, then $V^i \cdot V$ will equal p plus 4 terms that are near 0. Therefore for high-dimensional p, the vector V allows the identification of each of its 5 constituents.

Document retrieval gives a good example of where the superposition property is useful. Suppose we represent every *word* by a high-dimensional p-vector. We can now represent a document by the (normalized) sum of the vectors for those words in the document, and similarly for a *query*. For retrieval we can simply find those document vectors having largest dot product with a given query vector. Note that by the superposition property a word appearing both in a document d and in the query will make a big positive contribution to the dot product of d with the query. The final ingredient needed to make our system work well is to have the p-vector representation for words reflect similarity of meaning, so that 'car' and 'driver' have closer vectors than 'car' and 'hippopotamus'. Document retrieval using neural network techniques is a rapidly developing area for current research.

We will see more on superposition in chapter 5.

2.2.4 Learning

Returning to the first example of recognizing 1,000 images on a noisy 16×16 retina, we can see how distributed representations can be a big help in learning. If we use a local representation for this problem then we have one big 1,000-output learning problem. By contrast if we use a distributed representation consisting of 100 cells that represent key features, then we can learn each of these feature cells *independently* (and in parallel, hardware permitting). Thus we have decomposed the original problem into 100 independent and easier problems. (For the actual recognition of the 1,000 images we can pattern match on the activations of the 100 key feature cells using the linear machine model of chapter 4 or use an autoassociative model from chapter 5.) It would be very interesting to apply this representation and this approach to recognition of kanji characters.

2.3 Feature Spaces and ISA Relations

We have seen how neural network models can represent Boolean *functions*; now we will look at how networks can represent concepts. The most natural approach for this involves feature spaces, a type of representation that is closely related to the distributed representations from the previous section. Feature space representations also give us a nice unification of functions and concepts.

2.3.1 Feature Spaces

A *feature space* consists of a fixed set of phrases or predicates that act as coordinates for representing concepts. For example a tiny feature space might consist of

{*animal, living, big, pretty, walks, aggressive*}.

A *feature vector* is a vector having one component per feature. In our tiny feature space we could represent *nice-doggie-1*, *mean-dog-4*, and *Clyde* (an elephant) by the feature vectors

$$nice\text{-}doggie\text{-}1 = \langle +5 \quad +5 \quad -1 \quad +2 \quad +5 \quad -4 \rangle$$

$$mean\text{-}dog\text{-}4 = \langle +5 \quad +5 \quad +3 \quad -3 \quad +5 \quad +5 \rangle$$

$$Clyde = \langle +5 \quad +5 \quad +5 \quad -5 \quad +5 \quad -5 \rangle.$$

Several points are worth noting:

• Clearly we would need more features for actual applications, something on the order of several hundred. In fact *mean-dog-4* is closer to *Clyde* in this tiny feature space than it is to the other dog, *nice-doggie-1*.

• We have arbitrarily chosen integer feature values that lie in the range -5 to $+5$. Boolean or real-valued features could have been used instead.

• There is much overlap among features. For example *animal, living, walks,* and *aggressive* have extensive overlaps. Therefore feature space representations will usually be distributed representations, with the advantages we saw in the previous section.

• It is possible to adjoin *random features*, i.e., additional features with values chosen at random. For example we could add 4 more random features to the 6 we are currently using. This would be helpful in distinguishing *nice-doggie-1* from *nice-doggie-2* by giving similar objects an individual "name" in the random features.[1]

---

1. On the other hand, if there are many features then any two objects will have at least slightly different feature vector representations. There may be no need for a separate name "field."

• Feature vectors can represent objects or *situations* (containing or per-taining to objects). One way to construct a situation feature vector is to sum the object vectors that comprise the situation. For example, a situa-tion where *nice-doggie-1* and *Clyde* are both present could be represented by their vector sum. (As noted in section 2.2.3, in large feature spaces the individual vectors that comprise such a vector sum are still individually recognizable.)

Feature space representations are very well-suited for neural network computations, because it is very easy to use them for network inputs or outputs. In the neural network models we use (and arguably for biological neural networks) every cell sees a fixed set of activation values for inputs. Thus every cell is locally acting on a feature space (although the individual features may themselves be results of subnetwork computations or other-wise abstract and hard to describe).

2.3.2 Concept-Function Unification

A pleasing aspect of feature space representations is that they nicely unify the representation of *concepts* and *functions*. A *concept* in a feature space representation consists of a subset of feature vectors. For example the concept of "dog" consists of those feature vectors that correspond to dogs.

For our tiny example the concept "dog" might be all feature vectors having either

• positive components for *animal, living,* and *walks* (living dog), or

• a positive component for animal and negative components for *living, pretty, walks,* and *aggressive* (dead dog).

Notice that the concept of dog is *not* simply a subset of *positive features.*[2] Defining concepts by subsets of *feature vectors* is more general, allowing many more concepts to be defined (exercise 13). In fact a huge number of concepts may be true and false *simultaneously* for a given feature vector; said differently, a feature vector may simultaneously be a member and a nonmember of many subsets of all possible feature vectors.

Our definition of concept also allows many concepts to "coexist," with-out the need to define a separate set of features for every concept. (This is a major drawback with equating concepts to subsets of positive features.)

---

2. This approach was taken in previous work by Hinton [98].

object   feature vector

situation   feature vector (possibly a sum of feature vectors)

concept $\begin{cases} \text{subset of feature vectors} \\ \text{Boolean function} \end{cases}$

context   restriction to a subset of feature vectors

ISA $\begin{cases} \text{subset inclusion} \\ \text{function implication} \end{cases}$

Figure 2.9
Some feature space correspondences.

It is easy to see that every concept corresponds to a unique Boolean function defined on feature vectors, namely the function that outputs $+1$ if and only if the feature vector is a member of that concept. Thus the dog function, f_{dog}, outputs $+1$ only when input features represent a dog. Similarly every Boolean function on a set of feature vectors corresponds to a unique concept. Therefore *in feature space representations, concepts are exactly equivalent to Boolean functions.*

In section 2.1 we saw how to represent Boolean functions by neural networks. Therefore these same networks can also represent concepts in feature spaces. Furthermore all of the neural network learning algorithms that apply to learning *Boolean functions* will equally well apply to learning *concepts.* To summarize:

$$\{\text{concepts}\} = \{\text{Boolean functions}\}$$
$$= \{\text{neural networks with Boolean outputs}\}$$

2.3.3   ISA Relations

ISA relations[3] are naturally represented in feature spaces by *subset inclusion.* For example, to say '*dog* ISA *mammal*' means that every feature vector in the 'dog' subset of feature vectors is also in the 'mammal' subset of feature vectors.

---

3. ISA's have a long and somewhat controversial history in AI. See, for example, the excellent articles by Brachman [28, 27]. They are generally used in semantic networks (Quillian [166]) to express relationships such as '*dog* ISA *mammal*' or '*Clyde* ISA *elephant*'. For more details see any introductory text on AI.

If we look at the corresponding Boolean function representations, *ISA* *is equivalent to implication*:

$$dog \text{ ISA } mammal \Leftrightarrow f_{\text{dog}}(\mathbf{V}) = +1 \Rightarrow f_{\text{mammal}}(\mathbf{V}) = +1$$

$$\Leftrightarrow \{f_{\text{dog}} \Rightarrow f_{\text{mammal}}\}.$$

We can generalize even further in a useful way. Suppose we define a *context* in a feature space to be a subset of the feature vectors where a certain concept is true. For example, a *child's-story* context would consist of those feature vectors that comprise the concept of *child's-story*. Then we can define a *contextual ISA relation* by subset inclusion on the restricted set of feature vectors corresponding to the context.

For example *bears* may not be *friendly-animals* in real life, but in a *child's-story* context they are always friendly. We can represent this situation using feature spaces by having every feature vector that represents a *bear* in a *child's-story* context also be in the *friendly-animals* concept, as illustrated by figure 2.10.

Notice that contextual ISA's are in a sense *automatically defined*; they arise directly and implicitly from the definitions without any additional computation required. For example suppose we trained three independent

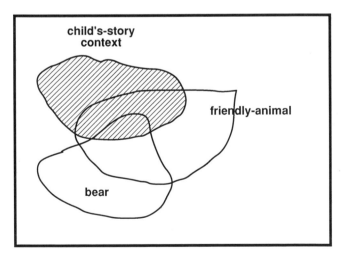

Figure 2.10
Contextual ISA: In a *child's-story* context *bear* ISA *friendly-animal*.

neural networks (using examples) to recognize *bear*, *friendly-animal*, and *child's-story*. Now whenever an input to the *bear* and *child's-story* networks produce +1 outputs then the *friendly-animal* net would also produce +1. This is the functional equivalent of contextual ISA.

2.3.4   Binding

We are still a long way from being able to represent complicated relationships such as

"George told Mary that John loves Sally, but Sally loves George."

Representing such relationships is very important for research, and several different approaches are currently being explored.

Much of this work focuses on the problem of *binding* objects. For example if we learn that "Clyde the elephant likes chocolate," how do we represent this? We can make some headway simply by using vector addition in a feature space representation to form a situation. For example, we could add the vector for *Clyde* to a typical vector from the concept class *likes-chocolate*. By the superposition property (section 2.2.3), the resulting vector would probably remain in the *likes-chocolate* class and also be close to *Clyde*.[4] This scheme breaks down, however, when we want to simultaneously represent that "Bertha the baboon likes coffee." A separate feature vector would be needed to avoid "cross-talk," such as "Clyde likes coffee." For some current approaches to this problem see Pollack [162], Dolan and Smolensky [43, 188], and Plate [159].

Ideally we strive for a neural network representation scheme that could take the statement "John threw the ball to Mary" and represent it so that the questions could be easily answered:

- Does John have the ball now?
- Does Mary have the ball now?
- Did John have the ball previously?
- Did Mary have the ball previously?

---

4. We can also consider Clyde as a concept class rather than an individual object. It seems reasonable to use different vectors to represent Clyde today, Clyde yesterday wearing his ballerina outfit, the astronaut that Clyde would have become had he not dropped out of flying school to protest the Vietnam war, etc. Thus objects can be viewed as narrow concepts with relatively few constituent vectors.

- Who is holding the baseball now?
- Who was holding the ball before?
- Does the ball weigh over 7 tons?
- Does John have any arms?

Doing so is a difficult and important research question.

2.4   Representing Real-Valued Functions

As previously noted, we will use the term *real number* somewhat loosely to mean a value that is typically represented by digital computers. More precisely, computers represent only about 2^{32} or 2^{64} rational points in some interval. These points are used to approximate real numbers in that same interval. Notice that digital computers use a *collection* of Boolean values (bits) to represent real values. This is exactly the approach we will take for *discrete* models; we will represent non-Boolean values by collections of discrete cells using one of several schemes.

Of course the most straightforward way of representing non-Booleans is with *continuous* connectionist models such as backpropagation networks (section 1.3.2). Here we only need adjust the representation interval from $[0, 1]$ to some desired interval $[a, b]$ by the transformation

$$\langle \text{value on } [a, b] \rangle = (b - a)\langle \text{value on } [0, 1] \rangle + a.$$

There is also a straightforward way to represent functions with Boolean outputs but real-valued inputs. We can use MLP models and simply allow the input activations to assume non-Boolean values. We then compute everything as before, for example

$$S_i = \sum w_{i,j} u_j$$

where the only difference is that u_j can take on real values.

The more difficult and interesting questions involve representing non-Boolean inputs and outputs by collections of discrete cells. In this section we will examine several ways to do this. We will also generalize the notion of separability and develop sufficient conditions to allow a single-layer network to represent a real-valued function of a single variable to arbitrary precision.

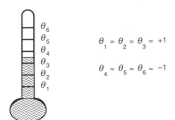

$\theta_1 = \theta_2 = \theta_3 = +1$

$\theta_4 = \theta_5 = \theta_6 = -1$

Figure 2.11
Cutoff representation of a number x where $\theta_3 \leq x < \theta_4$.

2.4.1   Approximating Real Numbers by Collections of Discrete Cells

There are several ways of approximating a real number x by a collection
of linear discriminant cells $\{u_1, \ldots, u_k\}$.

Cutoff Approximations
One simple representation is to make each u_i represent a *cutoff approximation* or 'thermometer code'.[5] Figure 2.11 illustrates the idea.

We can represent any number in an interval $[a, b]$ to arbitrary precision
as follows:

$$\left.\begin{array}{c} u_1 \\ u_2 \\ \vdots \\ u_k \end{array}\right\} = \text{true } (+1) \text{ iff } x \geq \left\{\begin{array}{c} \theta_1 \\ \theta_2 \\ \vdots \\ \theta_k \end{array}\right. \tag{2.7}$$

where the $\{\theta_i\}$ are called *cutoff values* and $\theta_i \leq \theta_{i+1}$. By convention we
define $\theta_0 = a$.

An *evenly spaced cutoff approximation* of the interval $[a, b]$ by k cells is
given by:

$$\left.\begin{array}{c} u_1 \\ u_2 \\ \vdots \\ u_k \end{array}\right\} = \text{true } (+1) \text{ iff } x \geq \left\{\begin{array}{c} a + \frac{1}{k+1}(b - a) \\ a + \frac{2}{k+1}(b - a) \\ \vdots \\ a + \frac{k}{k+1}(b - a) \end{array}\right. \tag{2.8}$$

5. The term was coined by B. Widrow.

For example, we could represent a probability in $[0, 1]$ within an interval of length 0.25 by an evenly spaced cutoff representation having 3 variables by defining $\{u_i\}$ thus:

$$\left.\begin{array}{c} u_1 \\ u_2 \\ u_3 \end{array}\right\} = \text{true}\ (+1)\ \text{iff}\ x \geq \left\{\begin{array}{c} 0.25 \\ 0.50 \\ 0.75 \end{array}\right.$$

Thus $x = 0.60$ would correspond to

$u_1 = +1$

$u_2 = +1$

$u_3 = -1.$

Since a cutoff representation R is a map from the interval $[a, b]$ to $\{+1, -1\}^k$, we can also define an *approximate inverse*

$$R^{-1} : \{+1, -1\}^k \to [a, b]$$

as follows:

$$R^{-1}(y) = \frac{1}{2}(a + \theta_k) + \frac{1}{2}\sum_{j=1}^{k}(\theta_j - \theta_{j-1})u_j.$$

If R is an evenly spaced cutoff representation and y is of the form

$$y = \langle \underbrace{+1, +1, \ldots, +1}_{i\ \text{terms}}, \underbrace{-1, -1, -1, \ldots, -1}_{k - i\ \text{terms}} \rangle \quad \text{for}\ 0 \leq i \leq k \tag{2.9}$$

and if we define Δ by

$$\Delta = \frac{b - a}{k + 1}$$

then this gives the simple form

$$R^{-1}(y) = \left\{a + \frac{k}{2}\Delta\right\} + \frac{\Delta}{2}\sum_{j=1}^{k} u_j = a + i\Delta = \theta_i. \tag{2.10}$$

Notice that it is not always desirable to make the cutoff values evenly spaced. For example, if we want to represent a quantity that has a normal distribution centered at 0 it would be reasonable to concentrate the cutoff values around 0 also. This way we could represent the smaller differences among the majority of values that are clustered around 0 with greater precision while distinctly representing the fact that some values are far from 0.[6] In section 7.3 we will see a way to use learning techniques to determine reasonable cutoff values.

An advantage of using cutoff approximations is that they are very insensitive to missing values, because removal of a number of cells leaves us with a usable representation; only the precision decreases. Similarly we can add cells to an already existing set of cells to increase precision.

Point Approximations

A second method for representing reals by a collection of discrete cells is by *point approximations*. We assign a value x_j in $[a, b]$ to each cell u_j and represent x by

$$u_j = \begin{cases} +1 & \text{if } x_j \text{ is the closest value to } x \\ -1 & \text{otherwise.} \end{cases}$$

If the values are evenly spaced and there are k cells, we let $\Delta = (b - a)/k$ and arrive at a representation such as:

$$\left.\begin{array}{c} u_1 \\ u_2 \\ \vdots \\ u_k \end{array}\right\} = \text{true } (+1) \text{ iff} \left\{\begin{array}{ccc} a & \leq x < & a + \Delta \\ a + \Delta & \leq x < & a + 2\Delta \\ \vdots & \vdots & \vdots \\ a + (k-1)\Delta & \leq x < & a + k\Delta = b. \end{array}\right.$$

Notice that point approximations require one more cell than a cutoff approximation uses to represent the same information. Also, point approximations are somewhat more sensitive to error. If we blank out several cells that include the single cell with a $+1$ activation, then we do not have much information left as to the value of x.

More importantly, every cell u_i in a point approximation depends upon other cells' values x_j in order to determine if x is closest to x_i or to some other x_j. Therefore adding new cells or removing cells requires changes in the interpretation of previously existing cells.

---

6. The human eye uses a similar arrangement (in two dimensions) by concentrating visual receptor cells to form the fovea, an area of high visual acuity.

Binary Representations

Another way to represent reals is to simply interpret a collection of cells as a (possibly fractional) binary number. This approach requires many fewer cells than previous methods. For example to represent the interval $[1, \ldots, 1{,}000]$ by subintervals of length 1, we could use only 10 cells if we interpret them as a binary number, whereas the cutoff and point approximation methods would require 999 and 1,000 cells respectively.

Binary representations are highly sensitive to error in individual cells; all the bits are important. It is difficult to remove cells, but new cells can be added to binary fractions in order to increase precision.

The main disadvantage of binary representations is that they are not well suited as network output representations because of the interdependency of the cells. This interdependency makes the learning task much harder. Consider, for example, individual output cells representing the numbers 15 and 16.

$$15 \Leftrightarrow \langle -1 \ +1 \ +1 \ +1 \ +1 \rangle$$
$$16 \Leftrightarrow \langle +1 \ -1 \ -1 \ -1 \ -1 \rangle$$

These are two adjacent integers, but the 5 output cells have a difficult task keeping things straight. By comparison, each cell in a cutoff representation only needs to respond to whether the quantity being represented is greater or less than that cell's cutoff value. If the cells $\{u_j\}$ have integer cutoffs $\theta_j = j$ then only 1 cell would change its output when going from 15 to 16, rather than 5 cells changing when binary representations are used.

For this reason binary representations are not often employed with connectionist models.

2.4.2 Precision

Precision plays a somewhat subtle role when comparing cells with continuous activations and cells with discrete activations. For example in a backpropagation network, what does it really mean when an intermediate cell has activation of .8971342 rather than .8971344? Do we want this difference to affect the output of the network? Does the compiler implementation we are using differentiate between these two quantities in its storage representation?

The answers to these questions vary with the particular problem being modeled and the particular compiler being used. It is clear, however, that

| Training | Inputs | | | | Correct output |
example	u_1	u_2	u_3	u_4	u_5
#1	1.172	+1	+1	+1	+1
#2	1.171	+1	+1	+1	+1
#3	1.169	−1	−1	−1	−1
#4	1.168	−1	−1	−1	−1

Figure 2.12
Effects of precision.

too much precision can be harmful if it overfits training data so that the resulting network does not generalize to new, unseen inputs.

Consider for example the training examples in figure 2.12.

If we now present a new example with inputs

$$\langle 1.67 \ +1 \ +1 \ +1 \rangle$$

what would we like the response to be? Common sense says it should be +1, but if precision of u_1 is too high relative to $u_2 - u_4$ then it is possible that a network could respond −1 instead.

On the other hand if $u_2 - u_4$ have continuous activations in the range of $[-10^6, 10^6]$, we might want the network to respond −1 because the differences for $u_2 - u_4$ are insignificant compared to u_1. The moral is that precision can be important.

Using collections of discrete cells to approximate real numbers may be more cumbersome than using continuous activations, but the groups of discrete cells have one definite advantage: *they allow (and force!) the person who creates the model to explicitly specify the precision of the data.*

Unfortunately it is not clear how to choose the best precision in general. For some problems the use of fewer cells and decreased precision might make for a better fitting (and faster running) model. One possible approach would be to generate several models from training data using different precisions and then to select the best model on the basis of a second set of *tuning* data drawn from the same population.

The biggest drawback of using a collection of discrete cells to represent continuous values is that the number of weights in the network grows. If there is not enough training data, this may cause overfitting of the data and poor generalization to unseen data. The analyses in chapter 9 are relevant to this issue.

2.4.3   Approximating Real Numbers by Collections of Continuous Cells

Another way to represent real numbers is by using a collection of continuous cells to represent a "hump" centered at the desired value. Figure 2.13 illustrates the idea.

Using more than one continuous-valued cell makes learning easier than had we used only a single cell, because the dimensionality of the representation is increased. (See also section 8.2.)

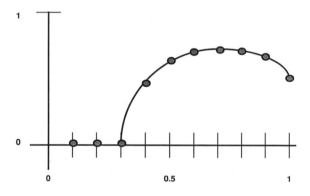

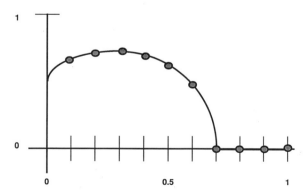

Figure 2.13
A hump representation of 0.7 and 0.31 using 9 continuous cells.

2.5   Example: *Taxtime!*

To illustrate several representations, consider the *Taxtime!* system for potential use by the IRS. The object of *Taxtime!* is to quickly scan income tax returns in order to find good candidates for IRS audits. The candidates selected by *Taxtime!* would then be screened by a human expert prior to a final audit decision. Because the IRS selects some returns for auditing at random, there is a readily available collection of good training examples.

A full *Taxtime!* system would look at hundreds of variables, but our illustrative prototype will examine only 3 inputs:

1. $\log_{10}$ *of total income*. It is natural to represent this variable as a real-valued input; it seems likely that the desirability of an audit would rise linearly with this index.

2. *Office in home*. This Boolean value is naturally represented by a discrete $\{+1, -1\}$ variable.

3. *Meals expenses as a percentage of total income*. Let us assume that there are only 4 interesting levels, which we can represent by a thermometer code:

Level			Code		
$0\% \leq$ expenses $\% \leq$		$.1\%$	-1	-1	-1
$.1\% <$	"	$\leq .5\%$	$+1$	-1	-1
$.5\% <$	"	$\leq 1.0\%$	$+1$	$+1$	-1
$1.0\% <$	"		$+1$	$+1$	$+1$

Finally suppose our collection of training examples has only 4 cases:

Name	Income	Office	Means			Audit candidate?
	u_1	u_2	u_3	u_4	u_5	u_6
Joyce Normal	4.2	-1	-1	-1	-1	NO (-1)
Ronald Dumpp	9.7	-1	-1	-1	-1	YES $(+1)$
Sally Sleaze	5.4	$+1$	$+1$	$+1$	$+1$	YES $(+1)$
Honest Hal	5.3	$+1$	$+1$	-1	-1	NO (-1)

In the next chapter we will see how to get weights $w_{6,0}, \ldots, w_{6.5}$, to fit this training data.

In this chapter we have seen some basic techniques for representing Boolean and real-valued numbers, Boolean functions and concepts using connectionist models. The most common way of representing sequences and signals is by a tapped delay line, which we will see in section 6.6.

Representation is an extremely important—yet frequently ignored—topic. In fact representation and learning appear to be the two most fundamental and important issues in neural network and AI research. It seems likely that a significant breakthrough in representation will be required for solving the really difficult AI problems.

2.6 Exercises

Assume that values of *unknown* are not allowed and assume $\{+1, -1, 0\}$ MLP models unless specified otherwise.

1. Give the formulas for transforming a $\{+1, -1, 0\}$ MLP model to a $\{1, 0\}$ MLP model corresponding to equation (2.1).

2. Consider a *modified* $\{1, 0\}$ *MLP* model where we change the activation computation as follows:

$$S_i = \sum_j w_{i,j}(2u_j - 1).$$

Given $\{w_{i,j}\}$ for such a modified $\{1, 0\}$ MLP, what would be equivalent $\{w'_{i,j}\}$ for the standard $\{+1, -1, 0\}$ MLP model?

3. Prove that no set of weights can satisfy the inequalities (2.2)–(2.5).

*4. Prove that no single-cell $\{+1, -1, 0\}$ model can represent the majority function on 2 inputs if we require correct behavior with respect to *unknown* inputs and outputs.

5. Show how to represent a majority function on p inputs (including behavior with *unknown* inputs) by an MLP with no more than $p + 1$ total intermediate and output cells (giving a total of $2p + 1$ cells).

6. Give single cell weights for the OR function defined on p inputs in both $\{+1, -1, 0\}$ and $\{1, 0\}$ models.

7. Give a multilayer perceptron that computes the following Boolean function:

$$F = \overline{B((\overline{C}A) \vee (\overline{D}CA))}$$

8. (a) Give a $\{+1, -1, 0\}$ MLP that computes the Boolean function

$G = (A\bar{B}CD \vee BD)\bar{E}F.$

(b) Give a $\{1,0\}$ MLP for the same function.

*9. Suppose that Boolean function $f(x_1, \ldots, x_p)$ can be represented by a single-cell model with weights $w_{p+1,0}, \ldots, w_{p+1,p}$. Define function

$f^*(x_1, \ldots, x_{p+1}) = f(x_1, \ldots, x_p) \; AND \; (NOT \; x_{p+1}).$

Give weights for a single-cell model that computes f^*.

10. List all nonseparable Boolean functions of 2 or fewer (Boolean) variables.

11. Show how to represent any Boolean function of p Boolean inputs with a flat network having at most 2^{p-1} cells in layer L_1.

*12. It has been suggested that error resistance is not really an issue in comparing local and distributed representations, because when using a local representation we can simply make copies of cells to improve behavior in the presence of noise. Suppose, then, we have 10 copies of each of 1000 $\{+1, -1\}$ cells and use these 10,000 cells to represent 1,000 concepts locally. Suppose 10 of the 10,000 cells give an incorrect reading. Estimate the probability that the resulting representation will be ambiguous or wrong, and compare it with the distributed case. Is some other comparison more appropriate?

13. For a feature space with p features that take on values $\{+1, -1\}$:

(a) How many distinct concepts are there?

(b) If instead we use the definition of a concept where a concept is a subset of features with value $+1$, how many concepts are there?

14. (research) How can semantic networks in conventional AI handle contextual ISA relations?

15. (a) Define a more realistic set of features for representing animals that uses at least 30 features.

(b) *(Foveation:)* The retina of the human eye allows increased detail in a small region called the *fovea* by simply increasing the density of receptors in that region. What is the feature space analogue of this? For example suppose in part (a) that the feature space representation was being used by a bear. Show how features could be added to give increased information for bear-specific problems, such as finding honey, finding sexually interesting bears, avoiding hunters, etc.

*16. Define a *separable concept* to be a concept that corresponds to a single-cell model. Suppose weight vectors W_1 and W_2 represent 2 separable concepts, $\mathscr{C}^1$ and $\mathscr{C}^2$, and that $\mathscr{C}^3$ is some other concept. Find necessary conditions on W_1, W_2 and $\mathscr{C}^3$ for the following relationship to hold:

$\mathscr{C}^1$ *ISA* $\mathscr{C}^2$ *in the context of* $\mathscr{C}^3$.

17. Prove that if R is a cutoff representation (not necessarily evenly spaced) and y is of the form

$$y = \langle \underbrace{+1, +1, \ldots, +1}_{i \text{ terms}}, \underbrace{-1, -1, -1, \ldots, -1}_{k - i \text{ terms}} \rangle \quad \text{for } 0 \le i \le k$$

then

$$R^{-1}(y) = \theta_i$$

where the approximate inverse is defined in section 2.4.1.

18. Is a cutoff approximation more of a distributed or a local representation? What about a point approximation?

19. Suppose you want to predict the yield of some crop raised in your area. Define useful temperature, rainfall, sunshine, and other factors and show how to represent them by input cells in an appropriate neural network model.

20. Define a set of cells to represent the temperature and rainfall using each of the following methods:

(a) (single) cells with continuous inputs

(b) cutoff approximations

(c) point approximations

(d) binary approximations

(e) hump approximations.

For each representation method show how 78 degrees and 0.3 inches of rainfall would appear.

21. *Fuzzy linguistic variables:* Show how to use a thermometer code to represent a fuzzy variable that can take on values of *very negative, slightly negative, intermediate, slightly positive,* or *very positive.*

22. For the *Taxtime!* system:

(a) Describe a reasonable thermometer code representation for income.

(b) Describe a reasonable hump representation for income.

2.7 Programming Projects

1. Extend the project from chapter 1 to allow backpropagation network computations. The user should see an initial menu that allows specification of the model, MLP or BPN.

There is a problem here because MLP's are most efficiently implemented using integer calculations, yet BPN's require manipulations of real variables. Possible solutions:

(a) *Store all values as real variables.* This slows down MLP calculations.

(b) *Keep separate copies of integer and real variables.* This uses up more storage and we must continually check which type of variable is currently in use.

(c) *Keep separate programs for real and integer calculations.* Here we must maintain two separate copies of essentially the same code.

(d) *Use conditional compilation facilities.* This is perhaps the best alternative, but it is not available for every language.

The first alternative is probably best if we are mainly interested in BPN's or in learning how the various methods work.

*2. Implement cutoff approximations to allow MLP's to work with real-valued functions. The intervals should be specified by an optional control line for every variable in the input file after the dimensions are given. For example:

$real(2) 4 0.2 0.4 0.6 0.8

specifies that u_2 is a real value represented by 4 cutoff cells with cutoff values 0.2, 0.4, 0.6, 0.8.

II LEARNING IN SINGLE-LAYER MODELS

3 Perceptron Learning and the Pocket Algorithm

At last we can begin our main topic for this book: machine learning in connectionist models. In this chapter[1] we will examine learning in single-cell networks. First we will study perceptron learning, the most important "early" learning algorithm, and then proceed to a recent extension of perceptron learning called the pocket algorithm that can handle non-separable problems.

Perceptron-based models are appealing because they are both fast and powerful in their ability to model data. Somewhat faster but less powerful algorithms will be presented at the beginning of chapter 5 and more powerful networks but slower algorithms will be the subjects of parts III and IV.

In this chapter we will only be looking at single-cell models. Therefore it is convenient to use an abbreviated notation. For a single-cell model with p inputs

$$W = \langle w_{p+1,0}, W_{p+1,1}, \ldots, w_{p+1,p} \rangle$$

we will sometimes represent individual weights and the weighted sum for a cell by the notation:

$$W_j = w_{p+1,j} \quad \text{and}$$

$$S = S_{p+1} \sum_{j-0}^{p} w_{p+1,j} u_j.$$

Also, if the context is clear, we will sometimes abbreviate a training example and its correct output by

$$E = E^k \quad \text{and}$$

$$C = C^k.$$

3.1 Perceptron Learning for Separable Sets of Training Examples

3.1.1 Statement of the Problem

Our goal is to compute network weights

$$W = \langle W_0, W_1, \ldots, W_p \rangle$$

1. Some of this research was performed while visiting the Knowledge Systems Lab, NTT Information Processing Labs, Yokosuka, Japan.

from a set of training examples. Recall that a supervised learning problem involves a set, **E**, of N training examples with corresponding correct responses

$$\mathbf{E} = \{\langle E^1, C^1 \rangle, \langle E^2, C^2 \rangle, \ldots, \langle E^N, C^N \rangle\}$$

where E^k is a p-vector of real numbers corresponding to the p inputs or features for a problem and C^k is the corresponding vector of correct responses. We will be especially interested in the special case where E_j^k is restricted to values in $\{+1, -1, 0\}$.

For our presentation of perceptron learning we will assume that only one (output) cell is involved, so that C^k is not a vector but a single number, either $+1$ or -1.

Note that by prohibiting C^k from assuming a value of 0 we are essentially throwing out any training example whose correct output is *unknown*. In fact we never attempt to train a cell to produce a 0 activation. This policy is due to the nature of the learning algorithms, but it seems quite reasonable for most supervised learning problems.

Figure 3.1 diagrams the situation for a single-cell problem in $\Re^2$ (i.e., $p = 2$). The hyperplane corresponding to W (here it is a line) is given by the equation

$$W \cdot x = W_0 + W_1 x_1 + W_2 x_2 = 0$$

and it separates the space into positive and negative points satisfying $W \cdot x > 0$ and $W \cdot x < 0$ respectively.

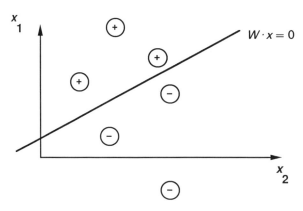

Figure 3.1
A separating hyperplane.

For the multicell (yet single-layer) models in chapter 4 we will seek a weight vector for each of the m trainable cells

$$\langle w_{i,0}, w_{i,1}, \ldots, w_{i,p} \rangle_{i=p+1,\ldots,p+m}.$$

3.1.2 Computing the Bias

Recall that the bias, W_0, is the constant term when computing

$$S = W_0 + \sum_{j=1}^{p} W_j u_j.$$

The perceptron learning algorithm assumes a bias of 0, but we can use an old trick to allow it to compute a nonzero bias. We simply add an additional 0th input with value $+1$ for every training example. After applying the perceptron learning algorithm, the weight $w_{p+1,0}$ will be the desired bias because a bias is exactly the same as a weight for an input that is always $+1$.

For example, consider a single-cell problem with 3 inputs where the training examples are

$$
\begin{array}{llll}
& u_1 \quad u_2 \quad u_3 & & u_4 \\
E^1 = \langle -1 \ -1 \ -1 \rangle & & C^1 = +1 \\
E^2 = \langle \ \ 1 \ -1 \ -1 \rangle & & C^2 = -1 \\
E^3 = \langle \ \ 1 \ \ \ 1 \ \ \ 1 \rangle & & C^3 = +1.
\end{array}
$$

Then before using perceptron learning we convert the problem by adding a column u_0 for the bias:

$$
\begin{array}{llll}
& u_0 \ u_1 \ u_2 \ u_3 & & u_4 \\
E^1 = \langle \ 1 \ -1 \ -1 \ -1 \rangle & & C^1 = +1 \\
E^2 = \langle \ 1 \ \ \ 1 \ -1 \ -1 \rangle & & C^2 = -1 \\
E^3 = \langle \ 1 \ \ \ 1 \ \ \ 1 \ \ \ 1 \rangle & & C^3 = +1.
\end{array}
$$

This transformation allows an algorithm such as perceptron learning to find an unrestricted separating hyperplane in p-space by computing in $(p + 1)$ space a separating hyperplane that passes through the origin.

By allowing a cell to have a nonzero bias we greatly increase the separating power of that cell. Figure 3.2 gives two examples of this in $\Re^2$. The nonbias weights for a cell form the normal vector that is perpendicular to

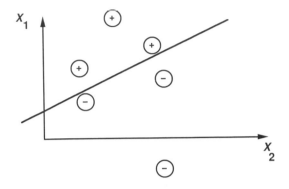

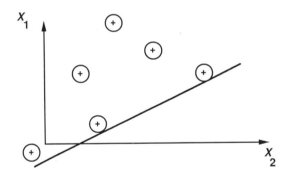

Figure 3.2
Two problems that are separable only if nonzero biases are allowed.

the corresponding separating hyperplane, and the bias gives the offset of that hyperplane from the origin. Restricting ourselves to a bias of zero is equivalent to only allowing separating hyperplanes that pass through the origin. This would have prevented the examples in figure 3.2 from being separable.

3.1.3   The Perceptron Learning Algorithm

The algorithm for perceptron learning is given in figure 3.3. We let W stand for the current vector of weights $\langle W_0, W_1, \ldots, W_p \rangle$ so that the corresponding weighted sum for example E^k is given by:

$$S = W \cdot E^k = \sum_{j=0}^{p} W_j E_j^k.$$

---

0. Set W to the 0 vector.

1. Select a training example E^k (with corresponding classification C^k). This may be done by cycling (in order) through the training examples, or by picking one at random.

2. If W correctly classifies E^k, i.e.,

   $\{W \cdot E^k > 0 \text{ and } C^k = +1\}$ or

   $\{W \cdot E^k < 0 \text{ and } C^k = -1\}$

   Then:
   2a. Do nothing

   Else:
   2A. CHANGE STEP: Modify W by adding or subtracting E^k according to whether the correct output C^k was $+1$ or -1:

   $W' = W + C^k E^k$.

3. Go to step 1.

Figure 3.3
The perceptron learning algorithm.

Each iteration might change the current weights, W, to new weights, W' (which become the current weights for the next iteration).

The change step (step 2A) merely adds or subtracts the example vector to the weight vector W according to whether the correct response, C^k, is $+1$ or -1. This will always improve W with respect to the particular training example that was misclassified, E^k, because

$$W' \cdot E^k = (W + C^k E^k) \cdot E^k$$

$$= W \cdot E^k + C^k (E^k \cdot E^k)$$

and $E^k \cdot E^k > 0$. In particular, if E^k consists of all ± 1 values, $W' \cdot E^k$ will improve by $p + 1$ units,[2] either positively or negatively as appropriate. Of course W' may be a *worse* set of weights for any other training example $E^i \neq E^k$. Therefore it is not immediately evident that perceptron learning should be a useful algorithm.

---

2. The bias raises the dimension to $p + 1$ from p.

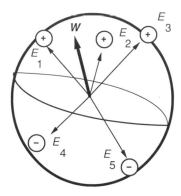

Figure 3.4
Geometrical interpretation of a single-cell learning problem.

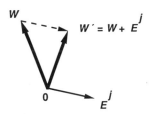

Figure 3.5
Geometrical interpretation of perceptron learning weight modification.

Geometrically we can picture what is going on as in figure 3.4. Each training example corresponds to a vector with "tail" at the origin and "head" at E^k. The set of weights is also a vector, with head at W. We seek a vector W that has *positive* projection (inner product) with all training examples labeled '+' and *negative* projection with all training examples labeled '−'.[3]

The change step in the algorithm amounts to vector addition (or subtraction) of a misclassified training example E^k to the current weights W, as illustrated in figure 3.5.

Let us now apply perceptron learning to the (modified) example given in section 3.1.2. For step 1 we will choose training examples at random

---

3. Equivalently, we seek a separating hyperplane that passes through the origin in $(p + 1)$ space. A normal to that hyperplane will be W. To get a separating hyperplane in p-space, we take $\langle w_1, \ldots, w_p \rangle$ as its norm and w_0 as its offset from the origin.

Iteration	Current W	Choice	OK?	Action
1.	$\langle 0 \quad 0 \quad 0 \quad 0 \rangle$	E^1	no	$W' = W + E^1$
2.	$\langle 1 \; -1 \; -1 \; -1 \rangle$	E^2	no	$W' = W - E^2$
3.	$\langle 0 \; -2 \quad 0 \quad 0 \rangle$	E^1	yes	no change
4.	$\langle 0 \; -2 \quad 0 \quad 0 \rangle$	E^3	no	$W' = W + E^3$
5.	$\langle 1 \; -1 \quad 1 \quad 1 \rangle$	E^1	no	$W' = W + E^1$
6.	$\langle 2 \; -2 \quad 0 \quad 0 \rangle$	E^3	no	$W' = W + E^3$
7.	$\langle 3 \; -1 \quad 1 \quad 1 \rangle$	E^1	yes	no change
8.	$\langle 3 \; -1 \quad 1 \quad 1 \rangle$	E^2	no	$W' = W - E^2$
9.	$\langle 2 \; -2 \quad 2 \quad 2 \rangle$	E^1	no	$W' = W + E^1$
10.	$\langle 3 \; -3 \quad 1 \quad 1 \rangle$			

Figure 3.6
Perceptron learning iterations.

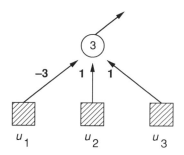

Figure 3.7
Final weights for the single-cell example.

rather than cycling through them in order, thereby producing the sequence of iterations given in figure 3.6.

The last set of coefficients works for all three training examples, so no more changes will take place. The corresponding network is pictured in figure 3.7, where $w_{p+1,0}$ has become the bias.

3.1.4 Perceptron Convergence Theorem

It is a remarkable fact that if any set of weights exists that correctly classify a finite set of training examples, then perceptron learning will come up with a (possibly different) set of weights that also correctly classifies all training examples after a finite number of change steps (2A) in the algorithm. Thus perceptron learning always succeeds in finite time for a finite, separable set of training examples.

We will prove this fact for training examples with components E_j^k that are arbitrary real numbers and then derive bounds for the special case where $E_j^k = \{+1, -1, 0\}$.

First notice that if the bias is required to be 0, then we can convert the problem of finding weights for a set of training examples having outputs of ± 1 to an equivalent problem where all correct outputs are $+1$; we merely replace each training example E_j^k having $C^k = -1$ by a revised training example $(-E^k)$ having $C^k = +1$. Geometrically in figure 3.4 we simply replace E^4 and E^5 by vectors pointing in the opposite directions labeled '+' rather than '−'.

This simplification gains very little in the actual computation of the perceptron learning algorithm, so we do not bother with it in practice. However, it does simplify the proof of the algorithm. Therefore we assume that every problem has been converted to one where all $C = +1$.

Our presentation of the perceptron convergence theorem is revised from Minsky and Papert [145]. Again recall that W stands for the current vector of weights $W = \langle W_0, W_1, \ldots, W_p \rangle$.

THEOREM 3.1 (Perceptron Convergence Theorem) *Let* **E** *be a (possibly infinite) set of training examples, each of which has length at most K. If there exists a set of weights, W^*, and a number $\delta > 0$ such that $W^* \cdot E^k \geq \delta$ for all $E^k \in$ **E** then the perceptron learning algorithm (figure 3.3) will execute the change step (2A) at most*

$$\left(\frac{K \|W^*\|}{\delta} \right)^2$$

times.

As an immediate corollary we have:

COROLLARY 3.2 *For a finite set of separable training examples, **E**, the perceptron learning algorithm will produce a set of weights, W, that satisfies $W \cdot E^k > 0$ for all $E^k \in$ **E** after a finite number of change steps.*

Proof of theorem: The idea of the proof is to show that the cosine of the angle θ between W and W^*,

$$\cos \theta = \frac{W^* \cdot W}{\|W^*\| \|W\|},$$

would become greater than 1 if too many change steps were executed, a contradiction.

Let us denote the set of weights achieved by the tth execution of the change step by W^t. Initially in the algorithm $W^0 = \langle 0, 0, \ldots, 0 \rangle$, but any other starting point would also work (with minor modifications).

After $t + 1$ weight modifications we have:

$W^* \cdot W^{t+1} = W^* \cdot (W^t + E^k)$ where example E^k caused the change step to be executed

$$= W^* \cdot W^t + W^* \cdot E^k$$

$$\geq W^* \cdot W^t + \delta.$$

Therefore

$$W^* \cdot W^t \geq t\delta. \tag{3.1}$$

Looking at the square of the length of W:

$\|W^{t+1}\|^2 = W^{t+1} \cdot W^{t+1}$

$= (W^t + E^k) \cdot (W^t + E^k)$ where example E^k caused the change step to be executed

$= W^t \cdot W^t + 2W^t \cdot E^k + E^k \cdot E^k$

$\leq \|W^t\|^2 + K^2$ because $W^t \cdot E^k \leq 0$ was what triggered the change step.

Therefore

$$\|W^t\|^2 \leq tK^2. \tag{3.2}$$

Putting it all together:

$t\delta \leq W^* \cdot W^t$ by equation (3.1)

$\leq \|W^*\| \|W^t\| \cos\theta$ where θ is the angle formed by the two vectors

$\leq \|W^*\| \|W^t\|$

$\leq \|W^*\| K\sqrt{t}$ by equation (3.2).

Hence

$$t \leq \left(\frac{K \| W^* \|}{\delta} \right)^2$$

as desired.   □

It is important to note that the perceptron convergence theorem depends upon the existence of some W^* that correctly classifies every training example; in other words the theorem only applies if E is a separable set of training examples.

Unfortunately, the bound given by the theorem is of little use in practice, because it requires us already to know a solution, W^*, in order to calculate $\| W^* \|$.

If we let $|E|$ denote the number of training examples in a finite set of training examples E, then we can state an important special case of perceptron learning:

COROLLARY 3.3   *Let E be a finite, separable set of training example, where each example has $p + 1$ inputs $E_j^k \in \{ +1, -1, 0 \}$. Then perceptron learning will produce a solution vector, W^*, having integral weights after executing at most*

$$(p + 1) \| W^* \|^2$$

change steps; moreover if examples are chosen consecutively in some fixed order, then at most

$$(p + 1) |E| \| W^* \|^2$$

iterations will produce such a solution.

Proof: Note that integer values for training examples allow us to take $\delta = 1$, and the fact that these values are restricted to $\{ +1, -1, 0 \}$ means $K^2 \leq p + 1$. Of course all weights produced from such training examples will have integer coefficients.   □

Thus for separable problems where solutions exist with bounded components ($|w_{p+1,j}| \leq C$), the algorithm will grow only polynomially with respect to the number of inputs p.

Looking back at the example in section 3.1.2, we see that $W^* = \langle 2, -2, 1, 1 \rangle$ is a solution (in addition to the one found in figure 3.6), so $\| W^* \|^2 = 10$. This gives a bound of $4(10) = 40$ change steps, when in fact 7 change steps were sufficient. Had we chosen examples in consecutive order, the iteration bound would have been $3(4)(10) = 120$ iterations.

3.1.5   The Perceptron Cycling Theorem

If the set of training examples is nonseparable, then for any set of weights, W, there will exist some training example, E^k, such that W misclassifies E^k. Therefore the perceptron learning algorithm will continue to make weight changes indefinitely.

This raises the question of what happens if we run perceptron learning on a nonseparable problem. Could the weights grow arbitrarily large? Surprisingly the answer is no, provided that the set of training examples is finite. The sets of weights that perceptron learning visits for any problem, separable or nonseparable, is bounded. More precisely:

THEOREM 3.4 (Perceptron Cycling Theorem)   *Given a finite set of training examples* **E**, *there exists a number M such that if we run the perceptron learning algorithm beginning with any initial set of weights, W^0, then any weight vector W^t produced in the course of the algorithm will satisfy*

$$\|W^t\| \leq \|W^0\| + M.$$

This theorem was first proposed independently by Nils Nilsson and Terry Beyer. The first reported proof by Efron [50] appears only in a technical report and is difficult to read. Minsky and Papert [145] published a proof that contained a gap that was later corrected by Block and Levin [22]. Their proof is somewhat lengthy and will not be included here.

For intuitive purposes figure 3.8 is useful for seeing why the perceptron cycling theorem holds. If the current weight vector is W^t, then a training

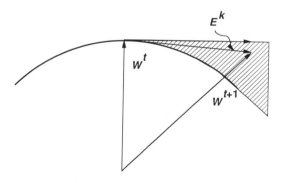

Figure 3.8
Geometric motivation for the perceptron cycling theorem.

example E^k that is incorrectly classified by W^t yet satisfies

$$\|W^{t+1}\| = \|W^t + E^k\| > \|W^t\|$$

must lie in the shaded region. Yet for large $\|W^t\|$ the circle approaches the tangent, so that it becomes hard for any E^k to satisfy this condition.

The following corollary is important:

COROLLARY 3.5   *If a finite set of training examples has integer (or rational) components E_j^k, then the perceptron learning algorithm will visit a finite collection of distinct weight vectors W^t.*   □

Unfortunately there is no known good bound on the number of weight vectors that the perceptron learning algorithm can visit.

Another important corollary gives a test for nonseparability:

COROLLARY 3.6   *For a finite set of training examples, **E**, with integer (or rational) components E_j^k, the perceptron learning algorithm will, in finite time, either*

*1. Produce a weight vector that satisfies all training examples (if and only if **E** is separable), or*

*2. Leave and revisit a weight vector (if and only if **E** is nonseparable).*

This test for separability, like most other such tests, has no known bound for how long it will take to reach a conclusion. (There is also the problem of storing previously visited weights, but this can be solved by hash coding techniques.) The only known polynomially bounded algorithm for separability testing is to first express the problem as a linear programming problem and then to use a polynomial linear programming algorithm.

See Duda and Hart [47] for other techniques for generating weights, including the Ho-Koshyap algorithm for determining separability.

3.2   The Pocket Algorithm for Nonseparable Sets of Training Examples

3.2.1   Problem Statement

If a set of training examples **E** is nonseparable, then by definition there does not exist a vector of weights, W, that correctly classifies all training examples in **E**. The most natural alternative is to find a vector of weights,

W^*, that classifies *as many training examples as possible* from **E**. We call such a set of weights *optimal*.

For example if we are solving the XOR problem defined in figure 2.5, then a set of optimal weights are:

$$\text{bias} = +1 \tag{3.3}$$

$$w_1 = +1 \tag{3.4}$$

$$w_2 = +1. \tag{3.5}$$

These weights correctly classify 3 of the 4 training examples, the best that is possible.

Finding optimal weights is a very difficult problem; about the best we can do is the pocket algorithm, which yields optimal weights with arbitrarily high probability, if the algorithm is run long enough. Unfortunately, in practice too many iterations are required for us to be certain of optimal weights. Therefore, the algorithm generates weights that are usually good but suboptimal.

As an alternative to finding optimal weights, we could try to solve a closely related problem that is easier computationally. In chapter 6 we will see such an approach involving minimizing the squared error.

3.2.2   Perceptron Learning Is Poorly Behaved

If we run perceptron learning on a nonseparable set of training examples, we quickly see that the algorithm can behave poorly. For example, if we are solving the XOR problem and the current weights are the optimal weights given in equations (3.3)–(3.5), then eventually the algorithm will select the single training example that is misclassified. After the weight change step the new weights will be:

bias $= 0$

$w_1 = 0$

$w_2 = 0.$

These weights misclassify *all* training examples! Thus the perceptron learning algorithm has gone from the best possible weights to the worst possible weights in one iteration. This is what we mean by calling perceptron learning *poorly behaved*: if we terminate the algorithm, even after a large number of iterations, we have no guarantee as to the quality of the weights that are produced.

3.2.3   The Pocket Algorithm

Evidently the problem with perceptron learning is that it only utilizes negative reinforcement, totally ignoring examples that are correctly classified. What is lacking is a way to add positive reinforcement to the algorithm so that good sets of weight vectors are rewarded.

The pocket algorithm takes correct classifications into account by keeping a separate set of weights, W^{pocket}, "in your pocket" along with the number of consecutive iterations for which W^{pocket} correctly classified the chosen training example. Now whenever the current perceptron weights, W, have a longer run of correct classifications, we replace the pocket weights W^{pocket} by W. Figure 3.9 gives the algorithm.

---

0. Set W to the 0 vector.
1. Select a training example, E^k, *at random* (with corresponding classification C^k).
2. If W correctly classifies E^k, i.e.,

   $\{W \cdot E^k > 0 \text{ and } C^k = +1\}$ or

   $\{W \cdot E^k < 0 \text{ and } C^k = -1\}$

   Then:
2a. If the current run of correct classifications with W is longer than the run of correct classifications for the weight vector W^{pocket} in the pocket:

   2aa. Replace the pocket weights W^{pocket} by W, and remember the length of its correct run.

   Else:
2A. CHANGE STEP: Modify W by adding or subtracting E^k according to whether the correct output C^k was $+1$ or -1:

   $W' = W + C^k E^k$.

3. Go to step 1.

Figure 3.9
The basic pocket algorithm.

For example, returning to the XOR problem, a typical sequence of iterations for training examples

$$E^1 = \langle +1 \ -1 \ -1 \rangle \qquad C^1 = -1$$

$$E^2 = \langle +1 \ -1 \ +1 \rangle \qquad C^2 = +1$$

$$E^3 = \langle +1 \ +1 \ -1 \rangle \qquad C^3 = +1$$

$$E^4 = \langle +1 \ +1 \ +1 \rangle \qquad C^4 = -1$$

is given in figure 3.10.

At iteration 9 we have reached the initial perceptron weights, $\langle 0 \ 0 \ 0 \rangle$. These misclassify every training example, whereas the pocket weights, $\langle 1 \ -1 \ -1 \rangle$, get 3 out of 4 correct. As we continue with iterations, changes to the pocket weights will become less and less frequent. The time between such changes increases exponentially with respect to $\text{Run}_{W^{pocket}}$. Most of these changes will replace one set of optimal weights by another; for example $\langle 1 \ 1 \ 1 \rangle$ is another set of optimal weights. From time to time, however, nonoptimal weights will appear in the pocket, but the following *pocket convergence theorem* states that this will happen less and less frequently as the number of iterations increases.

THEOREM 3.7 (Pocket Convergence Theorem) *Given a finite set of training examples, $\mathbf{E}$, and a probability $P < 1$, then there exists an N such that after any $n > N$ iterations of the pocket algorithm, the probability that the pocket coefficients, W^{pocket}, are optimal exceeds P.*

The proof is deferred until section 3.2.9.

Unfortunately the pocket convergence theorem gives no bound on the number of iterations required to guarantee optimal weights with probability at least P. This leads to some bad news and some good news.

The bad news is that for medium or large-size problems the pocket algorithm usually will not produce *optimal* weights after a reasonable number of iterations. In fact for nonseparable problems there is no known way of finding optimal weights except for procedures that grow exponentially with respect to the number of inputs.

The good news is that the pocket algorithm does produce *good* weights. For example this author [65] compared the algorithm with a standard statistical package (SPSS [180]) implementation of Wilks's method on 15 sets of training examples that included both natural and artificial data. (All

Iteration	W	Run_W	W^{pocket}	$\text{Run}_{W^{pocket}}$	Choice	OK?	Action
1	$\langle\, 0\ \ 0\ \ 0\ \ 0\, \rangle$	0	$\langle\, 0\ \ 0\ \ 0\ \ 0\, \rangle$	0	E^4	no	$W' = W - E^4$ $\text{Run}_W = 0$
2	$\langle\, -1\ -1\ -1\ -1\, \rangle$	0	$\langle\, 0\ \ 0\ \ 0\ \ 0\, \rangle$	0	E^4	yes	$\text{Run}_W = \text{Run}_W + 1$ $W^{pocket} = W$ $\text{Run}_{W^{pocket}} = \text{Run}_W$
3	$\langle\, -1\ -1\ -1\ -1\, \rangle$	1	$\langle\, -1\ -1\ -1\ -1\, \rangle$	1	E^2	no	$W' = W + E^2$ $\text{Run}_W = 0$
4	$\langle\, 0\ -2\ \ \ 0\, \rangle$	0	$\langle\, -1\ -1\ -1\ -1\, \rangle$	1	E^3	no	$W' = W + E^3$ $\text{Run}_W = 0$
5	$\langle\, 1\ -1\ \ -1\, \rangle$	0	$\langle\, -1\ -1\ -1\, \rangle$	1	E^4	yes	$\text{Run}_W = \text{Run}_W + 1$
6	$\langle\, 1\ -1\ \ -1\, \rangle$	1	$\langle\, -1\ -1\ -1\, \rangle$	1	E^2	yes	$\text{Run}_W = \text{Run}_W + 1$ $W^{pocket} = W$ $\text{Run}_{W^{pocket}} = \text{Run}_W$
7	$\langle\, 1\ -1\ \ -1\, \rangle$	2	$\langle\, 1\ -1\ \ -1\, \rangle$	2	E^3	yes	$\text{Run}_W = \text{Run}_W + 1$ $\text{Run}_{W^{pocket}} = \text{Run}_W$
8	$\langle\, 1\ -1\ \ -1\, \rangle$	3	$\langle\, 1\ -1\ \ -1\, \rangle$	3	E^1	no	$W' = W - E^1$ $\text{Run}_W = 0$
9	$\langle\, 0\ \ 0\ \ 0\, \rangle$	0	$\langle\, 1\ -1\ \ -1\, \rangle$	3	$\ldots$		

Figure 3.10
Pocket algorithm iterations.

of the data had Boolean inputs.) The pocket algorithm classified more training examples correctly for every set. The differences varied considerably according to the data, but the overall average reduction in misclassifications was about 20 percent. Note that generalization comparisons on unseen data were not performed here; only the ability of the algorithms to fit data to linear discriminant models was tested in these experiments. However, whenever two models are selected from the same family of models (with the same complexity) then the one that fits the training examples better should generalize better.[4] For some generalization tests see section 3.2.5.

3.2.4 Ratchets

When running the pocket algorithm there is nothing to prevent a bad set of weights from having a "lucky run" of correct responses and then replacing a good set of weights currently in the pocket. Even worse, if the lucky run is a long one then the bad weights can hang around in the pocket for a large number of iterations. We know that the probability of this happening becomes arbitrarily low as the number of iterations increases, but in practice it is common for such temporary retrogressive steps to occur.

Fortunately there is a simple way of guaranteeing that pocket weights strictly improve as changes are made, provided that the set of training examples is finite. Whenever a set of weights, W, is about to enter the pocket we can check to see whether W actually classifies more training examples than the current set, W^{pocket}. If not, we do not allow W into the pocket. (Thus the quality of the pocket weights *ratchets* up and never decreases.) Of course if there are many training examples then such a ratchet check is expensive, but as the run length of correct classifications for the pocket weights increases, the time between such checks goes up exponentially. This makes ratchets a big winner in practice, so for finite sets of training examples the ratchet version of the pocket algorithm should always be used.

Figure 3.11 gives the revised pocket algorithm with ratchet.

3.2.5 Examples

To give some idea of generalization differences, three recent experiments were run with results summarized in figure 3.12. The first used weather

---

4. With two models of differing complexity this need not hold, since the more complex model may overfit the data and generalize worse than the simpler model.

0. Set W to the 0 vector.
1. Select a training example, E^k, *at random* (with corresponding classification C^k).
2. If W correctly classifies E^k, i.e.,

   $\{W \cdot E^k > 0 \text{ and } C^k = +1\}$ or

   $\{W \cdot E^k < 0 \text{ and } C^k = -1\}$

   Then:
   2a. If the current run of correct classifications with W is longer than the run of correct classifications for the weight vector W^{pocket} in the pocket:

      2aa. If W correctly classifies more training examples than W^{pocket}:

         2aaa. Replace the pocket weights W^{pocket} by W, and remember the length of its correct run.

   Else:
   2A. CHANGE STEP: Modify W by adding or subtracting E^k according to whether the correct output C^k was $+1$ or -1:

   $W' = W + C^k E^k$.

3. Go to step 1.

Figure 3.11
Pocket algorithm with ratchet for a finite set of training examples.

	Perceptron learning		Pocket with ratchet	
	Train %	Test %	Train %	Test %
Weather data	71.3	67.0	80.9	76.6
	(11.0)	(10.0)	(0.5)	(1.8)
Financial data	54.4	51.3	62.5	63.6
	(3.6)	(7.5)	(1.0)	(1.6)
Parity-5 data	43.0	—	65.8	—
	(5.9)	—	(6.5)	—

Figure 3.12
Comparison of perceptron learning and pocket algorithm with ratchet. Averages and standard deviations (in parentheses) are computed over 10 trials each.

data of Ōsaka to predict if Tokyo would receive rain the next day.[5] The second set consisted of (proprietary) financial data.[6] The final test was parity-5, training only, using all 32 examples.[7]

Note in figure 3.12 the higher classification rates on both training and testing data for the pocket algorithm with ratchet as compared with perceptron learning. The standard deviations suggest greater stability for the former algorithm. To give some idea of speed, 30,000 iterations of the parity-5 problem consume about 30 seconds on a Sun 4.

3.2.6   Noisy and Contradictory Sets of Training Examples

We call a set of training examples *noisy* if a probabilistic process is involved in their generation. Noisy training examples are sometimes *contradictory*, meaning that there are training examples E^r and E^q where

$$E^r = E^s \quad \text{but} \quad C^r \neq C^s.$$

A nice feature of the pocket algorithm in this respect is that it converges to a set of weights that correctly classifies a randomly chosen training example with maximum likelihood. Therefore contradictory training examples are handled in a natural way. For example if C^r rather than C^s is the correct response for a greater number of the $E^r (= E^s)$ training examples, then the weight vector produced by the algorithm will produce C^r as its output when presented with input E^r, unless this causes too many other training examples to be misclassified. Therefore the pocket algorithm is a reasonable candidate to try on arbitrarily noisy and contradictory data.

If a simulated model of the noise is available, then figure 3.13 shows how to use the noise model to generate a single-cell network. Here noise-free training examples are corrupted by noise and then presented to the pocket algorithm along with correct classifications. Note that the classifications

5. Every three consecutive days for a year were randomly divided into two days for training and one for testing, giving 247 total training examples and 127 total test examples. Each example had 8 real-valued inputs, each of which were normalized and rounded to integers in the range $[-100, +100]$. The output was Boolean. 50,000 iterations were performed for each algorithm using 10 different random seeds (to change the order of selection of training examples). Data courtesy of R. Nakano and K. Saito of Knowledge Systems Lab, NTT Information Processing Labs, Yokosuka, Japan.
6. There were 1,564 training examples and 814 test examples, each with 29 Boolean inputs. Again 50,000 iterations were performed for each algorithm using 10 different random seeds.
7. 30,000 iterations were performed for each algorithm. Optimal performance in 69 percent, which the pocket algorithm with ratchet achieved on 8 of 10 trials.

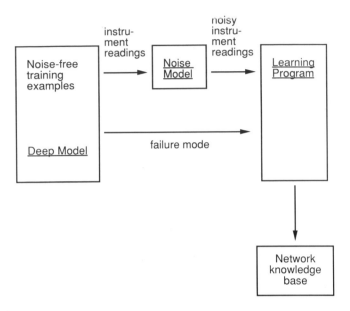

Figure 3.13
Using a noise model with the pocket algorithm.

are assumed to be noise-free.[8] No modification of the pocket algorithm is required, because it produces weights that correctly classify (nearly) as many training examples as possible, just what is needed here. For an example of generating weights for a noisy problem, see chapter 16.

3.2.7 Rules

Another important modification allows rules to be specified in addition to the training examples. Here we define a *rule* as an example E^r with corresponding classification C^r that *must* be satisfied by the resulting weights W. Normal training examples, on the other hand, need not be satisfied by W if they are noisy, contradictory, or no W exists that can simultaneously satisfy all training examples (i.e., nonseparable training examples). Thus we now seek W that:

1. Satisfies all rules.

8. This restriction can be relaxed, provided that noise corrupts less than 50 percent of the classifications and is uncorrelated with the noise that affects input values.

2. Satisfies as many training examples as possible without violating condition 1.

One way of meeting these conditions is simply to duplicate rules several times. This would mean that any set of weights that incorrectly classified a rule would make so many errors that it would be dominated by any other set of weights that classified all rules correctly.

Another way to handle rules is to modify the basic algorithm in figure 3.9 by changing step 2A to:

2A. CHANGE STEP: Modify W by adding or subtracting E^k according to whether the correct output C^k was $+1$ or -1:

$$W' = W + C^k E^k \tag{3.6}$$

2B. While W violates any rule E^r (with classification C^r), repeat step 2A using E^r and C^r.

Rules will be useful when we examine connectionist expert systems, because they give a way of guaranteeing the behavior of the network for especially important situations.

*3.2.8 Implementation Considerations

It is fairly straightforward to implement perceptron learning or the pocket algorithm with ratchet, but several points are worth noting.

At runtime with either algorithm we must decide when to stop iterating. A good practical solution is to let the user specify a number of iterations, say 10,000. After every 1/10 of these iterations are completed, the program should check the current pocket weights against the entire set of training examples and print the percentage that are correct. (Of course if there is an extremely large set of training examples then this will not be practical.) If the program finds that all training examples are correctly classified then the problem is separable, a solution has been found, and further iterations should be skipped. Thus for separable problems nothing would be lost by specifying 10 times as many iterations as actually required.

It is helpful for the program to print some character (e.g., '.') whenever the coefficients in the pocket are changed, and some other character (e.g., 'X') when a ratchet check prevents substitution of pocket weights. Now if the user calls for 10,000 iterations and some successful changes to the pocket occur after iteration 5,000, then it would probably be a good idea to do an additional 20,000 iterations to find a better solution. (The problem may even be separable.) Note that the pocket algorithm is relatively fast, so that 10,000 iterations should take well under one minute on a microcomputer. Otherwise the consequence proof fails to hold. On the other hand if the training examples are separable, perceptron learning can be speeded up by presenting often misclassified training examples more frequently.[9]

Please keep in mind that it is important for the pocket algorithm that training examples be chosen randomly (with replacement) rather than consecutively in order.

In practice it is not worth the trouble to verify conclusively that a set of training examples is nonseparable. It is easier simply to run iterations until it seems clear that further changes to the pocket weights are unlikely.

As a final point, when a ratchet check prevents a set of weights from entering the pocket, the easiest way to proceed is merely to reset the run length for these particular weights to some negative number (say $-1,000$) and continue iterating. Eventually a training example will be selected that causes a new set of weights to be computed by the change step (2A) in the algorithm.

*3.2.9 Proof of the Pocket Convergence Theorem

Restating the theorem more formally:

THEOREM 3.8   *Given a finite set of input vectors* $\{E^k\}$ *and corresponding desired responses* $\{C^k\}$ *and a probability* $p < 1$, *there exists an N such that after* $n \geq N$ *iterations of the Pocket Algorithm, the probability that the pocket coefficients are optimal exceeds p.*

The proof is in several steps:
I.   *Only a finite number of sets of coefficients can be reached using perceptron learning.* This is a restatement of the perceptron cycling theorem.
II.   *From any such set of coefficients there is a nonzero probability that perceptron learning will visit an optimal set of coefficients* (perhaps after several steps).

Let π be the current set of coefficients. Choose any optimal set of coefficients and the subset, K, of training examples for which it produces correct responses. By the perceptron convergence theorem, if inputs from

9. Richard Dixon, personal communication.

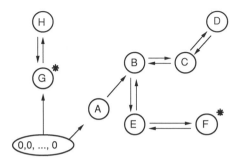

Figure 3.14
Learning coefficients visited in perceptron learning.

K are repeatedly chosen, in finite time perceptron learning will go from π to π' where π' are coefficients that give desired responses for all inputs in K. Therefore π' must be an optimal set of coefficients for all of $\{E^k\}$.

Since there is a nonzero probability that this exact sequence of vectors in K may be chosen when vectors from E are chosen randomly, an optimal solution can be reached from π with nonzero probability.

III. *As the number of iterations grows, perceptron learning will visit optimal sets of coefficients a nonzero fraction of the time.*

This follows directly from I and II. Figure 3.14 illustrating coefficient sets may be useful, where arrows indicate possible successor sets of coefficients from change steps of the pocket algorithm and where * indicates optimal sets.

Notice that the optimal sets (E, F, and G) may be visited less often than other sets (for example B).

IV. *Let set v be a nonoptimal set of coefficients that gives correct results for randomly selected inputs with probability P_v and let Ω be an optimal set of coefficients giving correct results with probability P_Ω ($> P_v$), and suppose v is visited M times for every time Ω is visited, where M is fixed and may be greater than 1. Then as the number of iterations n grows, the probability that*

{the longest run of consecutive correct responses with Ω is greater than the longest run with v}

approaches 1.

Proof: The probability that the longest run for v is $< k$ for N trials is easily seen to be:

$$(1 - P_v^k)^N \tag{1}$$

and similarly for Ω.

It suffices to show that given $0 < \sigma < 1$, there is an N and k satisfying:

1. $\text{Prob}\{\text{longest run for } v \text{ is } < k \text{ for } (MN) \text{ trials}\} > \sigma$

2. $\text{Prob}\{\text{longest run for } \Omega \text{ is } \geq k \text{ for } N \text{ trials}\} > \sigma.$

Let N be fixed. Condition 1 is satisfied for

$$k \geq \frac{\log(1 - \sqrt[MN]{\sigma})}{\log P_v} \tag{2}$$

For condition 2 we want

$$1 - (1 - P_\Omega^k)^N > \sigma \quad \text{or}$$

$$k < \frac{\log(1 - \sqrt[N]{(1 - \sigma)})}{\log P_\Omega} \quad \text{since } \log P_\Omega < 0. \tag{3}$$

Thus we must show that for large enough N,

$$\frac{\log(1 - \sqrt[MN]{\sigma})}{\log(1 - \sqrt[N]{(1 - \sigma)})} < \frac{\log P_v}{\log P_\Omega}. \tag{4}$$

Since $0 < P_v < P_\Omega < 1$ (because Ω is optimal),

$$\log P_v < \log P_\Omega < 0, \quad \text{so } 1 < \frac{\log P_v}{\log P_\Omega}.$$

Thus letting $C_1 = \sqrt[M]{\sigma}$ and $C_2 = (1 - \sigma)$, it suffices to show that:

$$\lim_{N \to \infty} \frac{\log(1 - \sqrt[N]{C_1})}{\log(1 - \sqrt[N]{C_2})} = 1.$$

This follows by two applications of l'Hôpital's rule.

V.   *I, III, and IV imply the Theorem.* If the problem is separable, the pocket algorithm will produce an optimal set of coefficients by the perceptron convergence theorem. Otherwise, perceptron learning will go from coefficient set to coefficient set, but eventually one of the repeatedly visited optimal sets will have a longer run of correct responses than any other particular nonoptimal set with arbitrarily high probability. Since there are only a finite number of nonoptimal sets of coefficients, as the number of iterations grows an optimal set will, with probability 1, have the longest run of correct responses.   □

It is important to note that for even medium-sized problems we are not likely to compute an *optimal* set of coefficients after any reasonable number of iterations. Thus the convergence to optimality is in theory only, and production of optimal weights is not to be depended upon for actual problems. Nevertheless experience has shown that the weights are very likely to be *good* weights that approach an optimal number of correct classifications. This makes the algorithm a good one for practical problems.

*3.3   Khachiyan's Linear Programming Algorithm

An important breakthrough in optimization theory was the discovery of linear programming algorithms that grow only polynomially with the precision of their inputs (Hačijan [83]; Aspvall and Stone [10]; Karmarkar [113]). We can use these algorithms to learn weights for separable sets of training examples, while guaranteeing a polynomial bound on learning time. (Computation for the perceptron learning algorithm can grow exponentially with respect to the input dimension × the number of training examples; see exercise 15.) Moreover, these algorithms give us a way of determining separability in polynomial time, and they tell us in advance the maximum number of iterations that might be required.

Unfortunately if the training examples are nonseparable then Khachiyan's algorithm will tell us only this fact; it will not provide us with any weights. This limits the usefulness of this approach for practical problems.

Recently A. J. Mansfield [135, 136] studied Khachiyan's algorithm for single-cell learning. In his simulations he found Khachiyan's algorithm had better *average* learning time than perceptron learning, as well as better *worst* case learning time for separable problems. For the special case where training example activations are in $\{+1, -1\}$, he also noted an improved upper bound on the maximum number of iterations.

Figure 3.15 gives Mansfield's presentation of Khachiyan's algorithm for single-cell learning with cell activations in $\{+1, -1\}$. The algorithm first sets W to the 0 vector and H to the $(p + 1) \times (p + 1)$ identity matrix, and then repeatedly seeks out a misclassified training example to adjust W and H. Recall that if Q is a vector, then $Q \otimes Q$ denotes the outer-product matrix of Q with itself given by $(Q \otimes Q)_{i,j} = Q_i Q_j$.

---

1. Set W to the 0 vector.

2. Set H to the $(p + 1) \times (p + 1)$ identity matrix.

3. Perform at most $(p + 1)^3 \ln(p + 1) + (p + 1)^2 \ln(\pi(p + 1))$ iterations:

   3a. If all training examples are correctly classified, i.e., every training example E^k having correct output C^k satisfies

   $$W \cdot E^k > 0 \text{ and } C^k = +1 \text{ or}$$

   $$W \cdot E^k < 0 \text{ and } C^k = -1,$$

   then training examples are separable; output W and quit. Otherwise let E^k be a training example that is not correctly classified.

   3b. Set vector $Q = HE^k$.

   3c. Set

   $$W = W + \frac{C^k}{(p + 2)\sqrt{Q \cdot E^k}} Q$$

   $$H = \frac{(p + 1)^2}{p(p + 2)} \left(H - \frac{2}{(p + 2)Q \cdot E^k} Q \otimes Q \right).$$

4. If no solution has been found, than the training examples are non-separable.

Figure 3.15
Khachiyan's algorithm for $\{+1, -1\}$ inputs.

Mansfield also showed how to modify a single-cell model so that it dynamically implements Khachiyan's algorithm.

3.4 Exercises

1. *Taxtime!:* Use hand simulation of perceptron learning to generate weights for the Taxtime! exercise of section 2.5.

2. If some weight vector W^* correctly classifies all training examples, show that there are an infinite number of weight vectors that also do this.

3. Use perceptron learning to find a cell (with 4 weights) that satisfies:

$$E^1 = \langle -1 \quad -1 \quad 1 \rangle \qquad C^1 = +1$$

$$E^2 = \langle -1 \quad 1 \quad -1 \rangle \qquad C^2 = -1$$

$$E^3 = \langle \quad 1 \quad -1 \quad +1 \rangle \qquad C^3 = -1$$

4. (a) What is the minimum number of training examples with p real-valued weights plus bias that can be nonseparable? (Assuming no 3 points lie on a line, no 4 points can line on a plane, etc.)

(b) What is the minimum number of training examples with p weights and bias of 0 that can be nonseparable? (Assuming no 3 points lie on a plane, etc.)

*(c) Prove your answer to either (a) or (b).

5. If perceptron learning is applied to the plurality function on p inputs and the 2^p inputs are chosen cyclically,

(a) Give a bound on the number of change steps that can be executed.

(b) Give a bound on the total number of iterations that can be executed before a solution is reached.

*6. If W^* is a solution vector (with integer components) for a separable problem with p inputs and perceptron learning finds solution $W \neq W^*$ (starting from $W^0 = \langle 0, 0, \ldots, 0 \rangle$), show that

$$\|W\| \leq (p + 1)\|W^*\|.$$

*7. (sloppy learning) Suppose we modify the perceptron learning algorithm as follows. Let $\{E^k\}$ and $\{C^k\}$ be a separable, finite set of training examples and corresponding classifications (where $C^k = \pm 1$). Now at iteration t if E^k is incorrectly classified, instead of adding $C^k E^k$ to current perceptron weights, suppose we add $\alpha(t) C^k E^k$ where $\alpha(t)$ is a positive number that may differ at different iterations (e.g., $\alpha(1) = .5$, $\alpha(2) = 27$, $\alpha(3) = 1.2, \ldots$). Here we might think of different learning rates at different times of day or of a sloppy learning algorithm.

For each of the following cases please determine whether a modified perceptron convergence theorem must hold so that we are still guaranteed that a perfect set of weights will be produced after only a finite number of mistakes. If perceptron convergence must hold, then please give reasons (outline a proof) why it is so. Otherwise give a counterexample ($\{E^k\}$, $\{C^k\}$, and $\{\alpha(t)\}$) where perceptron learning need not find a perfect set of weights after finite changes.

The cases are:

(a) $0 < A \le \alpha(t)$ where A is any fixed lower bound

(b) $0 < \alpha(t) \le B$ where B is any fixed upper bound

(c) $0 < A \le \alpha(t) \le B$ where A and B are bounds as above.

8. Suppose we modify perceptron learning so that the change step adds (or subtracts) *twice* the example chosen. Will the algorithm still find a solution for any separable problem making only a finite number of changes? If no, give a counterexample; if yes, give a proof and a bound on the number of change steps if inputs are restricted to $\{+1, -1\}$.

9. Suppose in the pocket algorithm, the current weights and run lengths are:

```
Perceptron Weights:   3 -5 -2  1;    Length of run:  4

Pocket Weights:        -6  2  3 -4;    Length of run:  4
```

Show what happens to weights and run lengths when the following two examples are the next ones selected (in order):

```
1  1 -1 -1    Correct output: -1

1 -1 -1  1    Correct output: -1
```

10. Suppose 20 iterations of the pocket algorithm have already been run, producing weights as indicated in the table below. For the next two iterations please give the correct ? entries in the following table where

$E^1 = \langle 1 \ -1 \quad 1 \ 1 \rangle, \quad C^1 = 1$ and

$E^2 = \langle 1 \quad 1 \ -1 \ 1 \rangle, \quad C^2 = -1.$

Iteration	π		run_π	W		run_W	Choice	OK?	Action
:	:		:	:		:			
21.	$\langle 1 \ -2 \ -1 \ 3 \rangle$		3	$\langle 2 \ 3 \ -2 \ 1 \rangle$		3	E^1	?	?
22.	$\langle$	?	$\rangle$?	$\langle$	?	$\rangle$?	E^2	?	?
23.	$\langle$	?	$\rangle$?	$\langle$	?	$\rangle$?	...		

11. (*learning AND functions with irrelevant features*) Consider the class of functions with p $\{+1, -1\}$ inputs of which r inputs are relevant. The function is computed as the AND function of the relevant inputs and the $p - r$ irrelevant inputs are ignored.

(a) Derive a bound on the maximum number of mistakes that perceptron learning can make before it learns this function.[10]

(b) Derive a bound on the maximum number of iterations that perceptron learning can make before learning the function.

*12. Describe a separable, infinite, unbounded set of real-valued training examples where perceptron learning need not produce a solution after any finite number of change steps.

13. How can the conclusions of the perceptron cycling theorem fail to hold for an infinite set of real-value training examples?

14. Suppose a finite set of training examples has solution

$$W^* = \langle w_{p+1,0}, w_{p+1,1}, \ldots, w_{p+1,p} \rangle$$

where each weight is an integer that satisfies $|w_{p+i,j}| \leq c$ for some integer constant c. If we run the perceptron learning algorithm starting from $W^0 = \langle 0, 0, \ldots, 0 \rangle$ show that the algorithm will make at most $(p+1)^2 c^2$ mistakes.

15. Consider the family of *AND-OR* functions:

$$A_1 = u_1 \ (u_i \in \{+1, -1\})$$

$$A_2 = u_1 \ AND \ u_2$$

$$A_3 = u_1 \ OR \ (u_2 \ AND \ u_3)$$

$$A_4 = u_1 \ AND \ (u_2 \ OR \ (u_3 \ AND \ u_4))$$

$$A_5 = u_1 \ OR \ (u_2 \ AND \ (u_3 \ OR \ (u_4 \ AND \ u_5)))$$

$$\ldots$$

(a) Show A_k is separable for all k.

*(b) Let W^k be any set of *integer* weights that correctly classifies A_k. Prove that the size of the largest component of W^k grows *exponentially* in k. In particular, show

$$W_0^k + W_1^k \geq f_k - 1$$

where f_k is the kth Fibonacci number $(1, 1, 2, 3, 5, 8, 13, \ldots)$. Hint: consider

---

10. For an algorithm with an improved bound for $r \ll p$, see Littlestone [131].

the family of training examples having k members exemplified by the following set for $k = 6$:

$$E^1 = \langle +1 \quad +1 \quad -1 \quad -1 \quad -1 \quad -1 \rangle, \qquad C^1 = +1$$

$$E^2 = \langle +1 \quad -1 \quad -1 \quad +1 \quad +1 \quad +1 \rangle, \qquad C^2 = -1$$

$$E^3 = \langle +1 \quad -1 \quad +1 \quad +1 \quad -1 \quad -1 \rangle, \qquad C^3 = +1$$

$$E^4 = \langle +1 \quad -1 \quad +1 \quad -1 \quad -1 \quad +1 \rangle, \qquad C^4 = -1$$

$$E^5 = \langle +1 \quad -1 \quad +1 \quad -1 \quad +1 \quad +1 \rangle, \qquad C^5 = +1$$

$$E^6 = \langle +1 \quad -1 \quad +1 \quad -1 \quad +1 \quad -1 \rangle, \qquad C^6 = -1.$$

*(c) Prove that for any $k \geq 2$ there exists a set of $k + 1$ separable training examples, each having k inputs in $\{+1, -1\}$, for which any set of integer weights, W^k, that correctly classifies these training examples *must* satisfy

$$\max_{j} W_j^k \geq 2^{\lceil k/2 \rceil - 1}.$$

(d) Prove that the number of change steps for perceptron learning can grow exponentially in ($p \times \langle \text{number of training examples} \rangle$).

16. (research) Can Khachiyan's algorithm be modified to handle separable and nonseparable training examples, perhaps by some sort of pocket technique?

3.5 Programming Projects

1. Implement perceptron learning. Assume an input format as follows:

• First line: number of input cells, p.

• Following lines: p input values followed by the correct output (± 1). Make the output compatible as input for your neural network simulator developed in previous chapters.

2. Use perceptron learning to find a cell (with 5 weights) that computes "*2 or more of 4 inputs true*" from the 16 training examples that define this function.

3. Modify your perceptron learning program to implement the pocket algorithm with ratchet using the above format.

4. Test either of the above programs on the following *addition* problem where the output is true whenever the sum is ≥ 8. There are 64 training examples.

6 {6 inputs}

-1	-1	-1	-1	-1	-1	-1	$\{0 + 0 = 0 < 8\}$
-1	-1	$+1$	-1	-1	-1	-1	$\{1 + 0 = 1 < 8\}$
$\vdots$			$\vdots$			$\vdots$	$\vdots$
-1	$+1$	$+1$	$+1$	-1	$+1$	$+1$	$\{3 + 5 = 8 \geq 8\}$
$\vdots$			$\vdots$			$\vdots$	$\vdots$
$+1$	$+1$	$+1$	$+1$	$+1$	$+1$	$+1$	$\{7 + 7 = 14 \geq 8\}.$

5. Test the pocket algorithm on parity-5 (32 training examples). How many of these training examples can be correctly computed by a single-cell model?

6. Run the pocket algorithm with ratchet to try to learn the *selector* function. For this function there are 6 $\{+1, -1\}$ inputs. The first two inputs are treated as a binary number that determines which of the remaining 4 inputs is taken as the desired input. For example,

select						output	remark
u_1	u_2	u_3	u_4	u_5	u_6		
-1	-1	$+1$	-1	$+1$	-1	$+1$	-1 -1 copies the first input, u_3.
$+1$	$+1$	$+1$	-1	$+1$	-1	-1	$+1$ $+1$ copies the last input, u_6.

What is the optimal single-cell performance?

7. Run perceptron learning for members from the class of functions described in exercise 11 and compare the actual number of mistakes and iterations with the theoretical maximum. Try $r = 2, 4, 8$ and $p = 5, 8, 10, 14$ (for $r \leq p$).

8. (research) Frean [58] has reported good results by modifying perceptron learning so that the weight change varies in size. Suppose there are

I total iterations. Then for iterations $i = 0, 1, 2, \ldots, I - 1$ we multiply the normal weight change by

$$\frac{I - i}{I} e^{-|S_i|/(I-i)}.$$

S_i is the weighted sum, and the basic idea is to penalize errors with large $|S_i|$ because they are difficult to correct without causing other errors.

Implement Frean's algorithm and run comparisons with the pocket algorithm with ratchet on noisy data.

4 Winner-Take-All Groups or Linear Machines

In this chapter we will examine *winner-take-all groups*, which are also called *linear machines*. Winner-take-all groups generalize single-cell models and are particularly useful for pattern recognition problems where inputs must be placed in one of several classes. After defining the winner-take-all group model we will extend perceptron learning and the pocket algorithm to generate weights for these networks.

Figure 4.1 illustrates the idea of a *winner-take-all group*. Such a group of intermediate or output cells is constrained so that for each set of inputs to these cells, exactly one cell from the group "fires" (i.e., has activation $+1$) and all other cells do not "fire" (i.e. have activations of -1). Having exactly one output cell fire makes winner-take-all groups ideal for pattern recognition problems; we simply identify each cell in the group with one of the possible pattern classes, and we interpret the single cell that fires for a set of inputs as the class recognized by the network. In the same way, winner-take-all groups are well suited to fault detection problems that assume no more than one fault is present at any one time.

To implement a winner-take-all group we compute the weighted sum for each cell in the group and define the cell that fires to be the the cell with the highest weighted sum:

$$S_i = \sum_{j \geq 0} w_{i,j} u_j$$

$$u_i = \begin{cases} +1 & \text{if } S_i > S_k \quad \text{for all } k \neq i \\ -1 & \text{if } S_i < S_k \quad \text{for some } k \neq i \\ 0 & \text{otherwise.} \end{cases}$$

For example in figure 4.1 when the inputs are $\langle +1, +1 \rangle$ then the outputs are $\langle -1, +1, -1 \rangle$, i.e., u_4 "fires."

In this formulation if two or more cells are tied for highest weighted sum, then all of the tied cells have activations of 0 (or *unknown*).[1] Note that a network can contain several winner-take-all groups, and that winner-take-all groups can mix intermediate and output cells.

Winner-take-all groups were called *linear machines* by Nilsson [149] because each cell computes its weighted sum S_i linearly with respect to its

---

1. We can also choose the cell with the lowest index among those with minimum S_i. This is appropriate in situations where any answer is better than no answer at all.

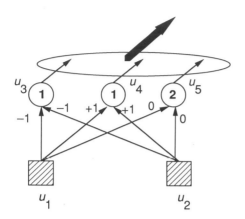

Figure 4.1
A winner-take-all group of cells.

inputs. The nonlinearities come in when the selection is made as to which cell fires.

Another name for winner-take-all groups is *choice groups*. This name emphasizes that exactly one out of a group of cells will be selected.

4.1 Generalizes Single-Cell Models

What is the relationship between winner-take-all groups and single-cell models? Given a single-cell model it is easy to construct an equivalent winner-take-all group; we merely add a second cell with every weight and bias equal to 0. Figure 4.2 illustrates this construction. It is clear that cell u_3' fires in the winner-take-all group whenever u_3 evaluates to false, u_4' fires whenever u_3 evaluates to true, and both u_3' and u_4' are unknown whenever u_3 is unknown. Therefore the winner-take-all group model is at least as powerful as the single-cell model in terms of representation.

For winner-take-all groups *with exactly 2 cells* we do not gain any representational power over single-cell models. This is because we can always transform a 2-cell winner-take-all group to a single-cell model by subtracting the weights of one of the cells from the other, as illustrated in figure 4.3. Therefore *2-cell winner-take-all groups and single-cell models are able to represent the same set of separable Boolean functions.*

Winner-take-all groups with 3 or more cells are able to represent functions that are not representable by an identical network of single cells. For

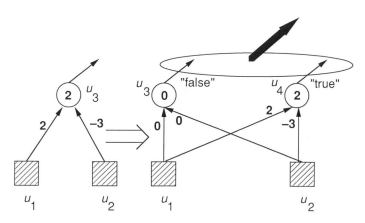

Figure 4.2
A single-cell model represented by a winner-take-all group.

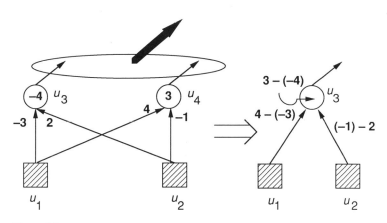

Figure 4.3
A 2-cell winner-take-all group represented by a single-cell model.

example cell u_5 in figure 4.1 computes an XOR function of its inputs, a nonseparable function. Moreover exercise 2 shows that we can construct a winner-take-all group in which one of its cells computes *any* specified Boolean function.

The next two sections show that perceptron learning and the pocket algorithm both have natural extensions to winner-take-all groups.

4.2   Perceptron Learning for Winner-Take-All Groups

To apply perceptron-learning to winner-take-all groups, we must modify the change step in figure 3.3 as follows. Suppose the current set of weights for the winner-take-all group misclassifies a training example E^k, putting it in class i when it belongs in class l (or the weighted sums are equal, $S_i = S_l$). Then we add the example E^k to the weights for u_l and subtract the example from the weights for u_i:

$$w_{l,j} = w_{l,j} + E_j^k$$

$$w_{i,j} = w_{i,j} - E_j^k.$$

Note that this adds 1 to the bias for u_l and subtracts 1 from the bias for u_i because E_0^k is always $+1$.

Such a change in weights clearly increases the weighted sum S_l and decreases S_i for example E^k, making E^k more likely to be correctly classified.

This brings up a subtle point: we might consider subtracting E^k not only from the weights for u_i but from *all* cells u_t satisfying $S_t \geq S_i$. This is a reasonable-sounding speedup, but unfortunately *it invalidates the algorithm!* Please avoid this pitfall.

Using the correct weight modification procedure, we can generalize the perceptron convergence theorem to winner-take-all groups (exercise 4).

4.3   The Pocket Algorithm for Winner-Take-All Groups

To extend the pocket algorithm to winner-take-all groups, we run perceptron learning for winner-take-all groups and keep a separate set of pocket weights for all cells in the group. We also keep a single run length for the entire group of cell weights in the pocket.

Now whenever the perceptron weights have a longer run of correct responses than the run length for the pocket weights, we replace *all* of the

INPUT: Training Examples $\{E^k, C^k\}$. E^k is a vector with $E_0^k \equiv 1$ and other components, $E_1^k, \ldots, E_p^k$, taking values in $\{+1, -1, 0\}$. C^k is an output vector with c entries, $C_{p+1}^k, \ldots, C_{p+c}^k$, one of which is $+1$ and the other $c - 1$ entries taking value -1.

OUTPUT: c cells, $\{W_{p+1}, W_{p+2}, \ldots, W_{p+c}\}$, where $W_i = \langle w_{i,0}, w_{i,1}, \ldots, w_{i,p} \rangle$ is a vector of integral "pocket" weights and $w_{i,0}$ is the bias.

TEMPORARY DATA:

$\pi = c$ vectors of integral perceptron weights, $\pi_{p+1}, \pi_{p+2}, \ldots, \pi_{p+c}$, where each vector $\pi_i = \langle \pi_{i,0}, \pi_{i,1}, \ldots, \pi_{i,p} \rangle$.

run_π = number of consecutive correct classifications using perceptron weights π.

run_W = number of consecutive correct classifications using pocket weights W.

num_ok_π = total number of training examples that π correctly classifies.

num_ok_W = total number of training examples that W correctly classifies.

Figure 4.4
Data for the pocket algorithm with ratchet for linear machines.

weights in the pocket by the current weights for winner-take-all group cells and update the pocket run length.

We can also implement a ratchet for the pocket algorithm applied to winner-take-all groups in the same way as we did for single-cell learning; we merely test a prospective set of weights against all training examples before bringing them into the pocket. Figure 4.4 gives the data and figure 4.5 summarizes the algorithm.

*4.4   Kessler's Construction, Perceptron Cycling, and the Pocket Algorithm Proof

In this section we examine a construction due to Kessler [47] that allows us to extend several theorems from single-cell models to winner-take-all groups. The basic idea is to show that a winner-take-all group problem is equivalent to an expanded single-cell problem.

1. Set $\pi_i = \langle 0, 0, \ldots, 0 \rangle$ for $i = p + 1, \ldots, p + c$;

   $\text{run}_\pi = \text{run}_W = \text{num\_ok}_\pi = \text{num\_ok}_W = 0$.

2. Randomly pick a training example E^k (with corresponding classification C^k).

3. If π correctly classifies E^k, i.e., if the correct class is i and

   $$\{\pi_i \cdot E^k > \pi_j \cdot E^k \text{ for } i \neq j\}$$

   Then:

   3a. $\text{run}_\pi = \text{run}_\pi + 1$.

   3b. If $\text{run}_\pi > \text{run}_W$

       Then:

       3ba. Compute num_ok_π by checking every training example.

       3bb. RATCHET: If $\text{num\_ok}_\pi > \text{num\_ok}_W$

           Then:

           3bba. Set $W = \pi$. Note that all c of the vectors are replaced at once.

           3bbb. Set $\text{run}_W = \text{run}_\pi$.

           3bbc. Set $\text{num\_ok}_W = \text{num\_ok}_\pi$.

           3bbd. If all training examples are correctly classified (i.e., $\text{num\_ok}_W = |\{E^k\}|$) then stop; the training examples are separable.

   Otherwise:

   3A. CHANGE STEP: Form a new vector of perceptron weights. Select one cell $j \neq i$ that satisfies $\pi_i \cdot E^k \leq \pi_j \cdot E^k$ and modify the weights of cells i and j as follows:

   $$\pi_i = \pi_i + E^k$$

   $$\pi_j = \pi_j - E^k.$$

   3B. Set $\text{run}_W = 0$.

4. End of this iteration. If the specified number of iterations has not been taken then go to step 2.

Figure 4.5
The pocket algorithm with ratchet for linear machines.

Consider a problem with 3 input cells (u_1, u_2, and u_3) and 3 output cells (u_a, u_b, and u_c) where the outputs form a winner-take-all group. As in the proof of perceptron learning, we will assume all 3 output cells have bias of 0. We will construct an equivalent single-cell problem consisting of 9 inputs ($u_1 - u_9$) and one output (u_{10}) where the 9 weights for the single-cell problem can be used for the original winner-take-all group.

We first construct modified training examples for the new single-cell problem. Suppose the desired classification for training example $E = \langle E_1, E_2, E_3 \rangle$ is cell u_b. Then for the modified single-cell problem we will have 2 training examples:

$$E' = \langle -E_1, \ -E_2, \ -E_3, \ E_1, \ E_2, \ E_3, \quad 0, \quad 0, \quad 0 \rangle, \quad C^1 = +1$$

$$E'' = \langle \quad 0, \quad 0, \quad 0, \ E_1, \ E_2, \ E_3, \ -E_1, \ -E_2, \ -E_3 \rangle, \quad C^2 = +1$$

E', the first single-cell training example, will be satisfied if and only if

$$\langle w_{10,4} \ \ w_{10,5} \ \ w_{10,6} \rangle \cdot E > \langle w_{10,1} \ \ w_{10,2} \ \ w_{10,3} \rangle \cdot E \tag{4.1}$$

and E'' if and only if

$$\langle w_{10,4} \ \ w_{10,5} \ \ w_{10,6} \rangle \cdot E > \langle w_{10,7} \ \ w_{10,8} \ \ w_{10,9} \rangle \cdot E. \tag{4.2}$$

In general if there are c output cells, then every training example for the original winner-take-all group becomes $c - 1$ training examples for the modified single-cell problem. The weights for the single-cell problem, $\langle w_{10,1}, \ldots, w_{10,9} \rangle$, can be converted to weights for the 3 output cells in the original winner-take-all group problem as follows:

$w_{a,1} = w_{10,1}$

$w_{a,2} = w_{10,2}$

$w_{a,3} = w_{10,3}$

$w_{b,1} = w_{10,4}$

$w_{b,2} = w_{10,5}$

$w_{b,3} = w_{10,6}$

$w_{c,1} = w_{10,7}$

$w_{c,2} = w_{10,8}$

$w_{c,3} = w_{10,9}.$

This condition then says that if training example E is presented to the winner-take-all group then cell u_b will be the one to fire.

Equation (4.1) and equation (4.2) imply that weights exist for the new single-cell problem that correctly classify E' and E'' if and only if weights exist for the original winner-take-all group problem that correctly classify E. We can continue this construction for all of the training examples in the original winner-take-all group problem. Thus we have succeeded in our goal of converting a winner-take-all group problem to an expanded single-cell problem.

A detailed look at winner-take-all group versions of perceptron learning and the pocket algorithm show something stronger, namely that when these learning algorithms are applied to winner-take-all groups, they are isomorphic to the single-cell versions of the algorithms. Therefore it follows that the perceptron convergence theorem, the perceptron cycling theorem, and the pocket convergence theorem all extend to winner-take-all groups.

Kessler's construction has been a big help from a theoretical point of view, but does it also give a practical way to solve winner-take-all group problems by first converting them to single-cell problems? Unfortunately the answer appears to be no. We end up with the same number of weights in the two models, but the number of training examples for Kessler's construction is multiplied by $c - 1$. This introduces redundant computations into the learning algorithms.

4.5 Independent Training

A technique worth remembering is to treat a winner-take-all group problem as a standard learning problem with c *independent* output cells. We then train the outputs *independently*, and treat the collection as a winner-take-all group using the same weights.

Independent training is useful when there is a limited supply of training examples, because it gives a way of overtraining in order to help generalization. If a problem is independently separable, then in the corresponding winner-take-all group the correct cell will not only have a higher weighted sum than any other cell, it will have *the only positive weighted sum*.

We can now interpret the independently trained cells as a winner-take-all group. This will guarantee that exactly one output cell will fire, whereas the independent cells might have some other number of cells firing.

4.6 Exercises

1. (a) Show that adding an identical constant to the biases of every cell in a winner-take-all group does not change the functionality of the group.

(b) Show that multiplying every weight of every cell in a winner-take-all group by a positive constant does not change the functionality of the group.

2. Show that a winner-take-all group can be constructed so that one of its cells computes any given Boolean function.

3. Let cell i be one of the output cells in a winner-take-all group with c output cells. Show how to construct an equivalent winner-take-all group where cell i has every weight and bias equal to 0.

*4. State and explicitly prove an extension of the perceptron convergence theorem (theorem 3.1) for winner-take-all groups by adapting the proof of that theorem.

*5. For the previous exercise, derive a bound on the number of change steps when all inputs are $\{+1, -1\}$.

4.7 Programming Projects

1. Extend your neural network shell to handle the case where all output cells form a winner-take-all group. Indicate this by the presence of a '$W' control field on the first input line.

2. Extend your implementation of the pocket algorithm with ratchet to a single-layer winner-take-all group. Make the output format compatible with your neural network simulator input.

*3. Pattern recognition: On a 5 × 5 grid of Boolean values, first define images of the digits from 0 to 9 as patterns in these 25 pixels.

(a) Train a winner-take-all group with 10 output cells to recognize the patterns.

(b) Repeat with independent training of the output cells.

(c) Create 1,000 noisy versions of the patterns (100 for each pattern) by picking one of the basic digit patterns and inverting each bit with probability 0.15. Does the winner-take-all group from (a) or (b) give better performance on the noisy pattern?

(d) Now train on the 1,000 noisy patterns using both winner-take-all group and independent learning with the pocket algorithm. Compare generalization of the two models using a second set of 1,000 noisy patterns.

5 Autoassociators and One-Shot Learning

Autoassociators differ from the recurrent models we mentioned in chapter 1 by having different dynamics. Figure 5.1 gives the basic idea. Some or all of the cells are initialized at the beginning of the computation, then at each step all of the cells recompute their activations before simultaneously posting their new activations for the next step. Computation continues until the system reaches either a steady state or a limit cycle. (In practice computation is halted after a prespecified number of iteration steps.)

Autoassociators are trained to *reproduce their inputs* for some set of N training examples, $\{E^1, \ldots, E^N\}$. In other words if nodes are initialized to training example E^k, then we desire that after several (or one) iterations the outputs of the network cells will again be E^k. In this sense the network has *stored* the set of training examples.

What makes autoassociators especially interesting is their behavior if they are initialized to inputs that differ slightly from a stored training example E^k. The network tends to reproduce E^k. Thus the stored training examples can be viewed as memories and the autoassociator as a *content-addressable memory* that can recover a full memory from a partial or noisy version of a memory.

Some important early work using autoassociators was done by T. Kohonen [117]. Figure 5.2 shows a famous experiment where stored pictures of faces were able to be recovered using only a small fraction of the stored image. (Note, however, that the image was represented by a position-dependent collection of bits, so that a small shift of the image would cause severe degradation.)

Historically most of the learning algorithms used for autoassociators have been one-shot learning algorithms. Therefore it is natural in this chapter to examine some of the principal autoassociative models together with one-shot learning algorithms.

5.1 Linear Autoassociators and the Outer-Product Training Rule

The simplest autoassociators are *linear autoassociators*, characterized by continuous models whose cells are strictly linear:

$$u_i = S_i = \sum_j w_{i,j} u_j.$$

In this model we sometimes allow cells to be connected to themselves so

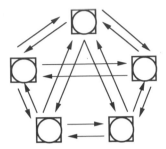

Figure 5.1
Autoassociator memory: cells serve as both input and output cells.

Figure 5.2
Recovery of a full memory from a partial memory using an autoassociator (Kohonen [117]).

that $w_{i,i}$ may be nonzero. However, we must require that each training example, E^k, have approximately unit length,

$$\|E^k\| \approx 1,$$

and that the inner product of any two different training examples be close to 0,

$$E^k \cdot E^l \approx 0 \quad \text{for } k \neq l.$$

Because these models are continuous, we seek outputs that are *close* to inputs after one iteration rather than requiring an exact match.

We train the network by summing the outer products of each training example with itself to produce a matrix of connection weights, W:

$$W = E^1 \otimes E^1 + E^2 \otimes E^2 + \cdots \quad \text{or}$$

$$w_{i,j} = \sum_k E_i^k E_j^k.$$

See figure 5.3 for an example using this one-shot learning algorithm.

The proof that this training algorithm works involves a bit of algebra. If a training example, E^l, is presented to the trained network, then cell u_i will assume activation

$$u_i = S_i = \sum_j w_{i,j} E_j^l \tag{5.1}$$

$$= \sum_j \sum_k E_i^k E_j^k E_j^l \tag{5.2}$$

$$= \sum_{k \neq l} \sum_j E_i^k E_j^k E_j^l + \sum_j E_i^l E_j^l E_j^l \tag{5.3}$$

$$= \sum_{k \neq l} E_i^k \left(\sum_j E_j^k E_j^l \right) + E_i^l \left(\sum_j E_j^l E_j^l \right). \tag{5.4}$$

The first parenthesized sum, $\sum_j E_j^k E_j^l$, is approximately 0 by our assumption on the inner product of different training examples, so that the entire left term is close to 0. The second parenthesized term, $\sum_j E_j^l E_j^l$, is just $\|E^l\|^2 \approx 1$ because we assume all training examples have length 1. Therefore

$$u_i \approx 0 + E_i^l = E_i^l$$

Training examples:

$$E^1 = \langle .42 \quad .80 \quad -.42 \rangle$$

$$E^2 = \langle .58 \quad -.58 \quad -.58 \rangle$$

$$\|E^1\| \approx \|E^2\| \approx 1$$

$$|E^1 \cdot E^2| \approx .02 \approx 0$$

Weight matrix:

$$W = E^1 \otimes E^1 + E^2 \otimes E^2$$

$$= \begin{bmatrix} .18 & .34 & -.18 \\ .34 & .64 & -.34 \\ -.18 & -.34 & .18 \end{bmatrix} + \begin{bmatrix} .34 & -.34 & -.34 \\ -.34 & .34 & .34 \\ -.34 & .34 & .34 \end{bmatrix}$$

$$= \begin{bmatrix} .52 & 0 & -.52 \\ 0 & .98 & 0 \\ -.52 & 0 & .52 \end{bmatrix}$$

Correct behavior of W:

$$W \cdot E^1 = \langle .44 \quad .78 \quad -.44 \rangle \approx E^1$$

$$W \cdot E^2 = \langle .60 \quad -.57 \quad -.60 \rangle \approx E^2$$

Figure 5.3
A simple linear autoassociator.

and the ith cell reproduces its corresponding input for training example E^l, as desired.

Several comments are in order here. First the orthogonality condition

$$\sum_j E_j^k E_j^l \approx 0 \quad \text{for } k \neq l$$

is almost always necessary for the training examples to be learned. While a few randomly selected training examples could be expected to satisfy this condition, as the number of training examples increases the error tends to grow. Moreover if we have p cells we can have at most p mutually orthogonal vectors, so this serves as an approximate upper bound on the number of training examples that can be stored with perfect recall using this learning algorithm.

Second, notice that the weight matrix is symmetric:

$$w_{i,j} = \sum_k E_i^k E_j^k = w_{j,i}.$$

Third, the outer-product learning rule is close to Hebb's learning algorithm. Weight (connection) $w_{i,j}$ increases (strengthens) whenever a training example E^k has both E_i^k and E_j^k in agreement by sign, but decreases (weakens) whenever E_i^k and E_j^k have different signs. Thus this learning law is "biologically plausible."

Finally, when we allow self-connections in this model it would be easy to store *any* set of training examples by taking W to be the identity matrix. Unfortunately this would also eliminate the ability of recovering patterns close to a training example; every input would be copied exactly as output. Therefore taking W as the identity matrix is of little interest.

5.2   Anderson's BSB Model

James A. Anderson did early work on autoassociators, developing the *Brain State in a Box* (BSB) model [7, 9]. BSB is interesting as a psychological model, and it is a cross between continuous and discrete models. Activations are continuous in the interval $[-1, +1]$, but the system repeatedly iterates until all units eventually saturate out at either $+1$ or -1. The "Box" is the p-cube, $[-1, +1]^p$, of possible activations for the collection of p cells.

We compute activations as follows. Letting $u_i(t)$ be the value of cell i at iteration t, then the value of $u_i(t+1)$ is given by:

$$S_i = u_i + \sum_j w_{i,j} u_j(t) \tag{5.5}$$

$$u_i(t+1) = \begin{cases} +1 & \text{if} & S_i > +1 \\ S_i & \text{if } -1 \le & S_i \le 1 \\ -1 & \text{if} & S_i < -1. \end{cases} \tag{5.6}$$

The $u_i(t)$ term in equation (5.5) is what drives the system to saturation.

Anderson performed numerous experiments on the ability of BSB models to complete partly specified patterns. Programming project 1 illustrates this type of behavior.

5.3   Hopfield's Model

John Hopfield popularized another autoassociative model that was important in reviving interest in connectionist models. His model is purely
discrete with inputs and activations of $\{+1, -1\}$. (Hopfield actually used
activations of $\{1, 0\}$, but it is easier to use an equivalent model with
$\{+1, -1\}$ activations until we get to the traveling salesman problem.)
Learning is again by the outer-product algorithm, but self-connections are
not allowed (i.e., $w_{i,i} = 0$ for all i). Activations are computed using linear
discriminants:

$$S_i(t) = \sum_j w_{i,j} u_j(t) \tag{5.7}$$

$$u_i(t) = \begin{cases} +1 & \text{if } S_i \geq 0 \\ -1 & \text{if } S_i < 0. \end{cases} \tag{5.8}$$

Dynamic behavior is slightly changed from linear autoassociators; cells
are chosen at random according to a fixed distribution where each cell has
nonzero probability of being selected next. When chosen, a cell recomputes
its activation using the above formulas. An analysis similar to equations
(5.1)–(5.4) shows that the learning rule works for this model (see exercise 6).
The storage capacity for randomly generated vectors is about .15 times the
number of inputs.

Figure 5.4 gives an example to illustrate the Hopfield model.

5.3.1   Energy

Hopfield used the notion of energy to show that his networks always
converge to a steady state.

Define the energy after t changes in activation to be

$$\mathscr{E}(t) = -\sum_{i<j} u_i(t) u_j(t) w_{i,j}. \tag{5.9}$$

Thus for the example in figure 5.4, the training example $E = \langle 1\ 1\ 1\ -1\ -1 \rangle$ would have energy

$$\mathscr{E} = -(w_{1,2} + w_{1,3} - w_{1,4} - w_{1,5} + w_{2,3} - w_{2,4} - w_{2,5} - w_{3,4} - w_{3,5}$$

$$+ w_{4,5})$$

$$= -(-1 + 1 - 1 - 1 + 1 + 3 + 3 + 1 + 1 + 3)$$

$$= -10.$$

Training examples (column vectors):

$E^1 = \langle \ \ 1 \ -1 \ -1 \ \ \ 1 \ \ \ 1 \rangle$

$E^2 = \langle \ \ 1 \ \ \ 1 \ \ \ 1 \ -1 \ -1 \rangle$

$E^3 = \langle -1 \ \ \ 1 \ -1 \ -1 \ -1 \rangle$

$E^1 \cdot E^2 = -3$

$E^1 \cdot E^3 = -3$

$E^2 \cdot E^3 = \ \ \ 1$

$\|E^k\|^2 = p = 5$ for all training examples

Weight matrix:

$$
W = \begin{bmatrix} 0 & -1 & -1 & 1 & 1 \\ -1 & 0 & 1 & -1 & -1 \\ -1 & 1 & 0 & -1 & -1 \\ 1 & -1 & -1 & 0 & 1 \\ 1 & -1 & -1 & 1 & 0 \end{bmatrix} + \begin{bmatrix} 0 & 1 & 1 & -1 & -1 \\ 1 & 0 & 1 & -1 & -1 \\ 1 & 1 & 0 & -1 & -1 \\ -1 & -1 & -1 & 0 & 1 \\ -1 & -1 & -1 & 1 & 0 \end{bmatrix}
$$

$$
+ \begin{bmatrix} 0 & -1 & 1 & 1 & 1 \\ -1 & 0 & -1 & -1 & -1 \\ 1 & -1 & 0 & 1 & 1 \\ 1 & -1 & 1 & 0 & 1 \\ 1 & -1 & 1 & 1 & 0 \end{bmatrix}
$$

$$
= \begin{bmatrix} 0 & -1 & 1 & 1 & 1 \\ -1 & 0 & 1 & -3 & -3 \\ 1 & 1 & 0 & -1 & -1 \\ 1 & -3 & -1 & 0 & 3 \\ 1 & -3 & -1 & 3 & 0 \end{bmatrix}
$$

Therefore

$$
W \cdot E^1 = \begin{bmatrix} 2 \\ -8 \\ -2 \\ 8 \\ 8 \end{bmatrix} \text{ yielding activations } \begin{bmatrix} 1 \\ -1 \\ -1 \\ 1 \\ 1 \end{bmatrix} = E^1
$$

and similarly for training examples E^2 and E^3. (Not every example is stored perfectly.)

Figure 5.4
An example of the Hopfield model.

Note that the energy does not depend upon cell numbering because $w_{i,j} = w_{j,i}$. Now if cell k is chosen to reevaluate its activation, it will keep the same value (and leave energy unchanged) unless:

1. $u_k(t) = -1$ and $S_k(t) \geq 0$. Then $u_k(t + 1)$ becomes $+1$.

2. $u_k(t) = +1$ and $S_k(t) < 0$. Then $u_k(t + 1)$ becomes -1.

In either case the energy changes by

$$\Delta \mathscr{E} = \mathscr{E}(t + 1) - \mathscr{E}(t) \tag{5.10}$$

$$= -(u_k(t + 1) - u_k(t)) \sum_{j \neq k} u_j(t) w_{k,j} \tag{5.11}$$

$$= -2u_k(t + 1)S_k(t) \tag{5.12}$$

$$\leq 0. \tag{5.13}$$

Notice that we needed the facts that weights are symmetrical, ($w_{i,j} = w_{j,i}$), and that $w_{k,k} = 0$ in equation (5.11) above, plus the fact that $u_j(t + 1) = u_j(t)$ for $j \neq k$. Thus energy in a Hopfield model can never increase, and whenever a cell changes activation to -1 the energy strictly decreases. Since there are only finitely many states a discrete system can assume, this suffices to prove that a Hopfield system must reach steady state rather than cycling.

Hopfield's use of the notion of energy had an important influence on Hinton, Sejnowski, and Ackley in their development of the Boltzmann machine model (chapter 13).

5.4   The Traveling Salesman Problem

Hopfield and Tank [102] were the first to try neural network techniques on the traveling salesman problem, one of the most famous optimization problems.

Given n cities with intercity distances $d_{ij} = d_{ji}$, the (symmetric) traveling salesman problem seeks a valid *tour* that minimizes total trip length. A tour is an ordering of all n cities, and the length of the tour is given by the total distance traveled in starting at the first city, visiting all other cities exactly once, and returning to the first city. (Of course the starting city of a tour and the direction of the tour make no difference in total trip length.)

We can express the traveling salesman problem by an energy minimization problem as follows. Define cell u_{ij} (note the double subscript) for $1 \le i, j \le n$ by

$$u_{ij} = \begin{cases} 1 & \text{if city } i \text{ is the } j^{\text{th}} \text{ city visited in the tour} \\ 0 & \text{otherwise.} \end{cases}$$

Note that a valid tour corresponds to a permutation matrix. For example the tour

$$1 \to 4 \to 3 \to 5 \to 2 \to 1$$

is equivalent to

$$u_{ij} = \begin{bmatrix} 1 & 0 & 0 & 0 & 0 \\ 0 & 0 & 0 & 0 & 1 \\ 0 & 0 & 1 & 0 & 0 \\ 0 & 1 & 0 & 0 & 0 \\ 0 & 0 & 0 & 1 & 0 \end{bmatrix}.$$

For notational convenience, we let subscripts be cyclic so that

$$n + 1 = 1 \quad \text{and} \quad 1 - 1 = n.$$

Then for positive constants A, B, C, F the energy formula is

$$\mathscr{E} = A \sum_{x=1}^{n} \sum_{i=1}^{n} \sum_{j \neq i} u_{xi} u_{xj} + B \sum_{i=1}^{n} \sum_{x=1}^{n} \sum_{y \neq x} u_{xi} u_{yi} + C \left(\sum_{x=1}^{n} \sum_{i=1}^{n} u_{xi} - n \right)^2$$

$$+ F \sum_{x=1}^{n} \sum_{y \neq x} \sum_{i=1}^{n} d_{xy} u_{xi} (u_{y,i+1} + u_{y,i-1}). \tag{5.14}$$

We first want to verify that minimizing $\mathscr{E}$ will produce a valid tour. The A term penalizes any set of values where a city appears at 2 or more positions, and similarly the B term gives a penalty for having 2 or more cities at the same position. The C term applies pressure for the sum of all u_{ij} to be exactly n. Finally the F term brings in the distances, and penalizes longer tours.

Now suppose we consider the network equations (5.7)–(5.8) and the energy equation (5.9) as abstract systems. By defining $w_{xi,yj}$ appropriately, Hopfield and Tank were able to derive a continuous neural network model that finds a local minimum to the traveling salesman problem energy equation. The definitions of $w_{xi,yj}$ follow with brief comments on the terms. Here $\delta_{ij} = 1$ if $i = 1$ and is 0 otherwise.

$$w_{xi,yj} = -A\delta_{xy}(1 - \delta_{ij}) \qquad \text{inhibitory connections within a row}$$

$$-B\delta_{ij}(1 - \delta_{xy}) \qquad \text{inhibitory connections within a column}$$

$$-C \qquad \text{global inhibition}$$

$$-Dd_{xy}(\delta_{j,j+1} + \delta_{j,j-1}) \quad \text{distance term}$$

$$w_{xi,0} = Cn \qquad \text{bias} \approx \text{global excitation}$$

Hopfield and Tank used a continuous model for u_{ij}:

$$u_{ij} = \frac{1}{1 + e^{-S_{ij}K}} \quad \text{for constant } K \gg 0.$$

Making K large forces the activations to be close to 0 or 1.

We are now ready to have the network compute a solution:

1. Set u_{ij} to small random positive values to break symmetry.

2. Iterate the network until it converges by picking a cell at random and recomputing its activation. (Because we are using continuous activations, the network will not reach an exact steady state.)

The values for constants A, B, C, F, and K were found by some initial trial and error. Hopfield and Tank used

$$A = B = 250$$

$$C = 100$$

$$F = 250$$

$$K = 50.$$

Although Hopfield and Tank reported good success at finding valid tours that were near optimum, others (Wilson and Pawley [209], Van den Bout and Miller [195]) have encountered difficulty with this formulation and have introduced various modifications. It should be emphasized, moreover, that the Hopfield and Tank approach to the traveling salesman problem is *not* competitive with specialized algorithms developed for this problem. Its main contribution is to show that the general technique of energy minimization + neural network simulations can be used to find *approximate* solutions to NP-Complete problems.

In more recent work Xu and Tsai [215] have explored *combining* neural network algorithms with conventional traveling salesman problem approaches, and they report improvements over conventional approaches used alone. Combining neural network techniques with standard algorithms is an appealing idea.

5.5   The Cohen-Grossberg Theorem

Hopfield was not the first person to use energy to prove that a system reaches equilibrium. A standard tool of those who study dynamic systems has been the Liapunov function, a generalization of the notion of energy. If for a system of differential equations a Liapunov function exists that is monotonic decreasing along trajectories of the system, then this gives a way to prove that the system cannot cycle.

Cohen and Grossberg [39] have proven an even stronger result for certain continuous neural network models that have symmetric, nonnegative weights and where cells are mutually inhibitory. More specifically, suppose we have n cells, u_i, whose activations over time satisfy

$$\frac{du_i}{dt} = a_i(u_i)\left[b_i(u_i) - \sum_{j=1}^{n} w_{i,j} d_j(u_j) \right]$$

where

- $w_{i,j} = w_{j,i} \geq 0$ (symmetric, nonnegative weights)
- $d_j(\ )$ is a differentiable, nonnegative, nondecreasing function
- $a_i(\ )$ and $b_i(\ )$ are continuous functions and $a_i(x) > 0$ for $x > 0$.

Then Cohen and Grossberg have proven that the following function, $\mathscr{E}$, is a Liapunov function that satisfies $\frac{d}{dt}\mathscr{E}(u_1(t),\ldots,u_n(t)) \leq 0$ on trajectories of cell activations:

$$\mathscr{E}(u_1,\ldots,u_n) = \sum_{j=1}^{n} \int_0^{u_j} b_j(x_j) d_j'(x_j)\, dx_j$$

$$+ \frac{1}{2}\sum_{i,j=1}^{n} w_{i,j} d_i(u_i) d_j(u_j).$$

After making several additional technical assumptions they showed that trajectories actually converge to limit points that satisfy $\frac{d}{dt}\mathscr{E}(u_1,\ldots,u_n) = 0$. Cohen and Grossberg also indicated how their results could be extended to cover systems with threshold discontinuities, such as Hopfield networks. However, they did not focus in on these systems in detail as Hopfield later did.

*5.6 Kanerva's Model

Kanerva [111, 112] has developed an interesting autoassociative model that he calls a *sparse distributed memory*. Suppose we have 1,000 training examples, $\{E^1,\ldots,E^{1,000}\}$, where $E_j^k = \{+1,-1\}$, and we want to be able to store and recall these training examples from partial or noisy approximations. To do this we generate c *reference sets*,

$$R^i = \langle R_1^i,\ldots,R_p^i \rangle, \quad i = 1,\ldots,c,$$

where each R_j^i also is $+1$ or -1. The reference sets are generated *at random* and remain fixed. Any training example, E^k, can be compared to a reference set, R^i, and the *Hamming distance* calculated by counting how many positions differ:

$$\text{distance}\,(E^k,R^i) = |\{j : R_j^i \neq E_j^k\}|.$$

We store the training examples by computing $p \times c$ integer weights, $w_{i,j}$, one for every entry of every reference set. (There are no bias weights in this model.) For each training example we modify only those weights that correspond to reference sets R^i that are within a fixed distance, D, of E^k:

If distance $(E^k,R^i) \leq D$ then

$$w_{i,j} = w_{i,j} + E_j^k.$$

This adds or subtracts 1 from the corresponding weights $w_{i,j}$ according to the value being stored, E_j^k. Of course this is a one-shot learning algorithm, and it is especially fast if weight modifications are performed in parallel.

We can now recover a stored E^k from a close approximation, E, by polling nearby reference weights:

$$S_j = \sum_{i:\text{distance}(E,R^i)\leq D} w_{i,j}$$

$$E'_j = \begin{cases} +1 & \text{if } S_j \geq 0 \\ -1 & \text{otherwise.} \end{cases}$$

We can also repeat this recall operation using E' to get E'' and so on.

Kanerva reports that for $p = 1,000$ and with $c = 1,000,000$ reference points and a distance bound of $D = 450$, that the capacity of the model is about 100,000 randomly generated training examples. If only about 10,000 (random) training examples are stored, recovery to a stored training example E^k is good starting from a vector E that is distance no more than 209 from E^k.

What makes Kanerva's model work is that random reference vectors in high-dimensional space are well separated. In the above example the expected distance from a reference vector to its nearest neighbor reference vector is 424 bits. Therefore the neighbors of a stored training example E^k will not change very much if the recovery vector E is at all close to E^k in Hamming distance. Once we know that the neighbors are about the same and that there are enough of them (about 1,000 reference vectors are neighbors for any training example in the case above), then the law of large numbers will make it very likely that a stored training example will be recovered, provided pairs of stored values are not themselves too close together.

Thus sparse distributed memories exhibit the typical properties of one-shot learning algorithms: very fast learning speed balanced by a required separation of stored training examples.

*5.7   Autoassociative Filtering for Feedforward Networks

Using autoassociators as data filters is a simple idea that deserves more study and more comparisons with other methods. For example it is not even known how much (if any!) such a model increases the functions that a single-cell model can recognize.

Figure 5.5 illustrates this architecture. Here all cell activations are discrete. The input values initialize the autoassociative cells, $u_1 - u_5$, and these cells recompute their activations t times. At each iteration cells $u_1 - u_5$ recompute their activations and post their new activations simultaneously. After the t iterations the current activations of $u_1 - u_5$ serve as input to u_6, which then computes the network output.

The learning algorithm has two steps. First $u_1 - u_5$ are trained as autoassociators on the set of training examples, $\{E^k\}$, by either a one-shot

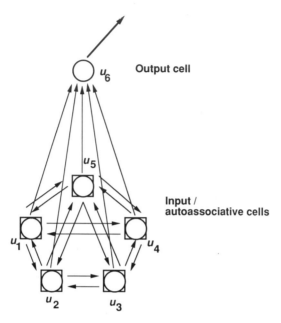

Figure 5.5
Autoassociative filter for a feedforward network

or an iterative method (see next section). This training occurs independently of correct outputs $\{C^k\}$.

Next we compute $\widehat{E^k}$, the activations of the autoassociative cells after t iterations when cells are initialized with training example inputs, E^k. Finally we train the top cell, u_6, using a single-cell algorithm such as the pocket algorithm operating on training examples $\{\langle \widehat{E^k}, C^k \rangle\}$.

While the idea of an autoassociative filter is appealing, it is not known whether it actually gains anything over simply training a single-cell model with training examples $\{\langle E^k, C^k \rangle\}$.

5.8   Concluding Remarks

It is important to note that we can use any learning algorithm for feedforward networks to train autoassociators. Figure 5.6 shows how to represent the autoassociator of figure 5.1 by such a feedforward network. We merely train each output cell to reproduce its corresponding input for each

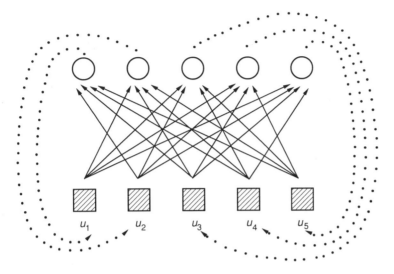

Figure 5.6
Feedforward network used for training an autoassociator.

of the training examples. The resulting weights are now suitable for the corresponding autoassociator.

By using more powerful learning algorithms, for example the pocket algorithm with ratchet, we can generate autoassociator weights with greater storage capacity than is normally possible using one-shot learning algorithms. We can also do away with the requirement that training examples be nearly orthogonal, so that even very similar training examples can be stored and recovered.

Finally, it is worth reemphasizing the advantages and disadvantages of one-shot learning algorithms versus iterative algorithms. One-shot learning algorithms are faster and are perhaps more "biologically plausible," but they do not fit the data as well as iterative algorithms. In cases where learning is performed only once and where the resulting weights are heavily used it is often advisable to use iterative algorithms, even for training autoassociators.

5.9   Exercises

1. Normalize examples, compute weights, and verify the behavior for a linear autoassociator given training examples

$$E^1 = \langle \quad 3 \; -2 \quad \; 4 \; 1 \rangle$$

$$E^2 = \langle -4 \; -7 \; -1 \; 3 \rangle.$$

*2. Generalize the outer-product learning rule of section 5.1 for auto-associators to be able to learn input-output vector pairs, $\langle E^k, C^k \rangle$, where $\{C^k\}$ are desired output *vectors* when input units are initialized to E^k. The C^k vectors need not be of the same dimension as the E^k vectors.

(a) What restrictions must be imposed upon E^k and C^k vectors?

(b) Give a simple one-shot learning algorithm based upon linear auto-associators and prove that it works.

(c) Try your algorithm with the following data:

$$E^1 = \langle \quad .35 \; .52 \; -.35 \; .70 \rangle, \quad C^1 = \langle \quad 5 \; -2 \; 3 \rangle.$$

$$E^2 = \langle -.94 \; .24 \quad \; 0 \; .24 \rangle, \quad C^2 = \langle -1 \quad \; 0 \; 4 \rangle.$$

3. For the Hopfield model in figure 5.4, suppose the current activations are $\langle 1 \; 1 \; 1 \; -1 \; -1 \rangle$ and the cell u_1 is chosen to recompute its activation. Will u_1 change and, if so, what will the new energy be?

4. Recalculate the Hopfield model in figure 5.4 where E^1 is replaced by $\langle 1 \; -1 \; -1 \; 1 \; -1 \rangle$. Which of E^1, E^2, E^3 are now correctly stored by W?

5. (a) Compute weights for a Hopfield model with training examples:

$$E^1 = \langle 1 \; -1 \quad \; 1 \; -1 \rangle$$

$$E^2 = \langle 1 \quad \; 1 \; -1 \; -1 \rangle.$$

Verify that E^1 and E^2 are correctly "stored" by the model.

(b) Calculate the energy for the above net.

(c) Repeat with

$$E^1 = \langle 1 \; -1 \quad \; 1 \; -1 \rangle$$

$$E^2 = \langle 1 \; -1 \; -1 \; -1 \rangle.$$

Are training examples correctly stored? Is this a surprise and why?

*6. (Hopfield) Show that the outer-product learning rule of section 5.1 (with $w_{i,i}$ defined to be 0 for all i) will work with linear discriminant activation computations (equations (5.7)–(5.8)).

7. (research) Are there interesting analytical results for autoassociator filtering for feedforward networks?

5.10   Programming Projects

*1. Consider a simple expert system knowledge base with names, jobs, and pay scales of the form:

E^1 = <FRANK . . . CONSTRUCTION . . MEDIUM . PAY . . >

E^2 = <SUSAN . . . EXEC . . VP . . . . . . BIG . BUCKS . . . >

E^3 = <GEORGE . . PLUMBER . . . . HUGE . BUCKS . . >

E^4 = <MARIE . . . POLICE . WOMAN . . SMALLISH . PAY>

Note that periods count as characters. Use the outer-product rule to train up an autoassociator where each letter is represented by some collection of bits (e.g., its 8-bit ascii code but using $\{+1, -1\}$ rather than $\{1, 0\}$). Now implement a BSB model that can answer queries such as:

<SUSAN . . . ???????????? . . BIG . BUCKS . . . > (What is Susan's big bucks job?)

<?????? . . PLUMBER . . . . ????????????> (Who's a plumber and with what salary?)

Hint: represent ? entries as 0 values for corresponding bits. (This program may be a separate, stand-alone program that is not integrated with the previously developed neural network shell.)

2. Implement a Hopfield model with 100 cells and experiment with how many random vectors can be stored and recalled with small error. (Stand-alone program.)

3. (research) Implement an autoassociative net for a feedforward network (section 5.7). Generate noisy data and examine its performance. Compare it with a single-cell model using pocket algorithm with ratchet or Widrow-Hoff (next chapter) or backpropagation (chapter 11).

6 Mean Squared Error (MSE) Algorithms

6.1 Motivation

Several considerations motivated researchers to look at mean squared error algorithms. Originally Widrow and Hoff [202] sought a better alternative to perceptron learning that could do a reasonable job with nonseparable data. Recall that perceptron learning can be very poorly behaved with such data (and this was long before methods given in section 3.2.3 came on the scene). A second motivation was to fit even separable data better than perceptron learning could. The idea here is that perceptron learning stops iterating as soon as any solution is found that correctly classifies every training example. Perhaps such a solution only "barely works," while another solution would be preferable, as illustrated in figure 6.1. A third goal was to improve the speed of perceptron learning by adjusting the magnitude of the change at each iteration. The Widrow-Hoff rule is a gradient descent algorithm with an adjustable learning rate. Finally Widrow and Hoff wanted a model that was better suited for output values that were continuous. Although approximations for continuous outputs are available with perceptron learning and the pocket algorithm, they require thermometer codes or some similar mechanism (see section 2.4.1).

6.2 MSE Approximations

When faced with a difficult problem it is natural to look at other closely related problems that are easier to solve. For a classification problem, the most popular alternative to finding an optimal set of weights is to find weights, W, that minimize the *mean squared error* (MSE). If there are N training examples $\{E^k\}$ with corresponding correct outputs $\{C^k\}$ then the MSE, $\mathscr{E}$, is given by

$$\mathscr{E} = \frac{1}{N} \sum_{k=1}^{N} (W \cdot E^k - C^k)^2. \tag{6.1}$$

(Note that $W \cdot E^k = S_{p+1}$, the weighted sum for the output cell u_{p+1}.)

The advantage of this error function is that its derivatives with respect to individual weights exist everywhere, in contrast to the count of the number of misclassifications. Therefore it is possible to apply gradient

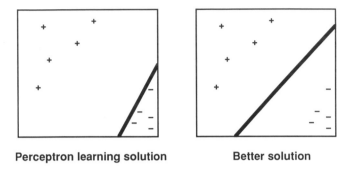

Perceptron learning solution   **Better solution**

Figure 6.1
A solution found by perceptron learning and a better solution.

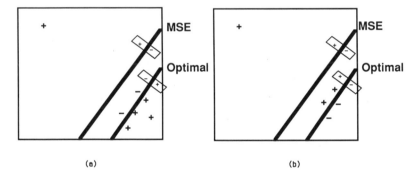

Figure 6.2
MSE classification is not optimal.

descent methods. Another difference with perceptron learning problems is that the correct answers, C^k, are allowed to be any real numbers; they are not limited to $\{+1, -1\}$.

The disadvantage of MSE is that it solves a distinctly different problem than finding weights that give the greatest number of correct classifications. For example in figure 6.2a the single '+' example out in left field severely distorts the separating hyperplane so that the majority of training examples are misclassified. Perhaps the isolated '+' example is even a spurious example due to noise. A major disadvantage of MSE is that such far-out points are overemphasized, even for separable sets of training examples (figure 6.2b).

6.3 The Widrow-Hoff Rule or LMS Algorithm

There is a fast, convenient gradient descent algorithm for minimizing MSE called either the *Widrow-Hoff rule* or *LMS* (least mean square) algorithm. Usually it is used in an *on-line* (also called *stochastic*) mode where the weights are updated after every iteration. Suppose we see example E with correct output C and the current weight vector is W. Then the squared error is

$$\mathcal{E}(W) = (W \cdot E - C)^2.$$

The gradient vector $\nabla \mathcal{E}$ is given by

$$\nabla \mathcal{E} = \left\langle \frac{\partial \mathcal{E}}{\partial W_0} \cdots \frac{\partial \mathcal{E}}{\partial W_p} \right\rangle \tag{6.2}$$

$$\frac{\partial \mathcal{E}}{\partial W_j} = 2(W \cdot E - C)E_j = 2(S - C)E_j \tag{6.3}$$

where $S = S_{p+1}$ is the weighted sum $(W \cdot E)$ for the cell.

Because we must specify a step size, ρ, for gradient descent, we can absorb the factor of 2 into ρ. Gradient descent now dictates that we take a step in the direction $-\nabla \mathcal{E}$, yielding the final form of the Widrow-Hoff algorithm:

$$W^* = W + \rho(C - S)E. \tag{6.4}$$

This updating procedure is also called the *delta rule* because δ is sometimes used to represent the error, $(C - S)$.

Equation (6.4) tells us to update by taking the signed difference between the correct output and the weighted sum, multiplying by the small step size ρ, and then taking a step in the direction of the cell's inputs (or the opposite direction if $(C - S) < 0$).

We can now compute the revised squared error for the new weights W^* with example E:

$$\mathcal{E}(W^*) = [W^* \cdot E - C]^2 \tag{6.5}$$

$$= [(W + \rho(C - S)E) \cdot E - C]^2 \text{ from equation (6.4)} \tag{6.6}$$

$$= [(W \cdot E - C) + \rho(C - S)E \cdot E]^2 \tag{6.7}$$

$$= [(S - C) + \rho(C - S)E \cdot E]^2 \tag{6.8}$$

$$= \mathscr{E}(W) - 2\rho\mathscr{E}(W)(E \cdot E) + \rho^2\mathscr{E}(W)(E \cdot E)^2 \tag{6.9}$$

$$= \mathscr{E}(W) + \rho\mathscr{E}(W)(E \cdot E)[\rho(E \cdot E) - 2]. \tag{6.10}$$

Note that $\mathscr{E}(W) \geq 0$. Thus for small step sizes ρ that satisfy

$$0 < \rho < \frac{2}{E \cdot E} \tag{6.11}$$

the bracketed term in the last equation will be negative, and $\mathscr{E}(W^*)$ will be less than $\mathscr{E}(W)$. Thus equation (6.11) gives a stability condition for ρ.

From equation (6.8) it is easy to see that setting $\rho = 1/E \cdot E$ brings the error to 0 for the current example. In the discrete case where $E_j = \{+1, -1\}$, this works out to $\rho = 1/(p + 1)$. Any larger setting overcorrects the error. Widrow suggests that a practical range for ρ is

$$\frac{.1}{E \cdot E} < \rho < \frac{1}{E \cdot E}.$$

A very nice property of using MSE is that there are no local minima to worry about (problem 3). Therefore gradient descent algorithms must converge to a global minimum, provided the step size is small enough.

6.3.1   Number of Training Examples Required

Widrow and Hoff also studied how many training examples are needed for good approximate solutions. They define a *misadjustment* or *slack* parameter s that tells how far a system with MSE $\mathscr{E}$ is from the optimal mean squared error, $\mathscr{E}^*$

$$s = \frac{\mathscr{E} - \mathscr{E}^*}{\mathscr{E}^*}.$$

They then show that for N randomly selected training examples consisting of p inputs,

$$s = \frac{p + 1}{N}.$$

This formula assumes that the actual errors $\{(C^k - W^* \cdot E^k)\}$ are Gaussian-distributed with mean 0 and are uncorrelated; however, Widrow and Hoff note that the formula is insensitive to distribution shape and little affected by correlation less than 0.8.

In practice the Widrow-Hoff algorithm works very efficiently for single-cell models to minimize $\mathscr{E}$. Notice however, in equation (6.4) that as the error decreases, the magnitude of the change decreases. This leads to an asymptotic convergence that is a characteristic of gradient descent algorithms (section 1.4).

6.4 ADALINE

Widrow and Hoff used LMS to train the weights for a discrete single-cell model and called the result ADALINE. Originally this stood for ADAptive LInear NEuron, but it was changed to ADAptive LINear Element when neural networks were unpopular.[1]

It is interesting to compare the Widrow-Hoff algorithm with perceptron learning for this model. From equation (6.4) it is clear that perceptron learning is a gradient descent algorithm with constant step size:

$$W^* = W \pm E$$

where the sign is the same as $(C - S)$.

For *separable* sets of training examples, the perceptron convergence theorem (theorem 3.1) guarantees an optimal solution after finite mistakes for perceptron learning. The fact that the step size has a lower bound is necessary for this convergence. By contrast the Widrow-Hoff rule exhibits asymptotic behavior that may converge more slowly than perceptron learning. In fact the Widrow-Hoff rule need not converge to an optimal solution, as illustrated in figure 6.2. On the other hand the Widrow-Hoff algorithm might find a solution that generalizes better, because it is training the weighted sum, S, to be ± 1, and is not satisfied if S merely has the correct sign. (See figure 6.1.)

For *nonseparable training examples* it would seem that the Widrow-Hoff algorithm would be preferable to perceptron learning (but not necessarily the pocket algorithm) because Widrow-Hoff is not unstable like perceptron learning. It would be interesting to compare the generalization

---

1. B. Widrow, historical talk at Neural Network for Computation conference, Snowbird, Utah, April 1987. Quoted in Anderson and Rosenfeld [8].

abilities of the pocket algorithm with the Widrow-Hoff algorithm, but apparently this has not yet been done.

Finally there is the question of how well mean squared error approximates minimizing misclassifications for discrete single-cell models (i.e., ADALINE). Widrow and Hoff point out that if errors between the training examples and an optimal set of weights W^* have a Gaussian distribution, then MSE is equivalent to minimizing misclassifications. (Note that this was not the case with the examples given in figure 6.2.) Therefore MSE would seem to be a good approximation in most practical cases.

6.5 Adaptive Noise Cancellation

Widrow and associates [203, 204] also pioneered the related field of adaptive filtering. One important case is where we seek a signal s but we have access to the *sum* of the signal plus uncorrelated noise $(s + n_0)$, as well as a separate source of noise n_1 that is correlated with n_0 but not s. For example if we are trying to detect a fetal heartbeat $(=s)$, it is easy to monitor the baby's heartbeat plus the mother's heartbeat $(s + n_0)$ as in figure 6.3. (For this task the mother's heartbeat is the noise—of course the mother might view things differently.) We can also place monitors close to the mother's heart to get a separate source of noise, n_1.

Now we use MSE to find weights W for n_1 (which may be a vector) to minimize "error" $\mathscr{E}$ defined by

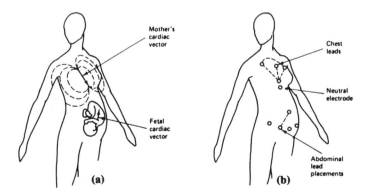

Figure 6.3
Canceling maternal heartbeat in fetal electrocardiography: (a) cardiac electric field vectors of mother and fetus; (b) placement of leads. (© 1988 IEEE.)

$$\mathscr{E} = s + n_0 - W \cdot n_1.$$

(The update step is $W^* = W + \rho(s + n_0 - W \cdot n_1)E$.)

Assuming that s, n_0, and n_1 have mean 0 and under the above dependence assumptions, Widrow showed that minimizing $\mathscr{E}$ causes $\mathscr{E}$ to be an MSE estimate of s. This, for example, would allow us to see the baby's heartbeat with the mother's heartbeat canceled out as in figure 6.4.

6.6 Decision-Directed Learning

Lucky [132] (see also Widrow and Winter [204]) introduced *decision-directed learning*, an interesting application of the LMS algorithm that is widely used for channel equalization in modems. The basic idea is to take advantage of our knowledge that an incoming signal should be *exactly* +1

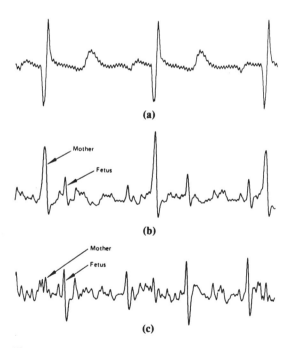

Figure 6.4
Result of fetal ECG experiment: (a) reference input (chest lead); (b) primary input (abdominal lead); (c) noise canceler output. (© 1988 IEEE.)

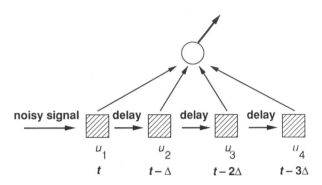

Figure 6.5
A single-cell model with tapped delay line input.

or -1 to learn to filter out noise that is distorting this signal. Thresholding the filtered signal will now be more reliable than thresholding the unfiltered signal.

We employ a *tapped delay line*, as illustrated in figure 6.5, to get signal inputs at time

$$t, t - \Delta, t - 2\Delta, \ldots, t - (p - 1)\Delta.$$

These in turn become inputs to a single-cell model with discrete $\{+1, -1\}$ outputs.

Learning is by LMS training, where the correct output, C, is taken as the thresholded ± 1 output of the filtered cell. For example if the weighted sum S is .9 then the output of the network would be $+1$ and the error, $(C - S)$, would be $+.1$. We can now update the weights using equation (6.4).

In order for this approach to work it is necessary that the raw signal not be too noisy. Typical telephone error rates of $\leq 10^{-1}$ are close enough. Initially the noise may cause some errors in the values of the desired outputs, C, but the system will quickly converge so that the output error rate drops to 10^{-6} or less.

It is impressive to note that the majority of modems use this technique. Also the tapped delay line technique is worth remembering as a way of representing continuous sequential inputs or *signals*. This allows us to train networks to recognize various classes of signals.

6.7   Exercises

1. Suppose a single-cell model computes its outputs by cubing the weighted sum of its inputs $u_i = (W \cdot E^k)^3$. Derive a mean squared error learning rule for such a unit.

2. Discuss how LMS can be used to find weights for a linear machine.

3. Show that the mean squared error given by equation (6.1) has a Hessian matrix of second order partial derivatives that are constant. In other words

$$\frac{\partial^2}{\partial W_i \partial W_j} = \text{constant.}$$

(This suffices to prove that any local minimum for $\mathscr{E}$ must be a global minimum.)

4. How few training examples are needed to compute weights that will give about 110 percent of the mean squared error generated from a very large sample? (This is sometimes referred to as *Bernie's rule*.)

6.8   Programming Projects

1. Implement the LMS algorithm as an option for your learning program.

2. Use the LMS algorithm to generate single-cell weights for the *Taxtime!* exercise in section 2.5.

3. Use the LMS algorithm to generate weights $w_{4,0} - w_{4,3}$ for the following set of training examples:

u_1	u_2	u_3	u_4 = output
-1	1	1.5	-2.0
-1	-1	-1.5	2.0
1	-1	1.5	2.0
1	-1	-1.5	-2.0

(If simulated by hand rather than by program, stop after 2 passes through the training examples.) What is the mean squared error? Do the weights separate the training examples?

4. (research) Do a thorough empirical comparison of ADALINE and the pocket algorithm with ratchet, with particular attention to generalization. Use separable and nonseparable sets of training examples. Try cases with

$\{+1, -1\}$ and real-value inputs, as well as cases that start as separable sets and then have noise added to the inputs.

5. *Time series prediction:* Collect average monthly sales for automobiles (or some other product) over 10 years. Construct a tapped delay line model to predict the next month's sales from the previous year's sales. Train the model using the first 8 years worth of data. (Notice how seasonal variations are automatically taken into account.) Now run your model to predict each month's sales in the ninth and tenth year based upon previous information, and evaluate its performance.

7 Unsupervised Learning

7.1 Introduction

Recall that in unsupervised learning there is no feedback as to correct classification; we see only examples $\{E^k\}$ but we are *not* given correct outputs $\{C^k\}$. Therefore the most that we can do is to cluster data into similarity groupings.

Clustering can be quite valuable, however, because it can drastically reduce the dimensionality of the data. For example if we are trying to understand speech, the input data usually consists of numerous measurements taken at various frequency and time intervals. If we can cluster such data into (say) 50 to 100 groups that roughly correspond with phonemes, then we will greatly ease the task of any further supervised learning. We will get better generalizations by having fewer relevant input parameters, provided the inputs are still sufficient to characterize the important aspects of the data. The use of clustering algorithms to preprocess data is a technique worth remembering.

A comprehensive overview of clustering algorithms is beyond the scope of this book, but for standard approaches and bibliographic information Anderberg [6] and Duda and Hart [47] are recommended. Recently there has also been some success by Cheeseman and associates [38] in giving clustering a foundation in Bayesian probability.

7.1.1 No Teacher

Although unsupervised learning uses no "teacher" to provide correct classifications, there must be some criterion for an algorithm's clustering decisions. Therefore some researchers (Barto [17]) even question the term *unsupervised learning*, pointing out that in fact such algorithms have a *fixed, built-in teacher*.

Also it is important to note that real-world problems usually involve sequential processes evolving over time. Although such sequential problems can be harder for learning algorithms if they require recurrent networks for representing the "state" of the system,[1] such problems have one great advantage. There is always a good source of supervised learning data for the important task of *predicting the next state of the model* (or for predicting the next input). Being able to predict future states makes it

---

1. Recall that a tapped delay line can also be used—see section 6.6.

possible to evaluate alternative actions and to *plan* several steps into the future.

7.1.2 Clustering Algorithms

In this chapter we will examine four clustering algorithms. First we will look at k-means clustering, a popular standard technique that can also serve as a baseline for comparing clustering algorithms that use neural networks. Then we will look at Kohonen's topology-preserving maps. These interesting algorithms use the topological arrangement of the *learning* cells to help capture information. Finally in sections 7.4 and 7.5 we will examine ART1 and ART2, biologically motivated algorithms due to Carpenter and Grossberg that dynamically determine the number of clusters based upon a "vigilance" parameter.

7.2 k-Means Clustering

One of the most popular clustering algorithms is k-*means clustering* due to MacQueen [134]. There are several variations of this algorithm, and we will look at *convergent k-means clustering* as described by Anderberg ([6], pp. 162–163). Anderberg's book provides a rich source for other standard clustering algorithms.

7.2.1 The Algorithm

We recall that the *centroid* of a set of N points (or training examples) $\{E^k\}$ is the vector where each component is the average of values for that component:

$$\text{centroid vector} = \frac{1}{N}\sum E^k.$$

k-means clustering operates by moving an example to the cluster with the centroid closest to that example, and then updating centroids for the revised clusters. Figure 7.1 illustrates the algorithm and figure 7.2 gives the details.

Anderberg suggests a proof that convergence will always occur along the following lines:

1. Each switch in step 2 decreases the sum of the squared distances from each training example to that training example's group centroid.

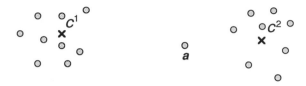

Figure 7.1
k-means clustering: point a leaves cluster C^1 and joins cluster C^2 and centroids are recomputed.

---

1. Begin with any initial partition that groups the data into k clusters. One way to do this is:

   1a. Take the first k training examples as single-element clusters.

   1b. Assign each of the remaining $N - k$ examples to the cluster with the nearest centroid. After each assignment, recompute the centroid of the gaining cluster.

2. Take each example E in sequence and compute its distance from the centroid of each of the k clusters. If E is not currently in the cluster with the closest centroid, switch E to that cluster and update the centroids of the cluster gaining E and the cluster losing E.

3. Repeat step 2 until convergence is achieved, that is until a pass through the training examples causes no new assignments.

Figure 7.2
Convergent k-means clustering (Anderberg [6]).

2. There are only finitely many partitions of the training examples into k clusters.

7.2.2 Comments

While the basic k-means clustering algorithm requires that the number of clusters, k, be chosen in advance, the algorithm is fast enough so that it is easy to experiment with different values of k. Another approach is to let the algorithm determine the number of clusters in accordance with user-specified parameters. Work along this line has been done by MacQueen [134], Wishart [212, 213], Ball and Hall [14, 12, 15, 13], and Wolf [214]. Also see writings on the ISODATA system by Sammon [182], Dubes [46], and Anderberg [6].

It is difficult to compare the variety of different clustering algorithms in the literature because comparisons are dependent upon the criteria used to evaluate the final clusters. However, it seems evident that k-means is a good algorithm if our criterion is to minimize the sums of squares of distances between training examples and corresponding cluster centroids. It also has the nice property that every example is in the cluster having a centroid closest to that example.

7.3 Topology-Preserving Maps

7.3.1 Introduction

Teuvo Kohonen [120, 119, 118, 122] has been the primary developer of *topology-preserving maps*. The main idea here is to consider the output cells as occupying positions in space, so that it makes sense to talk about those output cells that are *neighbors* of a particular cell. For example in figure 7.3 the output cells are arranged in a grid pattern, with the neighborhood of cell $u_{h,i}$ consisting of those cells at hamming distance less than or equal to 2 from $u_{h,i}$. Note that it is convenient to use two or more subscripts for cells, ($u_{h,i}$), rather than the usual single subscript (u_i) when dealing with a

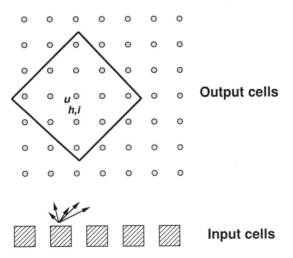

Figure 7.3
Output cells, showing neighbors of cell $u_{h,i}$.

grid of cells. Weights also pick up a subscript ($w_{h,i;j}$ rather than $w_{i,j}$), and we denote the vector of weights for a cell, $w_{h,i;*}$, by $W_{h,i}$.

We would like the behavior of the cells to be consistent with the neighborhood structure, so that similar inputs lead to output cells being activated that are close together. (In most models the output cells form a winner-take-all group, so that only one output cell will have activation $+1$.)

One motivation for such topology-preserving maps is the structure of the mammalian brain, where visual, auditory, and tactile inputs are mapped into a number of "sheets" (folded planes) of cells. Topology is preserved in these sheets; for example, if we touch parts of the body that are close together, groups of cells will fire that are also close together.

A second motivation arises from the problem of dealing with slight shifts in position and orientation. A grid of outputs with fewer cells than the number of cells in the input grid reduces the effects of such shifts.

7.3.2   The Algorithm

We will assume there is an $n \times n$ array of output cells, p input cells, and a set of training examples $\{E^k\}$.

We have two goals. First we want to *cover* the inputs by the output cells. In other words, for every training example E^k we would like at least one output cell, $u_{h,i}$, to have weights

$$W_{h,i} = w_{h,i;*}$$

that are close to E^k in Euclidean distance (i.e., $\|E^k - W_{h,i}\|$ is small). Our second goal is to have close output cells behave similarly (by having similar weighted sums). This will yield a topology-preserving map.

Note the important relationship between Euclidean distance and the dot product:

$$\|E^k - W_{h,i}\| = \sqrt{(E^k - W_{h,i}) \cdot (E^k - W_{h,i})}$$
$$= \sqrt{(E^k)^2 + W_{h,i}^2 - 2(E^k \cdot W_{h,i})}.$$

Hence if all $W_{h,i}$ are assumed to be normalized ($\|W_{h,i}\| = 1$), then for fixed E^k

$$\|E^k - W_{h,i}\| = \sqrt{\text{constant} - 2(E^k \cdot W_{h,i})}.$$

Therefore *the dot product determines the distance*, and *the minimum distance*

Let T be the total number of iterations. Define the *step size* for each iteration by $\alpha(t) = \left(1 - \dfrac{t-1}{T}\right)$.

0. Initialize weights for all output cells to random values.
1. At the start of iteration t, select an example E^k at random.
2. Find the output cell $u_{h,i}$ with weights $W_{h,i}$ closest to E^k in Euclidean distance.
3. Modify weights of *every cell $u_{h',i'}$ in the neighborhood of $u_{h,i}$*:

   $$W_{h',i'} = W_{h',i'} + \alpha(t)[E^k - W_{h',i'}].$$

   Cells not in the neighborhood of $u_{h,i}$ retain their weights.
4. Return to step 2 for the next iteration (with $t = t + 1$).

Figure 7.4
Algorithm for topology-preserving maps.

corresponds to the maximum dot product. Thus we can use a standard winner-take-all group network to compute the closest cell $u_{h,i}$, provided all $W_{h,i}$ are normalized.

Kohonen's algorithm is given in figure 7.4. For each training example E^k, we find the closest output cell $u_{h,i}$ and move the weights of $u_{h,i}$ *and weights of its neighbors* closer to E^k. The key to the algorithm is that weights of neighboring cells are also modified. If only the weights of the closest cell were modified, then there would be no relationship among neighboring cells.

At each iteration weights are modified using a decreasing step size, $\alpha(t)$; choice of this decreasing sequence $\{\alpha(t)\}$ can influence performance of the algorithm. Notice that we do not renormalize weight vectors in step 3, so we must use Euclidean distance in step 2 rather than the dot product.[2]

7.3.3 Example

To help clarify the algorithm, let us examine one iteration of a hypothetical problem.

2. This is because it is sometimes bothersome to be restricted to normalized weights. However, it is always possible to reformulate the problem by placing all inputs on the surface of a $p + 1$-dimensional hypersphere. (We can do this by adding an extra dimension and giving it values so that all training examples have the same length.) Then we could restrict ourselves to normalized weights and use a maximum inner-product test in step 2.

Suppose we have a 3×3 grid of output cells where a neighborhood consists of the 8 cells adjacent to a particular cell (*left, right, up, down, 4 diagonals*). Also, suppose at the start of iteration 501 (out of $T = 1,000$ total iterations) we have the following weights:

$i =$

$h =$	**1**	**2**	**3**
1	$\langle -3 \;\; +2 \rangle$	$\langle +5 \;\; +4 \rangle$	$\langle +7 \;\; -6 \rangle *$
2	$\langle -5 \;\; -5 \rangle$	$\langle +1 \quad 0 \rangle$	$\langle -1 \;\; +3 \rangle$
3	$\langle +4 \;\; -2 \rangle$	$\langle -3 \;\; -3 \rangle$	$\langle +5 \;\; -2 \rangle$

If the example at this iteration is $E = \langle 6 \;\; -5 \rangle$, then $u_{1,3}$ is closest and is marked by a '*'. The cells in the box are neighbors. At this iteration $\alpha(501) = 1/2$, so the new weights are:

$$W_{1,2} = \langle \;\; 5 \quad 4 \rangle + \tfrac{1}{2}[\langle 6 \;\; -5 \rangle - \langle \;\; 5 \quad 4 \rangle] = \langle 5.5 \;\; -.5 \rangle$$

$$W_{1,3} = \langle \;\; 7 \;\; -6 \rangle + \tfrac{1}{2}[\langle 6 \;\; -5 \rangle - \langle \;\; 7 \;\; -6 \rangle] = \langle 6.5 \;\; -5.5 \rangle$$

$$W_{2,2} = \langle \;\; 1 \quad 0 \rangle + \tfrac{1}{2}[\langle 6 \;\; -5 \rangle - \langle \;\; 1 \quad 0 \rangle] = \langle 3.5 \;\; -2.5 \rangle$$

$$W_{2,3} = \langle -1 \quad 3 \rangle + \tfrac{1}{2}[\langle 6 \;\; -5 \rangle - \langle -1 \quad 3 \rangle] = \langle 2.5 \;\; -1 \rangle$$

other weights = unchanged.

This completes the iteration.

7.3.4   Demonstrations

Kohonen has performed many beautiful experiments to demonstrate the "self-organizing" properties of his algorithm. We will sample a few in this section.

Grid of Cells Learning Inputs from a Square
Figure 7.5 shows how a grid of cells can self-organize when presented with inputs chosen at random from the unit square. Each cell has two weights, and the corresponding point on the plane is plotted in the figures. To indicate how cells are arranged in the output grid, we draw a line connecting the point for cell $u_{h,i}$'s weights to the points for the cell's four neighbors $(u_{h,i+1}, u_{h,i-1}, u_{h+1,i}, \text{and } u_{h-1,i})$.[3]

---

3. Note that different neighborhoods are used here and for the example in section 7.3.3.

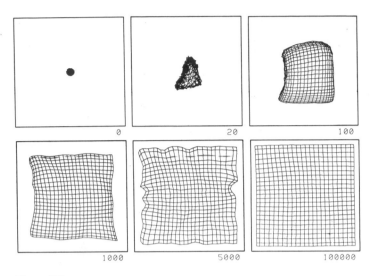

Figure 7.5
A grid of cells organizing into a square.

Initially (at iteration 0) the weights of cells are chosen at random near the center of the square. As iterations progress the weights of cells organize so that inputs that are close together activate output cells that are close.

Notice that there are symmetries involved, so we are not guaranteed that cell $u_{1,1}$'s weights will end up in the upper-left corner; they might just as well be any of the four corners. Similarly cell $u_{1,24}$'s weights can occupy either of the two corners adjacent to cell $u_{1,1}$'s corner.

Space-Filling Curves
Figure 7.6 shows an experiment where the output cells are arranged in a line rather than a grid. Inputs are points chosen at random from a triangle-shaped figure. As before, we plot the output cell weights, and we join neighboring pairs of cell weights by a line.

Notice how the cells organize themselves to cover (fill) the space while still preserving neighborhoods as best they can.

Grid of Cells Learning Inputs from a Cactus Pattern
Figure 7.7 shows a beautiful experiment that is similar to a grid of cells learning inputs from a square. Here, however, the inputs come from the irregular shape of a cactus. Covering a cactus shape with cells from a grid while preserving neighborhood relations presents a severe test. Yet the

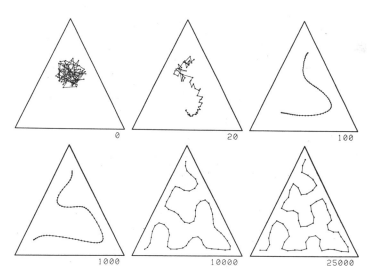

Figure 7.6
Cells can arrange themselves into a space-filling curve.

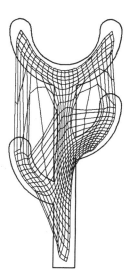

Figure 7.7
A difficult shape for a grid of cells.

algorithm produces a very reasonable solution. (Do you see where the four corners of the grid are mapped?)

Phoneme Maps

In another experiment Kohonen and associates [122] trained a grid of cells using spectral data from (Finnish) speech. Here the number of input dimensions, p, was 15 rather than 2 as in previous examples. Data was chosen at random times and was unlabeled.

After training, the phoneme map was calibrated with 50 samples of each phoneme. Each phoneme activated a small local group of cells most strongly, and these cells were then labeled with the corresponding phoneme.

After labeling, it was possible to trace the path of activated cells caused by any utterance, and to note the corresponding phoneme string that was traversed. Only areas occupying at least some minimum amount of time were labeled; these were likely to be phonemes, whereas the others were transitory sounds.

The phoneme string, once extracted, was then matched with string for words (using special string-matching algorithms developed for the task). The result was a *phonetic typewriter* that could produce words from utterances (Kohonen [121]).

7.3.5 Dimensionality, Neighborhood Size, and Final Comments

In practice, the dimensionality of the grid of output cells cannot be too high or else too many cells will be required. For example a 10-dimensional grid of cells with only 4 cells in each dimension would already require 4^{10} output cells.

The size of the neighborhood affects performance of the algorithm. In general the larger the neighborhood of cells, the easier for a group of cells to become correctly arranged (without "twists" or "folds"). However, the larger the neighborhood, then the greater the tendency for cell weights to group themselves near the centroid of the inputs and to move away from the borders of the region.

Let us consider the two extreme cases. If each cell has no other neighbors, then we lose any topology-preserving properties. Kohonen's algorithm is very similar to k-means clustering in this case. The other extreme has every cell as a neighbor of every other cell. In this case all cells gravitate toward the centroid of the training examples.

For an application such as speech processing, topology-preserving maps seem like a good way to reduce dimensionality of the input while preserving important information. An interesting approach to understanding multiple speakers would be to have an initial stage of topology-preserving cells that quickly adapt to a new speaker. If we picture a plane of such cells as a rubberized sheet, then we might think of deforming it to match the phonemes of a new speaker. This would allow higher-level processing of the speech input to proceed with minimal accommodation to the new speaker.

We will again see the idea that cell locations are important and the use of planes of cells when we examine work by Fukushima and by LeCun and associates in section 12.3.

7.4 ART1

ART1 is one of a series of architectures for unsupervised learning by Gail Carpenter and Steve Grossberg [33]. ART stands for *adaptive resonance theory*. These architectures are biologically motivated, with much attention to seeing how the collective actions of ensembles of cells can cause behavior that is analogous to cognitive phenomena in humans and animals. However, in keeping with our focus on functionality, we will examine only those aspects of ART1 that apply to problems of learning and classification.

7.4.1 Important Aspects of the Algorithm

ART1 clusters training examples $\{E^k\}$ with discrete coordinates, $E_j^k \in \{1, 0\}$. Each cluster is defined by a prototype, P_i, that may combine characteristics of more than one training example. There is no set number of clusters; clusters are created as needed. This solves what Grossberg refers to as the *stability-plasticity dilemma*, namely how to let a system adapt, yet prevent current inputs from destroying past training. ART1 allows a training example to modify a cluster only if that cluster is sufficiently close to the training example; otherwise a new cluster is formed.

As originally defined, ART1 does not treat 1 and 0 symmetrically; a 1 carries information whereas a 0 is definitely a second-class citizen. For example if a pattern is close to a prototype P_i with many 1's, then it is considered a member of P_i's cluster and differences are attributed to unimportant features or to noise. On the other hand if P_i has few 1's, then the same number of differences may be significant so that the pattern will not join P_i's cluster. Such asymmetry between 1 and 0 is reasonable for tasks such as recognizing isolated images against neutral backgrounds. We will see a way to introduce symmetry into ART1 in the next section.

Any clustering algorithm that does not prespecify the number of clusters must nevertheless have some parameter that controls cluster granularity. For ART1 this parameter is called the vigilance parameter, ρ. Regardless of the setting for ρ, ART1 is *stable* for a finite set of training examples, in that final clusters will not change with additional iterations from the original set of training examples. However, the order of the training examples may influence the final prototypes and clusters.

7.4.2   The Algorithm

Barbara Moore [147] has provided a concise review of ART1 from a functionality perspective, and we will follow much of her analysis. Every iteration consists of taking a training example E^k and examining existing prototypes that are sufficiently similar. Order of selection of prototypes is by the fraction of 1's in common with E^k. If a prototype P_i is found that is acceptable according to a test based upon the vigilance parameter, ρ, the example E^k is added to P_i's cluster and P_i is modified to make it closer to E^k. If no prototype is acceptable, then E^k becomes the prototype for a new cluster.

Details of the algorithm are given in figure 7.8. Several comments are in order. First note that for a vector X with components in $\{1, 0\}$,

$$\|X\|^2 = \text{number of 1's in } X.$$

$$X \cdot Y = X \cap Y = \text{number of 1's in common between } X \text{ and } Y.$$

Also the constant β in step 3 is a "tie breaker" that favors prototypes with more 1's over those with fewer 1's whenever all the 1's in the prototype are also in the example being searched.

In step 4 we are verifying that a sufficiently large number of the 1's are matched. Another way of viewing this step is that a 'default' prototype

$$P_0 = \langle 1 \ 1 \ \cdots \ 1 \rangle$$

is always available for matching.

Let:

β = small positive number
p = the dimension of the training examples and prototypes
ρ = vigilance parameter, with $0 \leq \rho < 1$.

1. Start with no prototype vectors.

2. Perform iterations until none of the training examples cause any change in the set of prototype vectors; at this point quit because stability has been achieved. For each iteration take the next training example, E^k, chosen in cyclic order.

3. Find the prototype P_i (if any) not yet tried during this iteration that maximizes

$$\frac{P_i \cdot E^k}{\beta + \|P_i\|^2}.$$

4. Test whether P_i is sufficiently similar to E^k:

$$\frac{P_i \cdot E^k}{\beta + \|P_i\|^2} > \frac{\|E^k\|^2}{\beta + p}?$$

    4a. If not, or there are no untried prototypes for this iteration, then:

        4aa. Make a new cluster with prototype E^k.

        4ab. End this iteration and return to step 2 for the next example.

    4A. If sufficiently similar, then test for vigilance acceptability:

$$\frac{P_i \cdot E^k}{\|E^k\|^2} \geq \rho?$$

        4Aa. If acceptable then E^k belongs in P_i's cluster. Modify P_i to be more like E^k

$$P_i = P_i \cap E^k$$

           and go to step 2 for the next iteration with the next example.

        4AA. If not acceptable, then return to step 3 to try another prototype.

Figure 7.8
The ART1 algorithm.

In step 4A we are testing that a sufficient fraction of the 1's in the current training example match the prototype. Increased vigilance will result in more clusters, and conversely.

Finally in step 4Aa, whenever a training example E^k joins a cluster we modify the corresponding prototype, P_i, by setting to 0 any component for which $E_j^k = 0$. Thus a new cluster can only have fewer and fewer 1's as iterations progress. Note that it is possible for a training example to form a new cluster but eventually to leave that cluster because other training examples have joined it.

Figure 7.9 gives a sample run of ART1 on letter patterns. Each row shows all existing prototypes and the order in which they are tried for each letter. RES (resonance) indicates the matching or new prototype (possibly after modification). When the patterns are presented a second time some prototypes will change. Eventually the system will reach equilibrium and no more prototype changes will occur.

Carpenter and Grossberg proved a number of theorems about ART1's behavior. The two most important are:

THEOREM 7.1 (Stability)   *ART1 will reach a stable set of prototypes for any finite set of training examples.*

THEOREM 7.2 (Direct Accessing)   *After stability has been reached, every training example E^k will directly access its prototype.*

Direct accessing means that the *first* prototype, P_i, produced in step 3 that maximizes

$$\frac{P_i \cdot E^k}{\beta + \|P_i\|^2}$$

is guaranteed to satisfy the tests in steps 4 and 4A.

Recently David Rosen has pointed out a simple way to make ART1 behave symmetrically with respect to 0 and 1 inputs. We can simply duplicate the inputs and switch 0's and 1's in the second copy. This makes all patterns have the same number of 0's and 1's.

7.5   ART2

Carpenter and Grossberg have gone on to develop ART2 for clustering continuous data (Carpenter and Grossberg [34]). We will look at ART2-A

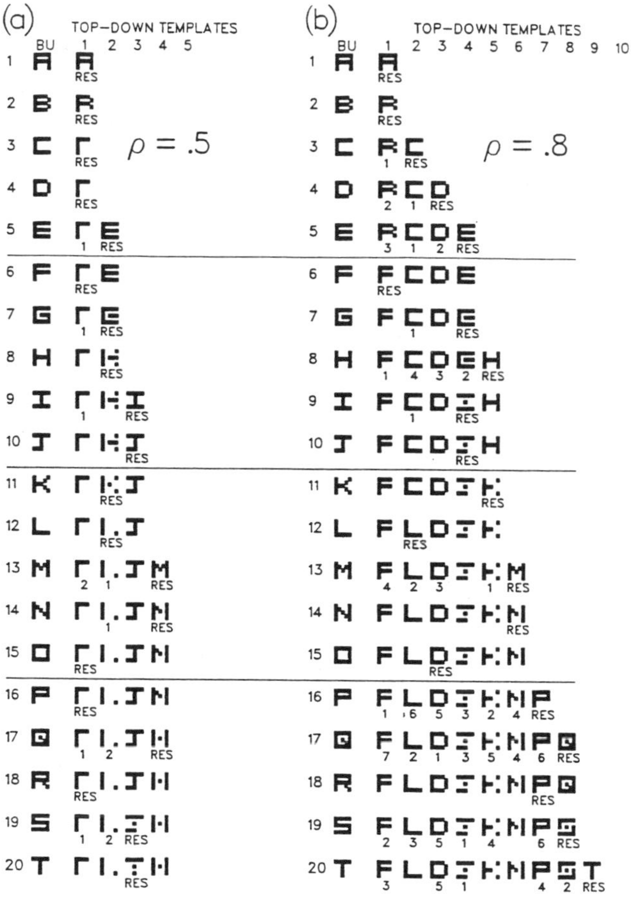

Figure 7.9
ART1 applied to letter patterns with two different vigilance values.

(Carpenter, Grossberg, and Rosen [37]), a version of ART2 that emphasizes functionality and speed. There are two basic differences between ART2-A and (the functional version of) ART1. First, the input data is preprocessed by normalization and by suppressing values below a certain threshold. This scales the data and helps eliminate small noise signals. Second, prototypes are updated by moving them a fraction β toward a new training example falling in that prototype's class; in the ART1 discrete case prototypes were simply intersected with the training example. Figure 7.10 gives the algorithm, and figure 7.11 gives an example.

Let: p = the dimension of the training examples and prototypes

α = positive number $\leq 1/\sqrt{p}$

β = small positive number

θ = normalization parameter, with $0 < \theta < 1/\sqrt{p}$

ρ = vigilance parameter, with $0 \leq \rho < 1$.

0. Preprocess all training examples using threshold θ:

   0a. Normalize all E^k.

   0b. Replace every component E_j^k that is $\leq \theta$ by 0.

   0c. Renormalize all E^k.

1. Start with no prototype vectors.

2. Perform iterations until none of the training examples cause any change in the set of prototype vectors; at this point quit because stability has been achieved. For each iteration take the next training example, E^k, chosen in cyclic order.

3. Find the prototype P_i (if any) not yet tried during this iteration that maximizes

   $P_i \cdot E^k$.

   (Break ties by arbitrary choice.)

4. Test whether P_i is sufficiently similar to E^k:

   $$P_i \cdot E^k \geq \alpha \sum_j E_j^k?$$

   4a. If not then:

      4aa. Make a new cluster with prototype set to E^k.

      4ab. End this iteration and return to step 2 for the next example.

   4A. If sufficiently similar, then test for vigilance acceptability:

      $P_i \cdot E^k \geq \rho?$

      4Aa. If acceptable then E^k belongs in P_i's cluster. Modify P_i to be more like E^k

      $$P_i = \frac{(1 - \beta)P_i + \beta E^k}{\|(1 - \beta)P_i + \beta E^k\|}$$

      and go to step 2 for the next iteration with the next example.

      4AA. If not acceptable, then make a new cluster with prototype set to E^k.

Figure 7.10
The ART2 algorithm.

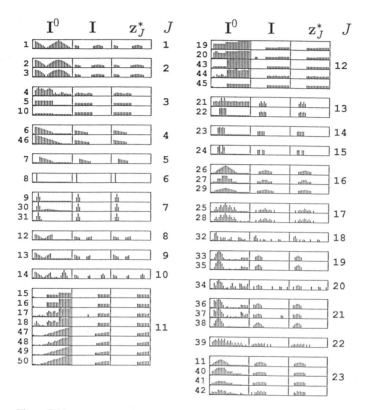

Figure 7.11
An ART2-A example. Columns represent original input, preprocessed input, and prototype after modification. Numbers at left are example numbers, and numbers at right are category numbers.

7.6 Using Clustering Algorithms for Supervised Learning

7.6.1 Labeling Clusters

It is possible to adapt any clustering algorithm to perform supervised learning. One way to do this is by merely labeling the clusters with the most common correct response (C^k) of elements in that cluster. This may not work very well, however, if clusters have significant mixtures of correct responses.

Robert Hecht-Nielsen [95, 96] has combined Kohonen's topology-preserving maps and the instar/outstar algorithm of Grossberg [80] into the *counterpropagation algorithm.* The basic idea is first to train a layer of cells using topology preserving maps (without regard to outputs). Then each cell outputs the *average desired output* for those training examples that get mapped into that particular cell. We can either compute this average output directly or iteratively using Grossberg's instar/outstar algorithm.

Another approach is first to group training examples according to correct response, and then to cluster each group. This provides several "pure" clusters for every classification. Now when a new input is presented, it is labeled with the label of the appropriate cluster. This approach can also break down if training examples with different classifications are intermingled to a large extent. Better to use supervised learning methods in such cases.

Note that all of these methods essentially construct a nearest neighbor lookup table, whose size equals the number of cells used for the topology-preserving map algorithm. A new input selects a closest entry in the table, and the corresponding correct output can then be read off.

7.6.2 ARTMAP or Supervised ART

A recent addition to the ART family is ARTMAP, a supervised version of ART (Carpenter, Grossberg, and Reynolds [36, 35]). The basic idea of the algorithm is to run ART1 or ART2 for the input patterns, but to keep prototype groups "pure" by temporarily increasing vigilance when necessary. Thus if a new example E^k is about to be placed into a prototype group with a different classification, then the vigilance is temporarily increased enough to rule out association with that prototype. (The next time the algorithm sees example E^k, the newly formed prototype will be closest.)

Intuitively this approach is appealing because it nicely integrates clustering with supervised learning. On the other hand problems caused by noise might be amplified by this approach. It will be interesting to see comparisons with backpropagation and other algorithms that will emerge over the next several years.

7.7 Exercises

1. Show how *k*-means clustering works for $k = 2$ on the following set of training examples:

$$E^1 = \langle \quad 1 \quad -1 \quad 1 \quad -1 \quad -1 \rangle$$

$$E^2 = \langle \quad 1 \quad -1 \quad 1 \quad 1 \quad -1 \rangle$$

$$E^3 = \langle -1 \quad 1 \quad -1 \quad 1 \quad 1 \rangle$$

$$E^4 = \langle -1 \quad 1 \quad -1 \quad -1 \quad -1 \rangle$$

$$E^5 = \langle -1 \quad -1 \quad -1 \quad 1 \quad -1 \rangle$$

2. Simulate ART1 for the training examples from the last exercise (after replacing -1 activations by 0). Use $\rho = 1/2$ and $\beta = 0.1$.

3. In k-means clustering, is it possible for a cluster to be emptied of training examples?

*4. Complete the proof outlined in section 7.2.1 that the convergent k-means clustering algorithm actually converges.

5. In Kohonen's algorithm for topology-preserving maps (figure 7.4), what happens if:

(a) $\alpha(t) < 0$?

(b) $\alpha(t) > 1$?

(c) $\alpha(t) > 2$?

6. Give a loose bound on the number of iterations that ART1 can make before reaching stability for N training examples, each having p inputs.

7. (research) Give a better bound on the number of iterations that ART1 can make before reaching stability for N training examples, each having p inputs, using parameters ρ and β.

7.8 Programming Projects

1. Implement convergent k-means clustering and try it on some data. One possible source of artificial data is to take k centers, and generate points at centers plus Gaussian noise. (Stand-alone code.)

2. Make a set of 26 training examples by representing letters of the alphabet on a 5×5 grid. Try k-means clustering on this data with $k = 4, 6, 8, 10$.

3. Implement Kohonen's topology-preserving maps and try a 10×10 grid of cells learning a square, as in section 7.3.4. Let the neighborhood of each cell be its 4 closest neighbors (except for cells on the edges or corners of the grid).

(a) When learning is completed, print out the 10×10 grid of coordinate pairs.

*(b) Program a graphical display to see the cell weights self-organizing, as in figure 7.5.

4. Program ART1 and try it on the data from project 2 above. Experiment with various settings for ρ to see how many clusters are generated and which letters are grouped together. (Stand-alone code.)

5. Generate additional *Taxtime!* training examples (see section 2.5) and cluster them using ART2.

III LEARNING IN MULTILAYER MODELS

8 The Distributed Method and Radial Basis Functions

We now begin the study of learning in multilayer networks.

Why use multilayer networks rather than single-layer networks? This important question is all too frequently overlooked in a rush to throw data into a backpropagation program or some other network learning algorithm. If we are primarily interested in constructing a model from training data that will generalize well, then the only reason to use a multilayer network is to fit the training data better than would be possible with a single-layer model so that better generalization might be achieved. Therefore if a single-layer model fits the training data as well as a multilayer network, *then by all means use the single-layer model!* In this case the single-layer model will be faster, simpler, quicker to (re)train, and it should give better generalization results. In fact it is good practice always to attempt to fit data with a single-layer model before trying any multilayer algorithms.

Our goal will be algorithms with as many of the following qualities as possible:

- good generalization to unseen data
- fast training speed
- suitability for large problems ("scaling up")
- ease of derivation of analytic bounds on performance, and
- models that are "robustness preserving" (see next chapter).

One key idea for algorithms in part III is to *take the difficult task of fitting data by a network and to somehow transform the problem into single-cell learning.* Any such approach is almost certain to be fast and to scale up for large problems; other goals may or may not be satisfied.

In chapter 8 we will look at the distributed method and radial basis functions. These algorithms create a layer of intermediate cells with very little effort, after which single-cell learning is used for the output cells. Section 9.3 gives an analysis of the distributed method. Finally, in chapter 10 we will look at *constructive algorithms* or *growth algorithms*. These algorithms grow a network as the learning progresses, using single-cell learning algorithms at each stage. Finally, we will look at backpropagation, currently the most widely used learning algorithm. For many people connectionist learning *is* backpropagation. We will also see several important applications of backpropagation and consider some significant NP-completeness results.

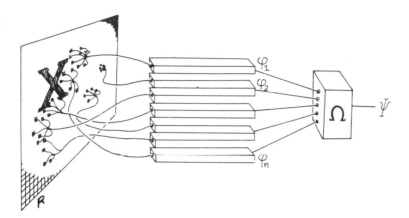

Figure 8.1
Rosenblatt's idea. The ϕ_i are randomly generated Boolean functions. (From Minsky and Papert [145].)

8.1   Rosenblatt's Approach

To fit data more closely than is possible with a single-cell model we need a network with intermediate cells. But how can weights be found for such cells? Even harder, how can we find weights without requiring excessive computation? In this chapter we will look at several 2-layer models where weights for intermediate cells are easy to compute. But first some historical background.

Frank Rosenblatt suggested using an intermediate layer of *randomly generated Boolean functions*, as illustrated in figure 8.1, and using the perceptron learning algorithm to train the top cell's weights. The idea was that each random cell[1] would have relatively few inputs, so that a large enough collection of such cells would include cells that computed the *critical features* for a problem. Having such critical features would assure the existence of a set of top-cell weights that correctly classify all inputs. Once we knew that such weights existed, the perceptron convergence theorem (theorem 3.1) would guarantee that perceptron learning would find some set of weights that correctly classified all inputs. Therefore the procedure would produce a correct network.

1. Strictly speaking, random function need not be representable as a single cell. However, for Rosenblatt's intermediate cells we can expand our notion of a cell to permit any possible function of its inputs.

The problem with Rosenblatt's approach was the requirement that intermediate cells have relatively few inputs. This turns out to be a severe limitation on their computational ability. For example Minsky and Papert [145] showed that the parity function on p inputs could not be computed by a strictly 2-layer network unless at least one intermediate cell had p inputs.

The alternative to limiting the number of inputs would be to allow intermediate cells to see all inputs, but Minsky and Papert pointed out that this would also present difficulties. The most severe problem would be that the combinatorics would become devastating. With p inputs there are 2^{2^p} possible functions; therefore there is very little chance of randomly selecting a particular feature detector if more than a few inputs are allowed. Moreover, if we were going to have an unrealistically large number of functions, why not let them see all inputs so that by chance one of the functions could compute the desired output for the entire network? Thus the alternative of allowing intermediate cells to see all inputs makes the problem trivial and/or impractical to solve.

Note that perceptron learning requires that *all* critical features be recognized by intermediate cells. If even one feature was not totally correct (or if the problem involved noisy data) then the data could become non-separable and we would no longer have confidence in perceptron learning's performance.

8.2   The Distributed Method

Figure 8.2 illustrates an alternative to Rosenblatt's approach that is called the *distributed method* (Gallant and Smith [74], Gallant [72]). The differences are as follows:

1. Every intermediate cell sees all inputs rather than a small subset.

2. We seek a *distributed representation* of the critical features in the activations of the collection of random cells, rather than individual cells that recognize critical features.

3. Each intermediate cell is a threshold logic unit (or linear discriminant) with randomly generated weights; thus only separable functions are allowed for intermediate cells.

4. For the trainable cell we use the pocket algorithm (with ratchet) rather than perceptron learning.

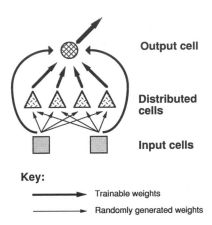

Figure 8.2
The distributed method.

---

1. Generate a layer of d intermediate cells (called *distributed cells*) just above the input layer as in figure 8.2. Each intermediate cell sees all p input cells and has integer weights and bias generated at random in some range $[-K, K]$. Once generated, these distributed cell weights do not change.

2. Remaining cells in the network use single-cell (or winner-take-all group) learning algorithms. Note, however, that their inputs now include the outputs from the newly added distributed cells.

Figure 8.3
Algorithm for the distributed method.

Figure 8.3 gives the algorithm.

The first and third points allow arbitrarily complex functions to be computed (see exercise 1 below).

The second point is the most important difference with Rosenblatt's method. Rather than hoping to generate individual cells that are feature detectors, we want the critical feature information to be available in the *collective pattern of intermediate cell activations*. These activations give a *distributed representation* of the features, as defined in section 2.2. The reason for naming this algorithm the distributed method was to emphasize this point.

Another way of seeing what is going on is to consider the situation from the perspective of the trainable top cell. Before intermediate cells are added, every training example consists of exactly p inputs. However, after the addition of d distributed cells, every training example is presented to the top cell as $p + d$ inputs. Thus we are increasing the dimension in which the training examples are represented, which makes the collection of training examples easier to learn and makes them more likely to be separable. This has been demonstrated by simulations and is consistent with a related result by Cover [41, 47].

8.2.1 Cover's Formula

Suppose there are N training examples, E^k, in Euclidean p space (i.e., E_j^k is real-valued) and assume the examples are in *general position*, meaning that every subset of p or fewer training examples is linearly independent. Suppose further that the training examples are labeled at random by $+1$ or -1. Then Cover showed that the probability that the set of training examples is separable is:

$$1 \qquad \text{if } N \le p + 1$$

$$\frac{2}{2^N} \sum_{i=0}^{p} \binom{N-1}{i} \quad \text{if } N > p + 1.$$

This of course is the probability that $N - 1$ flips of a fair coin will yield p or fewer heads. Therefore when $(N - 1)/2$ is smaller than p the probability is greater than $1/2$ that the training examples will be separable.

The situation with the distributed method is similar, in that the top cell is seeing N training examples in dimension $p' = p + d$ (where d is the number of distributed cells). This would suggest that enough distributed cells, $d \ge ((N - 1)/2) - p$, would give probability $\ge .5$ of separability. However, there is an important difference: distributed cell activations are in $\{+1, -1\}$ rather than continuous values. This makes it much less likely that the set of training examples will be in general position and makes it less likely that they will be separable. While a corresponding formula for the probability of separability is not known for such cases, Cover's formula nevertheless gives insight into why the addition of distributed cells gives increased probability of separability.

8.2.2 Robustness-Preserving Functions

Recall that in the distributed method we use threshold logic units for the distributed cells rather than arbitrary Boolean functions (which might be nonseparable functions). The reason that nonseparable Boolean functions were excluded was to obtain a robustness-preserving network.

The term "robustness-preserving" requires some explanation. After generating a network from a set of training examples, suppose we present an unseen example E that is very close to one of the training examples, E^k. It would be desirable if the output from the network tended to be the same for E as for E^k. If a model has this property then we call it *robustness-preserving*, because if the training examples are dense enough in the inputs then we would expect robust generalization to unseen data. It is important to avoid overstrict application of this principle, however, or everything except nearest-neighbor[2] learning algorithms would be ruled out. Thus calling for robustness-preserving algorithms is a kind of inductive bias (see Utgoff [193]). It is an a priori constraint on learning that is expected to produce better generalization for most real-world problem classes.

To see why some restriction on the intermediate cells is necessary, consider the case where we choose intermediate cells from all Boolean functions on p inputs (rather than restrict the selection to separable functions). Suppose E is an input that differs from training example E^k in only one position. Because the intermediate cells are arbitrary Boolean functions, then with probability exactly 1/2 any intermediate cell will give *differing* outputs for E and E^k. Therefore the patterns of activations of the intermediate cells will be *totally uncorrelated* for E and E^k, and the two outputs from the entire network will differ with large probability.[3] This contradicts our notion of robustness-preserving.

Now consider the distributed method where intermediate cells are restricted to separable functions (i.e., threshold logic units). If two inputs are close, then the outputs from any distributed cell will very likely be identical for the two examples. This was nicely demonstrated by Amari [3, 4] as follows. Suppose we have p inputs and d distributed cells. Now let D_I be the input distance defined to be

$$D_I = 1/p \times \text{hamming distance between two inputs}$$

---

2. The *nearest neighbor* learning algorithm is to remember all training examples and to classify an unseen input in the same way as the closest training example.
3. If weights from intermediate cells to the output cell dominate weights from input cells to the output cell, then the outputs will differ with probability approaching 0.5. Conversely, if the weights from input cells dominate (so that intermediate cells are effectively ignored) then outputs will be more likely to agree.

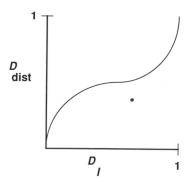

Figure 8.4
Distributed cell distance versus input distance.

and let D_{dist} be the output distance, defined to be

$D_{\text{dist}} = 1/d \times$ hamming distance of distributed cell activations.

Amari showed that if the distributed cell weights were normally distributed, then

$$D_{\text{dist}} \approx \frac{2}{\pi} \sin^{-1}(D_I).$$

This relation is graphed in figure 8.4.

Note that small D_I means small D_{dist}, so that output patterns of distributed cells will be similar for similar inputs.

Another way of seeing this result is to consider the weighted sum S_i that any cell computes. If we start with some input E^k and change a few bits at random, this will perturb S_i but would only make S_i change sign if S_i were already close to 0 and the perturbations were in the appropriate direction. However, the larger the input dimension p, the less likely that S_i will be close to 0 (for a randomly selected input), because we have a situation analogous to a random walk where the expected magnitude of S_i grows with $\sqrt{p}$. Therefore two close inputs to any threshold logic unit are likely to produce the same output, which in turn implies that the pattern of activations for the distributed cells will be similar for two close inputs.

Finally we can apply this same argument to an output cell. For two close inputs an output cell will see two close patterns of activations in the distributed cells, along with the raw inputs that are also close. Therefore

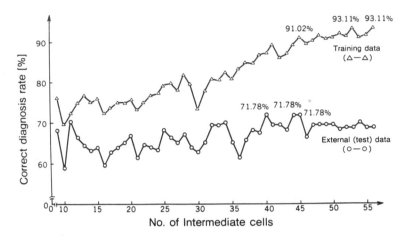

Figure 8.5
Performance versus number of intermediate cells.

the same output is likely to be produced for two close inputs, satisfying the definition of robustness-preserving.

We have shown that using threshold logic units for intermediate cells is *sufficient* to guarantee a robustness-preserving model, but it is not *necessary*. Section 8.6 offers one of several other possibilities for robustness-preserving intermediate cells.

8.3   Examples

8.3.1   Hepatobiliary Data

Yoshida, Hayashi, and Imura [216] used the distributed method to build a model for diagnosing hepatobiliary disorders based upon actual patient data. They reported 71.8 percent generalization results, as compared with 63.2 percent using a statistical linear discriminant package ('DISCRIM' of SAS [179]). One of their graphs is given in figure 8.5. Notice that as the number of intermediate cells is increased the model fits the training data better and better.[4] Testing results also tend to improve up to the point where the model begins to "overfit the data." From this point on, general-

4. For 0 cells, training was 70.1 percent and generalization was 59.5 percent (personal communication).

ization declines slightly. For a good discussion on fitting and overfitting data in the context of decision trees, see Breiman et al. [29].

8.3.2 Artificial Data

To explore how well the distributed method could fit difficult artificial data, Donald Smith and this author experimented with some classical problems proposed by Minsky and Papert [145] and by others:

1. *Parity:* the output is true if an odd number of inputs are true.

2. *T-C:* differentiating T figures from C figures among images on a 5 × 5 or 6 × 6 retina with wraparound. Every image is either a T or a C.

3. *Multiplexor:* the first 2 inputs are interpreted as an index that selects one of the remaining 4 inputs to be copied to the output [16].

4. *Symmetry:* true if feature pairs {1,6}, {2,5}, and {3,4} all agree.

5. *Shiftleft:* of 14 features, features 8–14 are features 1–7 after either: shifting right one position (with wraparound), shifting left one position, or no change. The output is true for the 128 cases involving shift left. Errors are unavoidable for some inputs, such as all 1's.

6. *Random:* a randomly selected Boolean function on 7 Boolean inputs.

Figure 8.6 summarizes the results. For N training examples, this type of data required $\frac{2}{3}N$ to N distributed cells if the output cell was not connected to the input cells. Many fewer cells usually suffice if the output cell sees the input cells or for real-world rather than artificial data. These tests demonstrate that the distributed method can fit the most difficult classical training data.

8.4 How Many Cells?

In practice, how can we determine an appropriate number of distributed cells for good generalization?

The first step is to try 0 cells! Surprisingly often, even noisy data turns out to be separable. Another reason to try 0 cells is that in some cases distributed cells do not improve generalization, so again it would be best to use a single-layer model.

Once we have established a 0-cell baseline, we can try adding various numbers of intermediate cells. Two good methods for determining how many to add are *pruning data* and *leave-one-out* (or *n*-fold cross validation).

Problem and number of features	Number of training examples	Number of random cells	Approximate percent correct	Comments
parity 7	128	40	83	
		80	100	
		20	100	$-1, +1$ coefficients only
T-C 25	200	130	100	
T-C 49	392	95	65	
		190	84	
		380	100	
		230	100	using 2 random layers with 230 cells per layer
multiplexor 2, 4	64	50	100	
symmetry 6	64	50	100	only 8 examples +1
shiftleft 14	384	50	54*	*contradictory input data precludes 100% learning
		200	68*	
		300	76*	
		500	84*	
random 7	128	10	56	
		50	70	
		110	100	

Notes:

1. For each test 10,000 iterations were made.

2. Lines with 100 percent correct indicate fewest number of random cells needed to assure separability. This is an approximation.

3. Usually 3 to 6 trials were made to establish behavior.

4. The trainable output cell does not see the inputs, only the activations of the random discriminants. Better percentages are achieved if the inputs are also visible.

Figure 8.6
Distributed method results for difficult problems.

These are good techniques to remember for adjusting parameters, such as number of cells or number of training iterations, in many practical situations.

8.4.1   Pruning Data

If there is an abundance of training data, we can reserve some of it for determining how many distributed cells to use. We simply generate networks with various numbers of distributed cells from the remainder of the training data, and then check which number of cells gives best performance on the pruning data. This is exactly the approach that Hayashi et al. used for the hepatobiliary data in section 8.3.1. (We must be a little careful, however, about using the results from the pruning as an estimate for generalization to unseen data; strictly speaking we need a third set of (testing) data to get an estimate of generalization that is unbiased.)

8.4.2 Leave-One-Out

If there is less data, we can still compare generalization with different numbers of intermediate cells. Using a fixed set of intermediate cells, we train on all but one of the training examples and then test on that single training example. We repeat this process N times, leaving out one of the training examples each time, and use the average number of correct classifications (out of N) to estimate generalization. Now we can repeat this process for different numbers of distributed cells to decide how many to use. After determining the number of distributed cells, we retrain with all N training examples and this is our final network.

When trying more and more intermediate cells it is probably best to add to existing sets rather than generating completely new sets. For example if we try 10 distributed cells and next want to try 15, we should add 5 new cells to the previous 10 rather than generating 15 entirely new cells. This guarantees that the ability to represent functions is nondecreasing as the number of intermediate cells are increased.

As with pruning, we have to be careful about using the estimates from the leave-one-out runs as generalization estimates. However, Breiman et al. [29] report good estimates of generalization using this approach.

A faster alternative to leave-one-out is *n-fold cross validation*. Here we divide the training examples into n equal-sized groups, then train on $n - 1$ groups and test on the remaining group. We do this n times, once for each group, to get a generalization estimate for a set of distributed cells. By obtaining such estimates for various numbers of distributed cells we can decide how many to use for the final network (which is trained using all the training examples). Of course leave-one-out is the special case of n-fold cross validation when $n = N$. Breiman et al. report that 10-fold cross validation usually gives sufficiently reliable results.

8.5 Radial Basis Functions

Another constructive algorithm for generating a network from data is the *radial basis functions (RBF) method* that is illustrated in figure 8.7. This method was originally proposed by Powell [164], but see also Niranjan and Fallside [150].

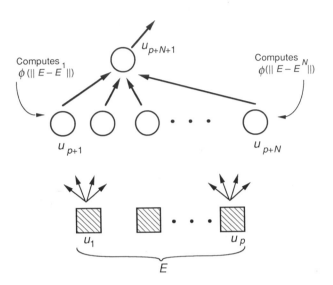

Figure 8.7
For each training example, radial basis function output cells receive $\Phi(\ )$ applied to distances between E and E^1 through E^N.

Suppose we have N real-valued training examples $\{E^i\}$ for p input cells. Letting ϕ be some real-valued function, for each training example E^i we can generate an intermediate cell u_{p+i} that, when presented with input vector E, gives activation

$$u_{p+i} = \phi(\|E - E^i\|).$$

Here $\|E - E^i\|$ is the Euclidean distance between E and E^i. A common choice for ϕ is

$$\phi(x) = (x^2 + c)^{1/2} \text{ for some constant } c \geq 0.$$

(Of course for $c = 0$ the intermediate cell activations are the Euclidean distances.)

We can use the intermediate cells as a basis to represent real-valued outputs $\{C^k\}$ for the N training examples $\{E^k\}$ if there are weights

$$W = \langle W_{p+1} \ldots W_{p+N} \rangle$$

that satisfy

$$\sum_{j=1}^{N} W_{p+j} \phi(\|E^k - E^j\|) = C^k. \tag{8.1}$$

Thus if the output cell was linear (see exercise 11 of chapter 1) so that

$$u_{p+N+1} = S_{p+N+1} = \sum_{j=1}^{N} W_{p+j} u_{p+j}$$

then u_{p+N+1} would compute correct activations C^k for every training example E^k.

We can always find such W if the $N \times N$ matrix

$$\Phi = \{\phi(\|E^k - E^j\|)\}_{i,j=1,\dots,N}$$

is nonsingular, that is, if and only if the vectors

$$V^k = \langle \phi(\|E^1 - E^k\|), \phi(\|E^2 - E^k\|), \dots, \phi(\|E^N - E^k\|) \rangle$$

form a basis. In practice Φ is usually nonsingular; in fact for $c > 0$ Miccheli [141] showed Φ is always nonsingular.

Turning to neural network problems where the top cell produces activations in $\{+1, -1\}$ and C^k is $\{+1, -1\}$, we would like to be able to use fewer than N RBF's in the intermediate layer. This is usually possible because we no longer require that the sum in equation (8.1) be exactly C^k, only that it have the same sign. Using fewer RBF's also decreases the tendency to overfit the data by reducing the number of adjustable parameters. There are efficient ways to find best mean squared error solutions to such problems, but they are outside the scope of this book. (See matrix algebra texts such as Golub and van Loan [79].)

A number of researchers have looked at RBF methods, particularly with speech data, including Niranjan and Fallside [150] and Renals and Rohwer [169].

8.6 A Variant: The Anchor Algorithm

Recall that the distributed method uses intermediate cells consisting of linear discriminants with randomly chosen weights. This allows speedy network learning while maintaining a robustness-preserving model. However, there are other possibilities for intermediate cells that accomplish these same goals.

A RBF approach has been developed by Renals and Rohwer and a later variant explored by Ryohei Nakano[5] and this author. The idea is simple.

5. Knowledge Systems Laboratory, NTT, Yokosuka, Japan.

We pick at random d of the training examples to serve as *anchor* points and measure how far (Euclidean distance) any set of inputs is from each of these points. This gives us d distances for each input, which we consider as activations from d anchor cells. As with the distributed method, these additional activations boost the representation of network inputs from p to $p + d$ to help learning. The pocket algorithm with ratchet is used to train the output cells.[6]

Several observations are in order here.

• Activations from anchor cells are real-valued numbers, rather than numbers in $\{+1, -1, 0\}$. This causes no problem because the pocket algorithm with ratchet can accept real-valued inputs.

• The correct classification for the training example is not used in the distance computation for anchor cells.

• It is important that Euclidean distance is a nonlinear function (exercise 3).

• A bias may be computed for output cells in the anchor algorithm.

Both the distributed method and the anchor algorithm require approximately the same time for learning. Therefore the key question is how the two algorithms compare with respect to generalization. Several experiments have been run by the author, but the results are inconclusive. For some data the anchor algorithm performed better and for other data the distributed method seemed preferable. More experiments are needed with this algorithm, but it is clear that the anchor algorithm should be considered a viable alternative to the distributed method, and that it may prove helpful for some problems.

8.7 Scaling, Multiple Outputs, and Parallelism

8.7.1 Scaling Properties

By design, the distributed method, radial basis functions, and the anchor algorithm all scale up to large networks. For the distributed method it is easy to generate random weights for intermediate cells, and we can use

---

6. For problems with real-valued outputs, it is also possible to use the Widrow-Hoff algorithm of section 6.3 to train the top cell. See also Poggio and Girosi [160, 161].

single-cell learning algorithms for the output cells. This makes learning much faster than with comparable fixed-network algorithms (such as backpropagation, chapter 11). By cutting the time required for learning by a factor of 100 to 1,000, we can tackle larger problems with more input features or more training examples. Being able to process a large number of training examples can be very important, because the amount of training data that can be modeled is often the main factor that governs how well the resulting model generalizes. In this way *training speed* of an algorithm affects its *generalization ability*.

8.7.2 Multiple Outputs and Parallelism

The algorithms in this chapter are especially efficient when several different output cells compute (possibly unrelated) functions of the network inputs. For example we could think of many interesting functions to compute on a set of inputs that comprise a grid of pixels. Because the distributed cells (or RBF cells) are not tuned to any particular output cell, the same set of intermediate cell activations can be reused for any number of output cells, as illustrated in figure 8.8 (this is especially useful when output cells comprise a winner-take-all group). We need only the same number of intermediate cells as the single output function that requires the greatest number of such cells. Once we have invested in a layer of distributed cells to boost the representational dimensionality of the training examples, these cells

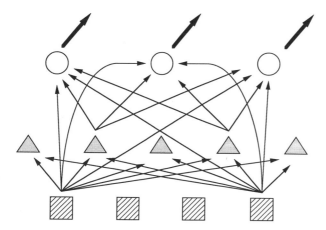

Figure 8.8
The distributed method used with several output cells or with a winner-take-all group.

will help any number of learning problems having the same set of network inputs.

Notice that we can learn weights for each output cell independently of all other outputs. This makes it easy to parallelize learning for multioutput problems. Of course the computation of intermediate cell weights is easy to do in parallel for both training and execution of the network.

8.7.3   A Computational Speedup for Learning

There is an important trick that greatly speeds up learning when there are a finite number of training examples. In fact if there are d distributed cells in the network, then this technique will reduce learning time to about $1/(d + 1)$ what it would have been otherwise. We simply precompute distributed cell activations for all training examples and store them. Now whenever we select a training example in the pocket algorithm or pocket algorithm with ratchet, we need only compute the top-cell activations using the saved activations for the distributed cells; we never need to recompute distributed cell activations.

8.7.4   Concluding Remarks

The constructive methods in this chapter seek to reduce a difficult problem, learning in networks, to an easier problem, learning in single-cell models. This gives significant gains in speed, thereby allowing large amounts of training data to be handled. More training examples usually means better generalization.

For smaller problems where training speed is not an important consideration, network learning approaches such as backpropagation (chapter 11) can sometimes give better generalization. However it is not clear which small problems are more suitable for backpropagation and which for the methods of this chapter, except that backpropagation seems preferable for problems that must compute real-valued outputs.

For an interesting recent comparison of radial basis functions and backpropagation, see Lee [129].

8.8   Exercises

1. Show that for any Boolean function f on p inputs there exists integers $K(p)$ and $d(p)$ depending only upon p so that a distributed network having $d(p)$ intermediate cells with randomly generated integer weights in the

interval $[-K(p), +K(p)]$ has positive probability of allowing f to be represented by a suitably chosen set of top-cell weights.

2. Give an argument for why the anchor algorithm of section 8.6 produces robustness-preserving models.

3. Why wouldn't the anchor algorithm work if a linear function of the input cells were used to compute anchor cell activations?

4. Use radial basis functions with $\Phi(x) = (x^2 + 9)^{1/2}$ to generate a network for the following set of training examples:

$$E^1 = \langle -7 \ +2 \rangle \qquad C^1 = +1$$
$$E^2 = \langle -4 \ -2 \rangle \qquad C^2 = -1.$$

8.9 Programming Projects

1. Implement the distributed method (with the speedup from section 8.7.3) in your learning program. Try your code on the parity-5 problem. How many distributed cells are required to reliably fit this data (i.e., to produce a network that classifies all training examples correctly)?

2. Modify the previous project to use the anchor algorithm. (This will also require a change in the simulator to compute distances between points.)

3. Add enough training examples to the *Taxtime!* examples in section 2.5 to make the problem nonseparable. Then generate a network using the distributed method or anchor algorithm.

*4. Combine the distributed method and Kohonen's topology-preserving maps.

For inputs start with a Booleanized representation of the square with corners

$$\langle 0,0 \rangle, \langle 0,10 \rangle, \langle 10,0 \rangle, \langle 10,10 \rangle.$$

Use an evenly spaced cutoff representation for each of the two coordinates with 9 variables per coordinate. Thus the point $\langle 3,5 \rangle$ would look like

$$\langle +1 \ +1 \ +1 \ -1 \ -1 \ -1 \ -1 \ -1 \ -1 \ -1 \ -1 \ -1,$$
$$+1 \ +1 \ +1 \ +1 \ +1 \ -1 \ -1 \ -1 \ -1 \ -1 \ -1 \ -1 \rangle.$$

There are 100 possible (discrete) inputs.

Now pass these inputs into a layer of 25 (linear discriminant) cells with random coefficients. The output from this distributed layer will be 25 values of ± 1, so we have represented our 100 training examples as 100 vectors with 25 values each. (Note that the original 18-value examples could have their coordinates shuffled with no effect!) That's the distributed part.

For the topological maps part take a 6×6 array of cells and do Kohonen learning with the 100 25-value vectors. Each cell has exactly 25 weights; the original 18 input values are *not* seen. Now when the array is self-organized we can take the original 100 examples (labeled $\langle 0, 0 \rangle$, $\langle 0, 1 \rangle, \ldots \langle 9, 9 \rangle$) and see which of the 36 cells is most strongly activated by each example. Present the results as 36 lists of points arrayed in a 6×6 grid.

The question is whether the final points are arrayed in a reasonable way. This will give evidence for or against the distributed method being "robust" in treating nearby points roughly the same.

*9 Computational Learning Theory and the BRD Algorithm

Deriving analytic generalization bounds is one of our goals for constructing algorithms. This is a difficult task, but for networks composed of simple threshold logic units we can derive some loose bounds that give us insight into the problem of fitting data with neural networks.

In this chapter[1] we will first examine a theoretical framework for analyzing algorithms called computational learning theory. Then we will look at a generalization of the distributed method called the BRD algorithm, and derive generalization bounds for both noise-free and noisy data. Here we will make use of some important results in computational learning theory. Finally we will be able to specialize these bounds and apply them to the single-cell algorithms of part II.

Please note that material in this chapter is optional and that future chapters do not depend upon it. If COLT is not your cup of tea, please feel free to gallop ahead!

9.1 Introduction to Computational Learning Theory

Recently there has been much interest in formalizing the study of machine learning to give it a more solid theoretical basis (Valiant [194]; Haussler and Pitt [88], Haussler [87]). This body of work is usually referred to as computational learning theory, learnability theory, or Valiant-style learning.

We will be using a lot of notation in the next few sections, so figure 9.1 is a symbol scorecard to help keep the players straight.

9.1.1 PAC-Learning

A *concept class* $\mathscr{C}$ is a set of Boolean functions f in which each function has a finite number of inputs, p. Usually a concept class is infinite, containing many functions for every value of p. Note that this definition generalizes the definition of *concept* used in chapter 2 by allowing the number of inputs, p, to vary.

As an example we might consider the concept class of *separable functions*. If we denote inputs by

$$X = \langle x_1, \ldots, x_p \rangle$$

where

1. Much of the material in this chapter is adapted from Gallant [71].

Symbol	Description	Page
p	number of input features	173
X	vector of inputs $\langle x_1, \ldots, x_p \rangle$, $x_i = \pm 1$	173
$\mathscr{C}$	concept class, a set of Boolean functions $\{f\}$	173
$P(X)$	probability distribution for input vectors	175
W	weight vector $\langle w_0, w_1, \ldots, w_p \rangle$; w_i is an integer	174
d	number of distributed cells in middle layer	176
K	bound for middle-layer weights: $|w_i| \leq K$	176
L	bound for length of top-cell weight vector: $\|W\| \leq L$	176
L'	$(p + d + 1)L$	179
γ, γ'	probability that a function will be representable by a bounded distributed network when intermediate-cell weights are set to random integers bounded by K	177, 180
f, f'	Boolean functions on p Boolean inputs; f' is the target function to be learned	173, 175
ε	allowed approximation error between target function f' and produced function f	175
ε'	revised error bound when the BRD algorithm fails	183
ε°	measured error of fallback network on training examples when the BRD algorithm fails	183
δ, δ'	bound on the allowed probability that f will not be an ε or ε'-approximation of f'	175, 183
s	*slack* between measured error, ε°, and error bound, ε', when algorithm fails: $\varepsilon' = \varepsilon^\circ/(1 - s)$ or $s = (\varepsilon' - \varepsilon^\circ)/\varepsilon'$	183
E	number of training examples called for	179
T	number of tries allowed to fit the training examples with a bounded distributed network	179
M	number of mistakes (change steps) allowed per try	179
$\mathscr{D}_p(d, K, L; \gamma)$	probabilistic bounded distributed concept class (of functions)	177
V	Vapnik-Chervonenkis dimension	184
$\ln(\ )$	natural logarithm	
$\log(\ )$	logarithm base 2	
e	the base of the natural logarithm	

Figure 9.1
A scorecard for symbols.

$$x_i = \begin{cases} +1 \Leftrightarrow i^{\text{th}} \text{ input is } \textbf{true} \\ -1 \Leftrightarrow i^{\text{th}} \text{ input is } \textbf{false,} \end{cases}$$

then a separable function, f_W, is given by an integer weight vector,

$$W = \langle w_0, w_1, \ldots, w_p \rangle$$

and the rule:[2]

---

2. For this chapter only it is convenient to modify our definition of separable for the case where the weighted sum is exactly 0.

$$f_W(X) = \begin{cases} +1 & \text{if } w_0 + \sum w_i x_i \geq 0 \\ -1 & \text{if } w_0 + \sum w_i x_i < 0. \end{cases}$$

PAC-learning, introduced by Valiant [194], formalizes the notion of learning from training examples. Given a concept class, $\mathscr{C}$, we want to be able to learn an approximation of any target function, $f' \in \mathscr{C}$, from training examples $\{X\}$ under any fixed probability distribution $P(X)$. It is often convenient to allow the approximation f to be chosen from a different concept class than the target function f'.

We measure how well a function f approximates f' by calculating the error probability that the function will not agree with an example selected according to the same distribution of inputs used in training

$$\sum_{X:f(X) \neq f'(X)} P(X).$$

We say that f is an ε-*approximation* of f' if such error is no more than ε.

Because a random process selects the set of training examples one by one (with replacement) according to distribution $P(X)$, there is always some chance that training examples will not represent f' well enough. Therefore we have to allow some probability δ that an algorithm will fail to produce a good approximation to f'. Thus we arrive at the notion of a *probably approximately correct* (PAC) learning algorithm that, given δ and ε, will, with probability at least $(1 - \delta)$, produce an approximation f that differs from f' by at most ε.

The bound on the error ε is *distribution-free* since it must hold for any distribution, $P(\ )$, of training examples. By contrast the usual practice in neural network research is to measure error with respect to one particular distribution, namely a uniform distribution over a set of training examples.

Now it is only reasonable that such an algorithm takes longer either to produce an approximation with higher certainty (i.e., smaller δ) or to produce a better approximation of f' (i.e., smaller ε). Also the concept class has target functions of varying numbers of inputs, p; certainly it will be harder to learn (or even output the representation of) a function involving more input dimensions than a function of fewer dimensions. Similarly we assume that we are working in a fixed representation (over a finite alphabet of symbols) and that we have to allow an algorithm at least enough steps to output the target function as determined by its size, $size(f')$, in that representation ($size(f')$ is the number of symbols required to represent f'

in our fixed representation). Finally, although we need to allow for arbitrarily long times for the algorithm, we prefer that the algorithm not grow exponentially in any of the foregoing parameters.

We capture these notions by defining a *polynomial learning algorithm* for a concept class C as an algorithm that is a PAC-learning algorithm for C and that takes time polynomial in $1/\delta$, $1/\varepsilon$, p, and $size(f')$. Roughly speaking such an algorithm is guaranteed with high *certainty* (small δ) to accurately *generalize* (small ε) for target functions chosen from C, and will *scale up* (large p, $size(f')$) *in a reasonable manner* (polynomially) with respect to the size of the target function.

By way of example, consider the class of *bounded separable functions* defined to be those separable functions for which there exists an integer weight vector W satisfying $\|W\| \leq L$ for some fixed constant L. For this concept class, perceptron learning [173] is a polynomial learning algorithm. This follows directly from results of Vapnik [196] and Blumer, Ehrenfeucht, Haussler, and Warmuth [25] and is also a special case of theorem 9.3 below.

Unfortunately the class of separable (single-cell) functions is too small; in practice we need to be able to work with nonseparable functions for real-world problems.

9.1.2 Bounded Distributed Connectionist Networks

Consider a distributed network as in figure 8.2 where the middle layer contains d *distributed* cells that are bounded separable functions with integer weights between $-K$ and K for some fixed integer K.

The top cell is of course a separable function of all network inputs and all activations (outputs) from the middle layer of cells. We also require that the length of the weight vector for the top cell, $\|W\|$, be bounded by another constant, L.

9.1.3 Probabilistic Bounded Distributed Concepts

We can now define the family of concept classes that are amenable to the learning algorithm to be presented in the next section. The basic idea is as follows.

Suppose f' is a function that can be computed by a bounded distributed network using some *particular* integer settings for the weights of the intermediate and output cells and that these weights are within the bounds K and L. However, if we generate intermediate-cell weights at *random* then we are no longer guaranteed that some set of top-cell weights, W, exists such that the resulting network computes f' and such that $\|W\| \leq L$. We can only say that a randomly chosen set of intermediate-cell weights will allow an L-bounded top cell to compute f' with some probability $\gamma > 0$. ($\gamma > 0$ since at least one such set of intermediate-cell weights exists by choice of f'.) Therefore probability γ serves as a measure of how easy it is to compute f' using bounded distributed networks.

By way of motivation, consider a brain as being partially genetically hard-wired, partially hard-wired but with some amount of randomness, and partially free to learn. Then some concepts would be easy for most people to learn because most people's hard-wired portions would permit these concepts to be learned. However, other concepts would be difficult (or impossible), since only a few people would have the necessary hard wiring to be able to learn them.

DEFINITION 9.1   *A function f' is a* probabilistic bounded distributed concept *with parameters p, d, K, L, and γ if*:

• *f' has p inputs*
• *the probability is at least γ that for a bounded distributed network (with d middle-layer cells having randomly generated integer weights bounded by K) there exists a vector W of top-cell weights satisfying $\|W\| \leq L$ and such that the resulting network computes the Boolean function f'.*

We denote a probabilistic bounded distributed concept class by $\mathscr{D}_p(d, K, L; \gamma)$. Using this notation, bounded separable functions are $\mathscr{D}_p(0, 0, L; 1)$. This is true since for any bounded separable function f, a distributed network with 0 intermediate cells will (with probability 1) allow a top-cell weight vector bounded by L to compute f.

Similarly, the exclusive-or function is in $\mathscr{D}_2(1, 1, \sqrt{7}; 4/9)$ since exactly 12 of the 27 possible sets of coefficients for the intermediate cell allow all of the training examples to be separated (using a top cell of length $\sqrt{7}$). Figure 9.2 gives an example of how this works. Whenever the distributed-cell weights $w_{3,1}$ and $w_{3,2}$ are both unequal to 0 (regardless of the $w_{3,0}$ bias value) then top-cell coefficients exist that satisfy $\|W\| = \sqrt{7}$ and such that the network computes XOR. When $K = 1$ then $w_{3,1}$ will be either $+1$ or -1 exactly two-thirds of the time, and similarly for $w_{3,2}$. Therefore XOR can be computed by such a bounded distributed network with probability $\gamma = \frac{2}{3} \times \frac{2}{3} = \frac{4}{9}$.

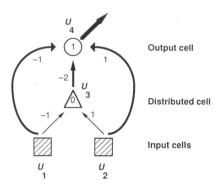

Figure 9.2
When $w_{3,1} = -1$, $w_{3,2} = +1$, and $w_{3,0} = 0$, then XOR can be computed using a top cell with length $\sqrt{7}$.

A similar enumeration shows parity -3 to be in $\mathcal{D}_3(1, 1, \sqrt{7}; 5/81)$. Probabilities for higher-parity functions can also be computed, but more than one distributed cell is required.

PROPOSITION 9.2

$$\mathcal{D}_p(d, K, L; \gamma) \subseteq \mathcal{D}_p(d^\circ, K, L^\circ; \gamma^\circ)$$

$$\text{for } d^\circ \geq d, L^\circ \geq L, \gamma^\circ \leq \gamma \tag{9.1}$$

$$\mathcal{D}_p(d, K, L; \gamma) \subseteq \mathcal{D}_p(\alpha d, K, L; 1 - (1 - \gamma)^\alpha)$$

$$\text{for integer } \alpha > 0 \tag{9.2}$$

Proof: The first relation follows directly from definitions. The second comes by dividing αd intermediate cells into α groups of d cells. The probability that some group will admit desired weights for the top cell is $1 - (1 - \gamma)^\alpha$.   □

Thus we know that exclusive-or is in $\mathcal{D}_2(d, 1, \sqrt{7}; 1 - (\frac{5}{9})^d)$ for integer $d \geq 1$.

9.2   A Learning Algorithm for Probabilistic Bounded Distributed Concepts

We now describe the *bounded, randomized, distributed algorithm* or BRD algorithm. It makes a number of tries at fitting the data using randomly

1. Accept δ, ε, p, d, K, L, and γ.

2. Based upon these parameters compute:

   $L' = (p + d + 1)L$

   T = number of tries to fit the data

   $= \ln(\delta/2)/\ln(1 - \gamma)$

   E = number of training examples called for

   $$= \frac{1}{-\ln(1 - \varepsilon)}\left[\ln T + \{(d + p + 1)\ln(2L' + 1)\} + \ln\left(\frac{2}{\delta}\right)\right]$$

   M = number of "mistakes" or change steps per try allowed in perceptron learning

   $= (p + d + 1)L^2$.

3. Collect E training examples (from the fixed unknown distribution).

4. Make no more than T tries to fit the examples as follows:

   4a. Generate a bounded distributed network with intermediate-cell weights consisting of randomly selected integers between $-K$ and $+K$.

   4b. Cycle through the training examples and do perceptron learning in an attempt to generate weights for the top cell. If a set of weights W is found before $M + 1$ mistakes (change steps) have been made that fits all training examples then

      4ba. Announce *success* and make no more tries.

      Otherwise
      4bA. This try fails.

5. If a successful try has been made, then:

   5a. Output the corresponding bounded distributed network (this is the approximation f).

   Otherwise
   5A. The algorithm fails.

Figure 9.3
The bounded randomized distributed (BRD) algorithm.

generated weights for intermediate cells and perceptron learning for the top-cell weights; see figure 9.3.

If the algorithm is successful, it will output an approximation f to the unknown target $f' \in \mathscr{D}_p(d, K, L; \gamma)$. However, f will lie in a different concept class, $\mathscr{D}_p(d, K, L'; \gamma')$, where

$$L' \equiv (p + d + 1)L \quad and \quad \gamma' > 0.$$

γ' may be larger or smaller than γ.

9.3   The BRD Theorem

The main theoretical result for the BRD algorithm is the following theorem.

THEOREM 9.3   *Given δ, $\varepsilon > 0$, a target function $f' \in \mathscr{D}_p(d, K, L; \gamma)$, and any fixed (unknown) distribution $P(X)$ of training examples, then the BRD algorithm will, with probability at least $(1 - \delta)$, produce an approximation*

$$f \in \mathscr{D}_p(d, K, (p + d + 1)L; \gamma'), \quad \gamma' > 0$$

that differs from f' by at most ε. Furthermore the computing time of the algorithm grows polynomially in p, d, $\ln K$, L, $1/\gamma$, $\ln 1/\delta$, and $1/\varepsilon$.

We need several propositions for the proof.

PROPOSITION 9.4   *The BRD algorithm will, with probability at least $(1 - \delta/2)$, have a successful run.*

Proof: A bounded distributed network (with randomly selected weights for intermediate cells) will, with probability at least γ, admit a top-cell weight vector W^* that computes the target, f', and that satisfies $\|W^*\| \le L$. If we make T tries, then the probability that none of the bounded distributed networks will admit such a top cell is $(1 - \gamma)^T$. Therefore setting $T \ge \ln(\delta/2)/\ln(1 - \gamma)$ means that with probability at least $(1 - \delta/2)$ one of the tries will have intermediate-cell weights that allow a W^* to compute f' where $\|W^*\| \le L$. Now when we run perceptron learning for such a set of intermediate cells, we are guaranteed by corollary 3.3 that the perceptron learning algorithm will produce a set of weights, W, that correctly classify all training examples and that satisfy $\|W\| \le L'$ while making at most $(p + d + 1)L^2$ mistakes. These are the conditions for the algorithm to announce success. $\square$

THEOREM 9.5 (Blumer, Ehrenfeucht, Haussler, and Warmuth [25]; see also Rivest [170])   *Let $\delta, \varepsilon > 0$ be given. If there are r functions in a concept class $\mathscr{C}$, and a target function f' (not necessarily in $\mathscr{C}$) is used to produce*

$$\frac{1}{-\ln(1 - \varepsilon)}(\ln r + \ln 1/\delta)\ \textit{training examples according to some fixed distri-}$$

bution $P(X)$, then with probability at least $(1 - \delta)$ any function f from $\mathscr{C}$ that fits all training examples will be an ε-approximation of f'.

Proof: Suppose $g \in \mathscr{C}$ is not an ε-approximation of f'. The probability that g would fit m randomly drawn training examples is less than $(1 - \varepsilon)^m$. Therefore the probability that one or more of r functions that are not ε-approximations of f' would fit the training data is less than $r(1 - \varepsilon)^m$. Thus even if all functions in $\mathscr{C}$ were not ε-approximations of f', the probability that at least one of them would fit all the training examples is less than

$$r(1 - \varepsilon)^{(1/-\ln(1-\varepsilon))(\ln r + \ln 1/\delta)} = re^{\ln(1-\varepsilon)(1/-\ln(1-\varepsilon))(\ln r + \ln 1/\delta)}$$

$$= re^{-(\ln r + \ln 1/\delta)}$$

$$= r(1/r)\delta$$

$$= \delta.$$

Therefore if one of the functions in $\mathscr{C}$ fit the data, it must be an ε-approximation with probability at least $1 - \delta$. $\square$

For the following proposition define the *space spanned by a set of T bounded distributed networks* to be those functions that can be expressed as networks using one of the T sets of random intermediate cells that the BRD algorithm creates along with any weight vector, W, for the top cell that satisfies $\|W\| \leq L$.

PROPOSITION 9.6   *Any function f produced by a successful run of the BRD algorithm will, with probability at least $(1 - \delta/2)$, approximate the target function f' to within ε.*

Proof: The BRD algorithm succeeds only when a function f is produced lying in the space spanned by the T bounded distributed network such that

f fits all E training examples. The number of distinct functions in this space is bounded by

$$T(2L' + 1)^{(d+p+1)} \tag{9.3}$$

since for each try there are $(d + p + 1)$ adjustable integer weights between $-L'$ and $+L'$ for the top cell. These weights totally specify any function computed by one of the networks because the random weights on intermediate cells do not change.

Then by proposition 9.5 any function in this space that fits

$$E = \frac{1}{-\ln(1 - \varepsilon)}[\ln T + \{(d + p + 1)\ln(2L' + 1)\} + \ln(2/\delta)]$$

training examples will, with probability at least $(1 - \delta/2)$, be an ε-approximation of f'.   □

Proof of theorem 9.3:   By proposition 9.4 the BRD algorithm will announce success and produce an f in $\mathscr{D}_p(d, K, L'; \gamma')$ with probability at least $(1 - \delta/2)$. By proposition 9.6 whenever this happens f will be an ε-approximation to the target function f' with probability at least $(1 - \delta/2)$. Therefore the algorithm can fail by not claiming success (with *probability* $\leq \delta/2$) or by claiming success but actually having too large an error (with *probability* $\leq \delta/2$). Thus the BRD algorithm will, with probability at least $(1 - \delta)$, produce an ε-approximation of f'.

All that remains is to verify that the work involved grows polynomially in the parameters.

$$T = \ln(2/\delta)/\ln(1 - \gamma)$$

$$= \frac{-\ln(2/\delta)}{[-\gamma - \frac{1}{2}\gamma^2 - \frac{1}{3}\gamma^3 \cdots]}$$

$$\leq 1/\gamma \ln(2/\delta).$$

E is also clearly polynomial in the various parameters, growing by no more than order

$$\frac{1}{\varepsilon}\left\{\ln T + (d + p)\ln((d + p)L) + \ln\frac{1}{\delta}\right\}.$$

(This scales by about $d \ln d$ for fixed p, δ, and ε and assuming K and L grow proportionally to d; there is no dependence upon γ.)

Finally $M = (p + d + 1)L^2$.

The total work grows by no more than $(p + d)TEM$ which is about

$$\frac{1}{\gamma} d^3 L^2 \frac{1}{\varepsilon}$$

if we assume $d > p$ and ignore ln terms. $\qquad\square$

9.3.1 Polynomial Learning

Under reasonable representations the size of a bounded distributed network is proportional to p, d, $\ln K$, and $\ln L$. In practice it would seem reasonable to limit L to some constant multiple of $(p + d)$. This gives the following corollary:

COROLLARY 9.7 *Under the assumption that L is bounded by some fixed polynomial in p and d, the BRD algorithm is a polynomial learning algorithm for the concept class $\mathcal{D}_*(*, *, *; \gamma)$ that finds approximations in $\mathcal{D}_*(*, *, *; *)$.*

$\qquad\square$

9.4 Noisy Data and Fallback Estimates

The BRD algorithm may fail to perfectly classify all E training examples in the allotted T tries. This might be caused by noisy data (i.e., data with inputs corrupted by a probabilistic process), overestimation of γ, or just bad luck in the generation of intermediate cells or training examples. Nevertheless we may extract a reasonable fallback function, f, from the algorithm by choosing from among the T networks the one having final coefficients that best fit the set of E training examples. We now must find bounds on what revised confidence, $(1 - \delta')$, we have that f approximates f' to within some revised error ε'. Note that ε' may be greater or less than the original error ε we used in the run of the BRD algorithm according to the revised confidence δ'.

Whenever the algorithm fails then the fallback network will have correctly classified only a fraction, $1 - \varepsilon°$, of the set of E training examples. Thus $\varepsilon°$ is the measured error on the training examples.

We cannot expect an error, ε', that is smaller than $\varepsilon°$ with any confidence $(1 - \delta') > 1/2$; therefore we assume $\varepsilon' > \varepsilon°$. It is convenient to define a *slack s*, $0 < s < 1$, to measure the difference between ε' and $\varepsilon°$ that satisfies

$$\varepsilon' = \frac{\varepsilon^\upsilon}{1 - s}.$$

We can now develop two fallback bounds for δ' and ε'.

9.4.1 Vapnik-Chervonenkis Bounds

The first set of fallback bounds involves the Vapnik-Chervonenkis dimension [197, 196], a generalization of the notion of capacity that was introduced by Cover [41]. For an overview of this theory see Blumer et al. [26]. This section is motivated by, and builds upon, work by Baum and Haussler [20].

For our purposes we can define the Vapnik-Chervonenkis dimension as follows. Let $\mathscr{C} = \{f^i\}$ be a set of functions (i.e., a concept class). A set of m training examples $\{E^k\}_{k=1,m}$ is said to be *shattered* by $\mathscr{C}$ if for each of the 2^m ways of labeling these examples ± 1 there is at least one function, f^i, that agrees with this labeling. Then the *Vapnik-Chervonenkis dimension*, V, of the set of functions, $\mathscr{C}$, is defined to be the maximum m for which there exists a set of m shattered training examples.

For example, let $\mathscr{C}$ be the family of half-planes. Then figure 9.4a shows that the Vapnik-Chervonenkis dimension of this family is at least 3 because these points can be separated into all 2^3 possible subsets. However, it can be shown that every set of 4 points cannot be separated into all 2^4 subsets. Therefore the Vapnik-Chervonenkis dimension of $\mathscr{C}$ is exactly 3.

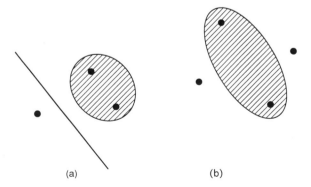

(a)   (b)

Figure 9.4
A set of 3 points that is shattered by half-planes (a); one subset is illustrated. A set of 4 points that is not shattered (b).

We can now make use of several theorems relating to the Vapnik-Chervonenkis dimension. All are either referred to or proven by Baum and Haussler [20].

THEOREM 9.8 *The Vapnik-Chervonenkis dimension of the class of separable functions with p inputs is p + 1.*

See Wenocur and Dudley [199] for a proof.

The following result is due to Baum and Haussler [20]. Recall that e is the base of the natural logarithm.

THEOREM 9.9 *Let $\mathscr{C}$ be the set of all functions computed by feedforward nets defined on a fixed underlying network with $N \geq 2$ intermediate and output cells and τ weights and biases.[3] Then the Vapnik-Chervonenkis dimension of $\mathscr{C}$ satisfies*

$V \leq 2\tau \log(eN)$.

The next theorem by Vapnik nicely quantifies the notion that if we pick enough training examples relative to the capacity of a set of functions, then we can expect that the best-fitting function will perform roughly as well on unseen data as it did on the training examples.

THEOREM 9.10 *Let $\mathscr{C}$ be a set of Boolean functions with Vapnik-Chervonenkis dimension V. Suppose m training examples are generated according to a fixed, unknown distribution P( ). The training examples are labeled $\{+1, -1\}$ by any probabilistic process that is constant over time. Let $0 < \varepsilon', \delta' < 1$, and let $0 < s \leq 1$ be a slack parameter. If m satisfies*

$$m \geq \max\left[\frac{8}{s^2\varepsilon'}\ln\frac{8}{\delta'}, \frac{16V}{s^2\varepsilon'}\ln\frac{16}{s^2\varepsilon'}\right]$$

then with probability at least $(1 - \delta')$ every function in $\mathscr{C}$ that disagrees with at most a fraction $(1 - s)\varepsilon'$ of these m training examples will correctly classify a new, unseen training example drawn according to distribution P( ) with probability at least $(1 - \varepsilon')$.

For a proof see Blumer et al. [26], theorem A3.3. Also see Vapnik [196], theorem A.3, p. 176.

We can now derive our first fallback bound.

---

3. We make no use of the fact that connections between intermediate cells are allowed.

THEOREM 9.11   *Suppose the BRD algorithm fails and that the best of the T networks misclassifies a fraction $\varepsilon° > 0$ of the training examples. For any $0 < \delta', \varepsilon' < 1$ and slack $0 < s < 1$ satisfying $\varepsilon°/(1 - s) \leq \varepsilon'$, if there are sufficient examples E so that*

$$E \geq \frac{8}{s^2 \varepsilon'} \max$$

$$\cdot \left[\ln \frac{8}{\delta'}, \min\{2(p + Td + 1), 4(pd + 2d + p + 1)\log(e(d + 1))\} \ln \frac{16}{s^2 \varepsilon'} \right]$$
$$(9.4)$$

then with probability at least $1 - \delta'$ the chance that the next training example will be misclassified is less than ε'.

Proof: We need only show that the Vapnik-Chervonenkis dimension of the collection of fallback functions produced by the BRD algorithm is bounded by $\min\{(p + Td + 1), 2(pd + 2d + p + 1)\log(e(d + 1))\}$ and apply the previous proposition.

Consider the T networks that the BRD algorithm generates. The weights for the intermediate (distributed) cells are chosen at random and do not depend upon the data. Any function computed by one of these networks could also be computed by a single big network with Td distributed cells with corresponding weights (as in the proof of proposition 9.2, equation (9.2)). But these Td fixed distributed cells only serve to project training examples from $\{+1, -1\}^p$ into $\{+1, -1\}^{p+Td}$ for the top cell. Therefore the Vapnik-Chervonenkis dimension for the set of top-cell functions is a bound for the entire network. Because the top cell is a separable function with $p + Td$ inputs, the Vapnik-Chervonenkis dimension is $p + Td + 1$ from theorem 9.8. This is the first Vapnik-Chervonenkis bound.

The second bound on the Vapnik-Chervonenkis dimension, $2(pd + 2d + p + 1)\log(e(d + 1))$, follows by applying the Baum-Haussler formula in theorem 9.9 to the class of all networks with d intermediate cells. The fallback network from the BRD algorithm is clearly a special case in this class. Such networks have τ weights where $\tau = d(p + 1) + (p + d + 1) = pd + 2d + p + 1$. □

Several comments are in order here. First, note that these bounds do not depend upon parameters K, L, or M. If the number of networks, T, is no more than about $2p$ then the first Vapnik-Chervonenkis bound $(p + Td + 1)$ holds. Otherwise we are trying so many networks that the more general Baum-Haussler bound, $2(pd + 2d + p + 1)\log(e(d + 1))$, which is independent of T, comes into play. Note that we are free to trade off improvements in δ' and ε' in equation (9.4), consistent with the total number of training examples.

9.4.2 Hoeffding and Chernoff Bounds

The second way to get fallback bounds is by applying Hoeffding's inequality [100] and Chernoff bounds (see Valiant [114], p. 287) in the proof of theorem 9.5. See also Devroye [42] and Pearl [153].

PROPOSITION 9.12 *Given a set of r Boolean functions $\{f^i\}_{i=1,r}$; $0 < \delta'$, $\varepsilon', s < 1$; and $\varepsilon° = (1 - s)\varepsilon'$, if some $f \in \{f^i\}$ misclassifies $\varepsilon°E$ out of a set of E (possibly noisy) training examples drawn according to a fixed distribution $P(\ )$ where*

$$E \geq \frac{\ln(1/\delta') + \ln r}{s^2\varepsilon'} \min\left\{\frac{1}{2\varepsilon'}, 2\right\}$$

then with probability at least $(1 - \delta')$ the function f will have error at most ε' on new training examples drawn according to the same distribution $P(\ )$.

Proof: The probability that any function f^i with actual error $> \varepsilon'$ would misclassify no more than $\varepsilon°E$ out of E training examples is bounded by the left tail of a binomial expansion

$$\sum_{k=0}^{\varepsilon°E} \binom{E}{k} \varepsilon'^k (1 - \varepsilon')^{E-k} \equiv lefttail(\varepsilon', E, \varepsilon°).$$

By Hoeffding's inequality,

$$lefttail(\varepsilon', E, \varepsilon°) \leq e^{-2(\varepsilon'-\varepsilon°)^2 E}.$$

Even if all $\{f^i\}$ had actual error $> \varepsilon'$, the probability that at least one of them would do better than error $\varepsilon°$ on the training examples is no more than $re^{-2(\varepsilon'-\varepsilon°)^2 E}$. Thus solving for E:

$$\delta' \leq re^{-2(\varepsilon'-\varepsilon°)^2 E} = re^{-2(s\varepsilon')^2 E}$$

$$E \geq \frac{\ln\frac{1}{\delta'} + \ln r}{2(s\varepsilon')^2}.$$

Using Chernoff bounds:

$lefttail(\varepsilon', E, \varepsilon°) \le e^{-s^2\varepsilon'E/2}$

leads to the other inequality.   □

Clearly Hoeffding bounds are preferable for $\varepsilon' > 1/4$ and Chernoff bounds for $\varepsilon' < 1/4$.

THEOREM 9.13   *Suppose the BRD algorithm fails and that the best of the T networks misclassifies a fraction $\varepsilon° > 0$ of the training examples. For any $0 < \delta'$, $\varepsilon' < 1$, and slack $0 < s < 1$ satisfying $\varepsilon°/(1 - s) \le \varepsilon'$, if there are sufficient examples E so that*

$$E \ge \frac{\ln\dfrac{1}{\delta'} + (d + p + 1)\ln(T(2L' + 1))}{s^2\varepsilon'} \min\left\{\frac{1}{2\varepsilon'}, 2\right\} \qquad (9.5)$$

then with probability at least $1 - \delta'$ the chance that the next training example will be misclassified is less than ε'.

Proof: As noted in proposition 9.6, $T(2L' + 1)^{(d+p+1)}$ is a bound on the number of possible networks that the algorithm can produce.   □

The above bound is usually better than equation (9.4) unless L' becomes quite large. Thus we expect the Hoeffding and Chernoff bounds to be more useful in practice than the Vapnik-Chervonenkis bounds.

It is interesting to note that if the fallback network classifies 90 percent of the training examples and we want to have confidence that it will at least generalize to 85 percent of unseen training examples (i.e., $\varepsilon° = .1$, $s = 1/3$, $\varepsilon' = .15$), then each new adjustable top cell weight (whether from an extra input to the network or an extra distributed cell) will require at most $120\ln(T(2L' + 1))$ additional training examples.

9.4.3   Pocket Algorithm

We can run the BRD algorithm using the pocket algorithm with ratchet rather than perceptron learning. If so then theorem 9.3 still applies, but now if the BRD algorithm fails we can use pocket coefficients rather than perceptron coefficients for the top cell and expect a better-fitting fallback model. The fallback bounds are not affected by the use of the pocket algorithm.

9.4.4 Additional Training Examples

Note that after a failure of the BRD algorithm it is possible to ask for additional training examples, then evaluate the T networks on the enlarged set of training examples and pick the best as a fallback. This allows a larger value of E, and Hoeffding or Vapnik-Chervonenkis bounds that require less slack.

9.5 Bounds for Single-Layer Algorithms

We can specialize the BRD bounds to derive bounds for the distributed method and for other single-layer learning algorithms. Here we examine only the noisy case, applying theorems 9.11 and 9.13. In particular:

1. For single-cell models (pocket algorithm with ratchet or ∞ training data or rules) specialize the theorems.

2. For linear machines with c output cells and p input cells it is known by Kessler's construction (section 4.4) that there exists an equivalent single-cell problem with $c(p + 1)$ input cells and bias of 0. The single-cell model can be further simplified by subtracting the first $p + 1$ weights from each of the sets of c weights, leaving a single-cell model with at most $(c - 1)(p + 1)$ adjustable weights and 0 bias. This allows substitution into the single-cell bound with $p' = (c - 1)(p + 1) - 1$ to derive generalization bounds for linear machines.

3. For the distributed method, use the theorems with $T = 1$.

Figure 9.5 summarizes the results.

As an example of how these numbers scale, the bounds for several typical cases are computed in figure 9.6. Note that distribution-free bounds are very conservative and that alternatives have been proposed, for example by Buntine [32].

9.6 Fitting Data by Limiting the Number of Iterations

There is an interesting case where theory can help us understand something that would otherwise appear strange. Several researchers have noted that it is sometimes better to limit the number of training iterations, because this produces better generalization. This observation seems to

Single-cell models:

- pocket algorithm with ratchet
- pocket algorithm for ∞ training data
- pocket algorithm with rules

Minimum of:

$$\frac{8}{s^2\varepsilon}\max\left[\ln\frac{8}{\delta},\min\{2(p+1),4(p+1)\log e\}\ln\frac{16}{s^2\varepsilon}\right]$$

or

$$\frac{\ln(1/\delta)+(p+1)\ln(2L+1)}{s^2\varepsilon}\min\left\{\frac{1}{2\varepsilon},2\right\}$$

Linear machine models

Minimum of:

$$\frac{8}{s^2\varepsilon}\max\left[\ln\frac{8}{\delta},\min\{2(c-1)(p+1),4(c-1)(p+1)\log e\}\ln\frac{16}{s^2\varepsilon}\right]$$

or

$$\frac{\ln(1/\delta)+(c-1)(p+1)\ln(2L+1)}{s^2\varepsilon}\min\left\{\frac{1}{2\varepsilon},2\right\}$$

Distributed method

Minimum of:

$$\frac{8}{s^2\varepsilon}\max\left[\ln\frac{8}{\delta},\right.$$

$$\left.\min\{2(p+Td+1),4(pd+2d+p+1)\log(e(d+1))\}\ln\frac{16}{s^2\varepsilon}\right]$$

or

$$\frac{\ln(1/\delta)+(d+p+1)\ln(T(2L+1))}{s^2\varepsilon}\min\left\{\frac{1}{2\varepsilon},2\right\}$$

Figure 9.5
Bounds for various algorithms: model and number of examples, E, required for confidence $(1-\delta)$ and error ε where $s=(\varepsilon-\varepsilon^\circ)/\varepsilon$.

Model	ε	ε°	s	δ	p	L	c	d	T	Examples
Single-cell	.20	.10	.50	.9	10	30	1	0	1	1813
Linear machine	.20	.10	.50	.9	10	100	3	0	1	4671
Distributed	.20	.10	.50	.9	10	50	1	5	10	4432
Single-cell	.15	.10	.33	.9	10	30	1	0	1	5439
Linear machine	.15	.10	.33	.9	10	100	3	0	1	14013
Distributed	.15	.10	.33	.9	10	50	1	5	10	13295
Single-cell	.10	.05	.50	.9	10	30	1	0	1	3626
Linear machine	.10	.05	.50	.9	10	100	3	0	1	9342
Distributed	.10	.05	.50	.9	10	50	1	5	10	8863

Figure 9.6
Some sample distribution-free bounds on the number of training examples required to ensure generalization.

apply to many algorithms (including backpropagation). A typical graph for training error and generalization error versus the number of training iterations is shown in figure 9.7.

One possible explanation for this phenomenon is as follows. When using a small number of iterations we are effectively limiting the concept class size, because fewer sets of weights can be *reached*. This produces better relative generalization, as in proposition 9.12. As more iterations are made, however, the bounds on the number of free parameters come into play (for example, Vapnik-Chervonenkis bounds). This explains why generalization stops getting worse as more and more iterations are made. Thus the top curve in figure 9.7 seems quite reasonable.

9.7 Discussion

This chapter has introduced computational learning theory, and we have seen some important theorems, particularly theorem 9.5, theorem 9.9, and theorem 9.10. These have been quite helpful in analyzing the BRD algorithm.

From a computational learning theory standpoint it is notable that the BRD algorithm is a slight variant of an algorithm for machine learning that is in current use with real-world data. For example Hayashi et al. [93] used a similar algorithm for recognition of multifont typed characters with good empirical results. Thus the BRD algorithm is one of the few learning algorithms to be shown polynomial within the computational learning theory framework that is close to an "industrial strength" algorithm.

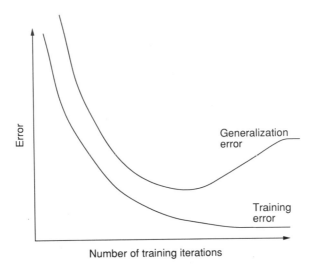

Figure 9.7
Training error and generalization error versus number of training iterations.

From a connectionist learning viewpoint we have gained several insights from the formal analysis that apply to real-world use. The tradeoff has been somewhat clarified between repeatedly trying to fit a set of training examples (i.e., increasing T) versus increasing the number of distributed cells, d. This is especially important if the set of training examples is limited in number. Since the number of training examples required for an ε-approximation grows by about $d \ln(dL)/\varepsilon$, it would be better to try many times to fit a fixed set of training examples rather than simply trying once and then increasing d to get a better fit. This is contrary to previous practice.

We should note that there are several criticisms of the computational learning theory approach. One of the most important is that the distribution-free bounds are extremely conservative [32]; standard statistical procedures can often do a much better job. For example, n-fold cross validation (section 8.4.2) generally produces much better bounds for practical problems.

It is likely that the computational learning theory analysis will prove most valuable in helping us understand the relationship between the power of models (size of concept class) and the amount of data required for generalization. The larger the family of models the easier it is to fit data, but the less certain we are of good generalization. Thus a small family of functions that is "biased" toward a particular set of data is best.

However, recent progress[4] indicates that the Vapnik-Chervonenkis dimension may be generalized to continuous models to give practical information on how many cells (or weights) to use for fitting data. This area certainly merits our attention.

9.8   Exercise

1. What is the probability that parity-3 will be separable for a distributed network of 10 intermediate cells having weights in $\{+1, -1, 0\}$?

9.9   Programming Project

1. Add the BRD algorithm to your learning program. Try to evaluate its performance with nonartificial data, if available.

4. For example the 1991 Neural Information Processing Systems (NIPS) Conference.

10 Constructive Algorithms

In this chapter we will examine several constructive algorithms, including the tower algorithm and pyramid algorithm of Gallant [64, 72],[1] the cascade-correlation algorithm of Fahlman and Labiere [52], the tiling algorithm of Mézard and Nadal [133], and the upstart algorithm of Frean [57]. The motivation for these algorithms is to transform the hard task of building a network into the easier problem of single-cell learning.

We will also look at easy learning problems, which are fixed-network learning problems that can be solved by single-cell or constructive methods. This type of network is especially useful for the connectionist expert system models in later chapters.

10.1 The Tower and Pyramid Algorithms

10.1.1 The Tower Algorithm

Figure 10.1 illustrates the idea of a tower network. The first (lowest) intermediate cell sees all the inputs; every other intermediate and output cell sees the input cells plus the single intermediate cell directly below it.

We train the network one cell at a time using the pocket algorithm with ratchet, working our way up the tower of cells. After a cell has been trained we freeze its weights; the activation from this cell now becomes input $(p + 1)$ to the next cell. Figure 10.2 gives the algorithm. Note that linear machines can be used at each stage in place of single-cell models.

10.1.2 Example

Parity-n was among the first tests that were presented to the tower algorithm. The author had thought that a tower with 1 intermediate cell would learn parity-2 (XOR), but that 2 intermediate cells would be required for parity-3, and in general $p - 1$ intermediate cells would be necessary for parity-p. It was quite a surprise when the algorithm produced a solution for parity-3 that used only 1 intermediate cell! An examination of this network showed that in fact $\lceil (p - 1)/2 \rceil$ intermediate cells suffice for parity-p (exercise 1).[2]

Figure 10.3 shows a typical solution to parity-5 found by the tower algorithm. There are many possible symmetrical solutions that differ only

---

1. The tower algorithm was also independently discovered by Nadal [148], and Frean [58].
2. The ceiling notation, $\lceil x \rceil$, means the smallest integer greater than or equal to x.

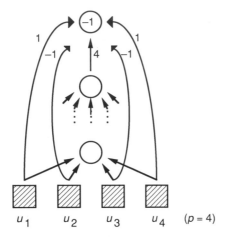

$u_1 \quad u_2 \quad u_3 \quad u_4 \quad (p = 4)$

Figure 10.1
The tower algorithm architecture.

1. Use the pocket algorithm to generate a single-cell model and freeze these weights.

2. Create a new cell that sees the p inputs to the network and the activation from the cell that was most recently trained. Run the pocket algorithm with ratchet to train the $p + 2$ weights (including bias) for this cell.

3. If the network with this added cell gives improved performance, then freeze its coefficients and go to step 2; otherwise remove this last added cell and output that network.

Figure 10.2
The tower algorithm.

	bias	in1	in2	in3	in4	in5	tv1	tv2
Tower Var. 1 for parity:	0	-2	-2	-2	-2	2	0	0
Tower Var. 2 for parity:	1	3	3	3	3	-3	6	0
parity (output):	0	-2	-2	-2	-4	2	0	9

Figure 10.3
Sample solution for parity-5 with two intermediate cells found by the tower algorithm.

by switching signs on weights. Solving this problem took under a minute on a Sun 3, illustrating the speed of constructive algorithms.

10.1.3 Proof of Convergence

The following theorem assures us that we can fit any discrete, noncontradictory set of training examples if enough iterations are taken at each stage.

THEOREM 10.1   *With arbitrarily high probability, the tower algorithm will fit noncontradictory sets of training examples with input values restricted to* $\{+1, -1\}$, *provided enough cells are added and enough iterations are taken for each added cell. Furthermore each added cell will correctly classify a greater number of training examples than any prior cell.*

Proof: The main step in the proof is to establish that an n-cell model that misclassifies example E^k can be made into an $n + 1$ cell model that correctly classifies E^k and leaves other classifications unchanged. To show this, let $C^k = \pm 1$ be the correct classification of E^k. Now set

$$w_{n+1,j} = C^k E_j^k \quad \text{for } j = 1, \ldots, p$$

$$w_{n+1,n} = p$$

$$w_{n+1,0} = C^k.$$

For example figure 10.1 gives a cell that copies the classification of the cell immediately below, except that $E^k = \langle -1, +1, +1, -1 \rangle$ now produces output $C^k = -1$.

The pocket algorithm converges on an optimal set of weights; therefore such an optimal set must correctly classify at least one more training example than the previous n-cell network because such a network has been constructed. This establishes the claimed theoretical convergence of the algorithm.   □

10.1.4 A Computational Speedup

There is a speedup for the tower algorithm that is analogous to the one for the distributed method presented in section 8.7.3. For a finite set of training examples we can speed the learning of cell u_i's weights by keeping track of the activations of cell u_{i-1} for each training example. Thus the work involved for learning each level of the tower algorithm will be exactly the same as solving a single-cell problem with $p + 1$ inputs.

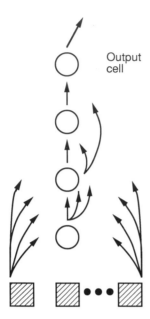

Figure 10.4
The pyramid algorithm.

10.1.5   The Pyramid Algorithm

The *pyramid algorithm* is identical to the tower algorithm except that each
newly added cell receives connections from all other cells, not just the cell
below. See figure 10.4. Although the additional connections and weights
would appear to increase learning power, simulations have been inconclusive on this point. The theoretical convergence of the algorithm can be
proven exactly as with the tower algorithm, and the computational speedup of section 10.1.4 is even more useful.

10.2   The Cascade-Correlation Algorithm

The third constructive algorithm in this chapter is the cascade-correlation
algorithm, which uses a network model similar to the pyramid algorithm.
Cascade-correlation utilizes continuous activations in a $\{+1, -1\}$ backpropagation network, where the output is computed by

$$u_i = -1 + \frac{2}{1 + e^{-s_i}} = \frac{1 - e^{-s_i}}{1 + e^{-s_i}}.$$

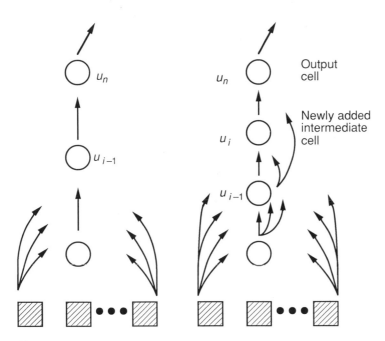

Figure 10.5
The cascade-correlation algorithm. The output cell and newly added intermediate cell are connected to all previous cells.

At each stage in cascade-correlation we add and train a new intermediate cell, and then we retrain the top cell (which now has one more input). See figure 10.5.

The key difference between cascade-correlation and pyramid algorithms is the way we train the newly added intermediate cell, u_i. For cascade-correlation we train u_i to maximize the correlation with the residual error of the output cell $\mathscr{E}(u_n)$. Letting u_i^k denote the value of u_i for training example k and $\bar{x}$ denote an average of the variable x taken over all N training examples, we seek to maximize[3]

$$\chi = \left| \sum_{k=1}^{N} (u_i^k - \bar{u}_i) \{ (C^k - u_n^k) - (\bar{C} - \bar{u}_n) \} \right|.$$

Letting κ be the bracketed term, we get

3. Fahlman and Labiere note that this is a covariance, not a true correlation.

$$\chi = \left| \sum_{k=1}^{N} (u_i^k - \overline{u}_i)\kappa \right|.$$

We now use a gradient descent approach. Differentiating with the chain rule and using $u_i^k = \tanh(\frac{1}{2}S_i)$ we get

$$\frac{\partial \chi}{\partial w_{i,j}} = \sum_{k=1}^{N} \frac{1}{2}\kappa\sigma u_j \frac{d}{dS_i}\tanh\left(\frac{1}{2}S_i\right)$$

where σ is the sign of $(u_i^k - \overline{u}_i)\kappa$.

We now use gradient descent to find weights $\{w_{i,j}\}$ that maximize χ. (Fahlman and Labiere now use a fast version of gradient descent called *quick-prop* for this task.) Next we freeze all of the weights to u_i and retrain the output cell u_n using either gradient descent, quickprop, pocket algorithm, etc. Note that u_n now has one additional input with corresponding weight $w_{n,i}$.

It is also possible to train a *pool* of (typically) 4 to 8 new intermediate cells starting from different random initial weights and, after training, to choose the one that maximizes χ. Fahlman and Labiere report that such pools help avoid generating useless intermediate cells. Presumably such a pooling technique would also benefit the tower and pyramid algorithms.

10.3 The Tiling Algorithm

Another interesting constructive algorithm due to Marc Mézard and Jean-Pierre Nadal is called the *tiling algorithm*. It constructs a strictly layered network where cells at layer L see only activations from cells at layer $L - 1$. Each layer contains a "master cell," and the master cell of layer L correctly classifies more training examples than that of layer $L - 1$. The master cell for the top layer gets all training examples correct, assuming noncontradictory data. See figure 10.6.

In addition to a master cell, every layer (except the last) contains "ancillary cells." The role of these units is to increase the number of cells for layer L so that no two training examples with *different classifications* have the *same set of activations* in layer L. Thus each succeeding layer has a different representation for the inputs, and no two training examples with different classifications have the same representation in any layer. Layers with this property are termed *faithful layers*, and faithfulness of layers is

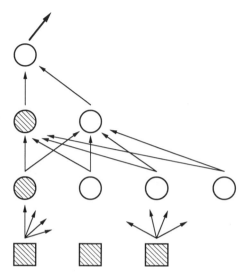

Figure 10.6.
A typical network for the tiling algorithm. Master cells are shaded.

clearly a necessary condition for a strictly layered network to correctly classify all training examples. Figure 10.7 gives the algorithm. The proof of convergence is similar to the proof for the tower algorithm.

10.4   The Upstart Algorithm

Marcus Frean [57] has developed an appealing constructive algorithm for which he reports favorable results compared with the tiling algorithm. Figure 10.8 illustrates the algorithm.

Inputs and activations are discrete in $\{+1, -1\}$. We first train a single cell, u_n, using the pocket algorithm with ratchet. Assuming nonseparability, we then train units u_{n+} and u_{n-} to *correct the mistakes of u_n*.

Unit u_{n+} is called upon to give positive reinforcement in cases where u_n incorrectly gives an output of -1. Letting u_n^k be the output of u_n for training example E^k, then positive training examples for u_{n+} are those examples where

$$C^k = 1 \quad \text{and} \quad u_n^k = -1.$$

The negative training examples for u_{n+} are those where

1. Set layer $L = 2$. (Layer 1 is the input layer.)

2. Use the pocket algorithm with ratchet to create the master cell for layer L using all activations from layer $L - 1$.

3. If the master cell for layer L correctly classifies all training examples, then quit.

4. Otherwise, continue to add ancillary cells ("tile") until layer L becomes faithful:

    4a. Find a maximum-sized subset of training examples with *more than one classification* that produces the *same activations* for all cells in layer L.

    4b. Use the pocket algorithm with ratchet to train a new ancillary cell for layer L using only the subset of training examples from step 4a.

5. Layer L is now faithful. Set $L = L + 1$ and go to step 2.

Figure 10.7
The tiling algorithm.

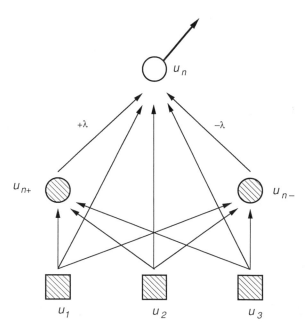

Figure 10.8
The upstart algorithm. Cells u_{n+} and u_{n-} are added to correct mistakes of cell u_n; λ is a large number.

$C^k = -1.$

Other training examples are ignored.

Similarly, for u_{n-} the positive training examples are the mistakes where

$$C^k = -1 \quad \text{and} \quad u_n^k = 1$$

and the negative training examples are those where

$$C^k = 1.$$

After training u_{n+} and u_{n-} we join them to u_n by connections with large positive and negative weights respectively. Thus if neither cell fires, then the weighted sum for cell u_n will be unchanged, but if one of them fires it will force u_n to be positive or negative. (If both cells fire it is an error, and u_{n+} and u_{n-} are effectively ignored.)

If u_{n+} and u_{n-} both correctly classify their respective sets of training examples, it is easy to see that u_n will correctly classify all of the original training examples. Otherwise we repeat the construction recursively for whichever of u_{n+} or u_{n-} is not correct, as in figure 10.9. Note that training is now with respect to problems for u_{n+} and u_{n-}, not the original problem. The final algorithm is given in figure 10.10. Once again we can prove convergence of the algorithm, assuming no contradictory training examples, similarly to the proof for the tower algorithm.

10.5   Other Constructive Algorithms and Pruning

With most of the algorithms in this chapter, as we add cells we can usually fit the training data better and better. Generalization should also improve, but only up to the point where we start overfitting the data. The situation is exactly analogous to increasing the number of cells with the distributed method, and we can apply techniques such as cross validation from section 8.4 to determine how many cells to add. Such pruning (or *destructive algorithms*) can be very important for fitting data, possibly even more important than the constructive part of the algorithm!

Currently there is much research activity in constructive algorithms, and further developments with these approaches is to be expected. One area in particular that bears watching concerns algorithms that combine decision trees and neural networks. Some exploratory work in this area has been done independently by Mario Marchand, J. P. Nadal, and this author. See

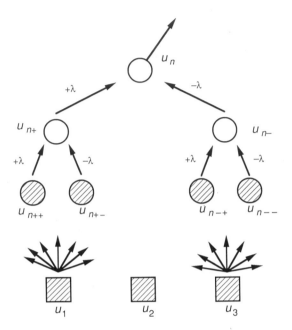

Figure 10.9
Adding cells to correct u_{n+} and u_{n-}.

also Golea and Marchand [78]. Michael Perrone [158] also has presented some interesting results recently. Pruning seems especially important with tree-based algorithms.

Other constructive algorithms of note have been investigated by Hanson [86] and Rujan and Marchand [175] (see also ARTMAP in section 7.6.2).

Finally, it is natural to consider *restricted coulomb energy (RCE) networks* as constructive algorithms. In this model we pick a training example and construct a hypersphere around its inputs. Any future input that falls within this hypersphere is given the same classification as the original training example. We now continue this process with the next training examples. When new training examples contradict a previously generated hypersphere, the hypersphere diameter is decreased to eliminate the clash. This approach is the basis of Nestor Corporation's learning systems, and they also market a type of expert system shell that gives some expert system functionality with these models. Details, however, are not public information. For additional information in the open literature, see Reilly

> 1. Construct an initial single-cell network with output cell u. Put u and all training examples on the TO-DO-LIST.
>
> 2. While the TO-DO-LIST is nonempty:
>
>   2a. Remove a node, u_i, and associated training examples, $E = \{E^k\}$, from the TO-DO-LIST.
>
>   2b. Run the pocket algorithm with ratchet to generate weights for u_i.
>
>   2c. If u_i incorrectly classifies one or more training examples with correct output of $+1$:
>
>   2ca. Create a new node u_{i+} linked to u_i with a large positive weight. u_{i+} sees all input cells.
>
>   2cb. Put u_{i+} on the TO-DO-LIST along with the following subset of examples from E:
>   positive examples: $\{E^k | u_i^k = -1, C^k = 1\}$
>   negative examples: $\{E^k | C^k = -1\}$.
>
>   2d. If u_i incorrectly classifies one or more training examples with correct output of -1:
>
>   2da. Create a new node u_{i-} linked to u_i with a large negative weight. u_{i-} sees all input cells.
>
>   2db. Put u_{i-} on the TO-DO-LIST along with the following subset of examples from E:
>   positive examples: $\{E^k | u_i^k = 1, C^k = -1\}$
>   negative examples: $\{E^k | C^k = 1\}$.
>
> 3. Output the final network.

Figure 10.10
The upstart algorithm.

et al. [168] and Scofield et al. [185]. For a controversial and somewhat critical review, see Hudak [103].

10.6   Easy Learning Problems

So far in this chapter we have examined constructive learning algorithms where there was freedom to choose any network to fit the data. Now we will look at *easy learning problems*. These are problems where we are given a network, and where the training examples specify input values and correct activations for all output *and intermediate* cells. What makes these problems "easy" is that we can decompose them into single-cell problems.

10.6.1 Decomposition

Knowing the correct activations for intermediate cells is a big help; it allows decomposition of the learning problem into independent single-cell learning problems. Consider an easy learning version of XOR in figure 10.11 with network given in figure 10.12. We can learn weights for cells u_3, u_4, and u_5 as three totally independent single-cell learning problems, as illustrated in figure 10.13. Note that cell u_5 does not see u_1 or u_2 at all because they are not directly connected in the fixed network of figure 10.12.

In order for all of the cells to fit all of the training examples in an easy learning problem, it is necessary and sufficient that the corresponding

| Training example | Inputs | | Correct intermediate cells | | Correct output |
	u_1	u_2	u_3	u_4	u_5
#1	−1	−1	−1	−1	−1
#2	−1	+1	+1	−1	+1
#3	+1	−1	+1	−1	+1
#4	+1	+1	+1	+1	−1

Figure 10.11
The XOR function, easy learning version.

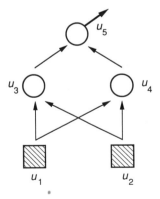

Figure 10.12
Prespecified network for XOR.

single-cell problems for each cell be separable. In such cases we can compute weights for the network by using perceptron learning at each intermediate and output cell. If separability is not assured, we can still compute a cell's weights using any of the single-cell learning algorithms, such as the outer-product training algorithm from section 5.1 or the pocket algorithm with ratchet from section 3.2.4. In many cases the pocket algorithm with ratchet is a natural choice because it is reasonably fast, powerful, and can handle noisy data.

10.6.2 Expandable Network Problems

For easy learning problems where some or all of the decomposed subproblems are nonseparable and where we need a closer fit of the training

Training example	Inputs		Correct output
	u_1	u_2	u_3
#1	-1	-1	-1
#2	-1	$+1$	$+1$
#3	$+1$	-1	$+1$
#4	$+1$	$+1$	$+1$

Training example	Inputs		Correct output
	u_1	u_2	u_4
#1	-1	-1	-1
#2	-1	$+1$	-1
#3	$+1$	-1	-1
#4	$+1$	$+1$	$+1$

Training example	Inputs		Correct output
	u_3	u_4	u_5
#1	-1	-1	-1
#2	$+1$	-1	$+1$
#3	$+1$	-1	$+1$
#4	$+1$	$+1$	-1

Figure 10.13
XOR decomposed into three single-cell problems.

examples, we can employ the distributed method or any constructive algorithm on the individual subproblems. We can think of such problems as *expandable network problems*. Expandable network problems allow us to generate new intermediate cells for a better fit, while still training by fast constructive algorithms. In general, whenever we know correct outputs for intermediate cells, the expandable network approach is better than ignoring this information and turning to the slower backpropagation algorithm. Expandable network approaches also can be quite useful for connectionist expert system models, as we shall see in part IV.

10.6.3   Limits of Easy Learning

Easy learning algorithms are a way to solve fixed-network problems as fast and as well as free-network problems. So why not use easy learning algorithms for *all* fixed-network problems? The answer is that it can be very difficult to determine what the correct activations should be for intermediate cells. In fact finding good intermediate cell functions is NP-complete, and seems no easier than solving the entire fixed-network problem.[4] Therefore if we are given a network of cells and must find weights without knowledge of correct intermediate cell activations, fixed-network algorithms such as backpropagation are the only option.

10.7   Exercises

*1. Let p be odd. For parity-p computed by a tower network with $(p - 1)/2$ intermediate cells, give weights for the first 4 intermediate cells, the last intermediate cell, and the output cell. (Hint: for any intermediate or output cell, u_i, the weights from network inputs, $\{w_{i,j} | j = 1, \ldots, p\}$, can be identical.)

*2. Using theorems from chapter 9, derive distribution-free generalization bounds for the tower algorithm.

3. Give a convergence proof for the tiling algorithm.

4. Give a convergence proof for the upstart algorithm.

---

4. This follows from Blum and Rivest's [24] NP-completeness demonstration for the problem of determining whether an arbitrary 3-layer network with 2 inputs and 2 intermediate cells has a solution. See chapter 11.

5. In the upstart algorithm some training examples are ignored when generating weights for u_{n+} and u_{n-}. Why is it permitted to do this and why is it desirable?

10.8   Programming Projects

1. Implement the tower algorithm in your learning program, and try it on parity problems. Use your pocket algorithm with ratchet code from previous projects and implement the computational speedup from section 10.1.4.

2. Implement the tiling algorithm and test it on some nonseparable data.

3. Implement the upstart algorithm and test it on some nonseparable data.

4. Add enough training examples to the *Taxtime!* exercise to make it non-separable. Then generate networks using the tower, tiling, and/or upstart algorithms. How do complexities of the generated networks compare?

5. (research) Compare at least three constructive algorithms using various sets of noisy training examples.

6. Modify your pocket algorithm code to be able to handle easy learning in fixed networks. To do this it is necessary to read in a description of the network. Use the following format for input:

line 1: $\langle$number of input cells, $p\rangle$ $\langle$number of intermediate cells, $d\rangle$ $\langle$number of output cells, $n - p - d\rangle$ (plus other keywords such as W)

line 2: $NETWORK (keyword for error checking on input data format)

lines 3 to $n - p + 2$: each row is the incidence vector for the corresponding cell

line $n - p + 3$: $EXAMPLES (keyword for error checking on input data format)

lines $n - p + 4$ to $n - p + N + 3$: one row for each training example.

For example the data for the sample problem in figure 10.11 and figure 10.12 would be

```
    2    2    1
$NETWORK
    1    1    0    0    0   {connections for cell 3}
    1    1    0    0    0   {connections for cell 4}
    0    0    1    1    0   {connections for cell 5}
```

\$EXAMPLES

−1	−1	−1	−1	−1	{training example #1}
−1	+1	+1	−1	+1	{training example #2}
+1	−1	+1	−1	+1	{training example #3}
+1	+1	+1	+1	−1	{training example #4}.

Test your code on this example. Can all cells fit all of the data?

11 Backpropagation

Backpropagation is currently the most important and most widely used algorithm for connectionist learning. Its rapid rise in popularity has been a major factor in the resurgence of neural networks, as discussed in section 1.5.

Backpropagation is an algorithm for learning in feedforward networks using mean squared error and gradient descent. Letting W be the set of all network weights, backpropagation employs a nice simplification that makes it easy to find the network's weight gradient $\nabla \mathscr{E}(W)$. This allows us to update the current W by a small step to form new weights W^* using

$$W^* = W - \rho \nabla \mathscr{E}(W).$$

The parameter $\rho > 0$ controls the step size.

In order to perform gradient descent we need a differentiable error function. Backpropagation accomplishes this by using mean squared error and by using continuous valued cells with activations given by

$$S_i = \sum_{j=0}^{i-1} w_{i,j} u_j$$

$$u_i = f(S_i) = \frac{1}{1 + e^{-S_i}}$$

(11.1)

The *sigmoid* function f is sometimes called a *squashing function* because it monotonically maps its inputs into $[0, 1]$, as illustrated in figure 11.1. Also see figure 1.10 for a graph of a squashing function into $[-1, +1]$.

It is interesting to compare backpropagation with the Widrow-Hoff algorithm of section 6.3. Backpropagation uses squashing functions and multiple cells, whereas Widrow-Hoff operates on a single-cell model with no squashing function (during training). As a result backpropagation error, $\mathscr{E}(\ )$, can have local minima, so we are no longer sure of finding a solution with global minimum squared error.

The next section will give details of the algorithm and a numerical example. This is followed by a more formal derivation of the calculations in section 11.2 and a look at some practical considerations in section 11.3. Finally we will look at some NP-completeness results and note their consequences.

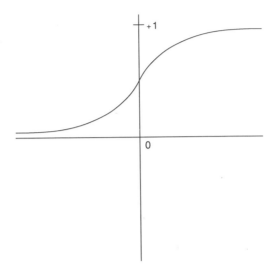

Figure 11.1
The sigmoid or squashing function.

Chapter 12 will present some variations and applications of backpropagation that emphasize its flexibility. Flexibility is a great strength of this approach.

11.1   The Backpropagation Algorithm

11.1.1   Statement of the Algorithm

We start with a backpropagation network as described in section 1.3.2 and a set of training examples with desired network outputs. As is customary, all activations u_i will lie in the interval $[0, 1]$. We compute them by

$$S_i = \sum_j w_{i,j} u_j$$

$$u_i = f(S_i)$$

where the activation function, $f(x)$, is

$$f(x) = \frac{1}{1 + e^{-x}}.$$

The derivative of this sigmoid function evaluated at x is

$$f'(x) = \frac{d}{dx}(1 + e^{-x})^{-1}$$

$$= -(1 + e^{-x})^{-2}e^{-x}(-1)$$

$$= \frac{1}{1 + e^{-x}}\left(1 - \frac{1}{1 + e^{-x}}\right).$$

Therefore we have the following handy identity:

$$f'(S_i) = u_i(1 - u_i). \tag{11.2}$$

Correct activations for intermediate cells are not specified (or else we could use the more efficient easy learning methods from section 10.6). Our goal is to determine weights and biases $\{w_{i,j}\}$ for the network that minimize the mean squared error.

The algorithm is given in figure 11.2. It begins by randomly assigning small initial weights, say in the range $[-0.1, 0.1]$. The reason for this is to break symmetry so that various intermediate cells can take on different roles.

Next we choose a training example (either in cyclic order or at random), and compute the gradient with respect to this single example. Computing the gradient involves a forward pass over the network to compute cell activations, followed by a backward pass that computes gradients. Once we know the gradient we can take a small step to update the weights. This process continues until changes become sufficiently small, i.e., the algorithm *converges*.

When computing the gradient it is also convenient to compute δ_i defined by

$$\delta_i = -\frac{\partial \mathscr{E}}{\partial S_i}. \tag{11.3}$$

This greatly speeds and simplifies the computation.[1]

Notice that in step 2c of the algorithm the backward pass through the network has computed all the necessary information when it comes time to compute δ_i. In particular, the summation for δ_i involves only cells that are *above* u_i in the network and to which u_i is connected. For other cells $w_{m,i} = 0$.

---

1. These deltas are not the same as the computational learning theory deltas in chapter 9; unfortunately both are standard usages for the same symbol.

1. Choose a small positive value for ρ, the step size, and assign randomly selected small initial weights $\{w_{i,j}\}$ to all cells.

2. Repeat until the algorithm converges, i.e., until weight changes and changes in the mean squared error, $\mathcal{E}$, become sufficiently small.

    2a. Take the next training example, E, with correct output C. (C may be a vector that gives the correct output for more than one output cell.)

    2b. *Forward propagation step:* Make a bottom-up pass through the network to compute weighted sums, S_i, and activations, $u_i = f(S_i)$, for every cell.

    2c. *Backward propagation step:* Starting with the outputs, make a top-down pass through the output and intermediate cells computing:

$$f'(S_i) = u_i(1 - u_i) \tag{11.4}$$

$$\delta_i = \begin{cases} (C_i - u_i)f'(S_i) & \text{if } u_i \text{ is an output unit} \\ \left(\sum_{m:\, m>i} w_{m,i}\delta_m \right) f'(S_i) & \text{for other units.} \end{cases} \tag{11.5}$$

    2d. Update weights:

$$w_{i,j}^* = w_{i,j} + \rho\delta_i u_j. \tag{11.6}$$

Figure 11.2
The backpropagation algorithm.

Before verifying that the computations in figure 11.2 actually compute $-\nabla\mathcal{E}(W)$, let us examine a numerical example to be sure that the algorithm is clear.

11.1.2 A Numerical Example

Consider the network of figure 11.3. We have assigned initial weights and biases rather arbitrarily and made most of them integers to ease the calculation a bit. (These weights are much too large for initial weights.)

We will explicitly compute all of the values needed for one iteration of the algorithm. This should both clarify the workings of backpropagation and serve as test data to check computer implementations.

Suppose the next training example has inputs and desired output of

$$u_1 = 1, u_2 = 0; u_5 = 1.$$

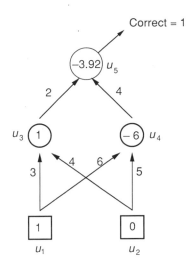

Figure 11.3
A backpropagation example. Weights and biases at the start of this iteration are given, as well as inputs and correct output.

We now make a forward pass computing

$$S_i = \sum_j w_{i,j} u_j \text{ and }$$

$$u_i = f(S_i) = \frac{1}{1 + e^{-S_i}}.$$

For example

$$S_3 = 1 + 3 = 4$$

$$u_3 = f(S_3) = 0.9820.$$

Filling in other values:

i	S_i	$u_i = f(S_i)$	Comment
1	—	1	input cell
2	—	0	input cell
3	4	0.9820	
4	0	0.5000	
5	0.04	0.5100	output cell

The single output u_5 takes value 0.51, whereas 1 is desired.

We now perform the backward pass, starting with output cell u_5.

$$f'(S_5) = u_5(1 - u_5) = (.51)(1 - .51) \approx .25$$

$$\delta_5 = (C_5 - u_5)(f'(S_5)) = (1 - .51)(.25) \approx 0.1225$$

Proceeding to intermediate cell u_4:

$$f'(S_4) = u_4(1 - u_4) = (.5)(1 - .5) = .25$$

$$\delta_4 = (w_{5,4}\delta_5)f'(S_4) = (4(.1225))(.25) = .1225$$

and similarly for the other intermediate cell u_3:

$$f'(S_3) = u_3(1 - u_3) = (.9820)(1 - .9820) \approx .0177$$

$$\delta_3 = (w_{5,3}\delta_5)f'(S_3) = (2(.1225))(.0177) \approx .0043.$$

Taking $\rho = 0.1$ for the step size, we can now compute new weights using

$$w_{i,j}{}^* = w_{i,j} + \rho\delta_i u_j.$$

For example

$$w_{3,0}{}^* = 1 + (.1)(.0043)(1) = 1.0004.$$

(Recall that the bias cell u_0 always has $+1$ activation.) Similarly

$$w_{3,1}{}^* = 3 + (.1)(.0043)(1) = 3.0004.$$

Filling in other values we find:

(i,j)	$w_{i,j}$	δ_i	u_j	$w_{i,j}{}^*$
3, 0	1	.0043	1	1.0004
3, 1	3	.0043	1	3.0004
3, 2	4	.0043	0	4
4, 0	−6	.1225	1	−5.9878
4, 1	6	.1225	1	6.0123
4, 2	5	.1225	0	5
5, 0	−3.92	.1225	1	−3.9078
5, 3	2	.1225	.9820	2.0120
5, 4	4	.1225	.5	4.0061

That is the end of the iteration. As a check, however, we can compute the new activations for the same input and verify that the error has been decreased.

$$u_3 = f(4.0008) \approx .9820$$

$$u_4 = f(.0245) \approx .5061$$

$$u_5 = f(-3.9078 + (2.0120)(.9820) + (4.0061)(.5061))$$

$$\approx f(.0955) \approx .5239$$

Therefore the error has decreased by about .014.

This example makes clear that backpropagation can be a very slow process.

11.2   Derivation

We need to show that the backpropagation algorithm as given in figure 11.2 actually performs a gradient descent in the direction $-\nabla \mathscr{E}(W)$.

We will do this by showing that

$$\frac{\partial \mathscr{E}(W)}{\partial w_{ij}} = -\delta_i u_j$$

where δ_j is as defined in the algorithm. The proof will be by induction on $\dfrac{\partial (W)}{\partial S_i}$ as well as $\dfrac{\partial \mathscr{E}(W)}{\partial w_{ij}}$.

THEOREM 11.1   *For $i = n$ down to $p + 1$, recursively define*

$$\delta_i = \begin{cases} (C_i - u_i)f'(S_i) & \textit{if } u_i \textit{ is an output unit} \\ \left(\displaystyle\sum_{m:\, m > i} w_{m,i} \delta_m \right) f'(S_i) & \textit{for other units.} \end{cases}$$

Let $\mathscr{E}(W)$ be half the squared error for the current example,

$$\mathscr{E}(W) = \frac{1}{2} \sum_{i \in output} (u_i - C_i)^2.$$

Then for all i and j the following two equations hold:

$$-\frac{\partial \mathscr{E}(W)}{\partial S_i} = \delta_i \quad and \tag{11.7}$$

$$-\frac{\partial \mathscr{E}(W)}{\partial w_{i,j}} = \delta_i u_j. \tag{11.8}$$

Proof: Working with half the squared error simplifies calculations. We first note that the δ_i are well defined in a backward pass over a feedforward network. We have already seen in equation (11.2) that $f'(S_i) = u_i(1 - u_i)$. Also we will frequently use the identity

$$\frac{\partial S_i}{\partial w_{i,j}} = \frac{\partial}{\partial w_{i,j}} \sum_m w_{i,m} u_m = u_j. \tag{11.9}$$

For output cells u_j, we derive

$$\frac{\partial \mathscr{E}(W)}{\partial S_i} = \frac{\partial}{\partial S_i} \frac{1}{2} \sum_{m \in \text{output cells}} (f(S_m) - C_m)^2$$

$$= (f(S_i) - C_i)f'(S_i) \qquad \qquad \text{by the chain rule}$$

$$= -(C_i - u_i)f'(S_i)$$

$$= -\delta_i.$$

Therefore equation (11.7) is verified for output cells. Turning to equation (11.8):

$$-\frac{\partial \mathscr{E}(W)}{\partial w_{i,j}} = -\frac{\partial}{\partial w_{i,j}} \frac{1}{2} \sum_{m \in \text{output cells}} (f(S_m) - C_m)^2$$

$$= -\frac{\partial}{\partial w_{i,j}} \frac{1}{2}(f(S_i) - C_i)^2 \qquad \begin{array}{l} \text{since } w_{i,j} \text{ only influences} \\ S_i \text{ because } u_i \text{ is an} \\ \text{output cell} \end{array}$$

$$= -(f(S_i) - C_i)\frac{\partial f(S_i)}{\partial S_i}\frac{\partial S_i}{\partial w_{i,j}} \qquad \text{by the chain rule}$$

$$= (C_i - u_i)f'(S_i)u_j \qquad \qquad \text{by equation (11.9)}$$

$$= \delta_i u_j.$$

Thus equation (11.8) is verified for output cells.

Now we need to verify these two equations for intermediate cells, which we will do by induction. Looking at cell u_i, we assume that equation (11.7) holds for all cells u_m where $m > i$. Letting m range over cells to which u_i is connected, we have by the chain rule

$$\frac{\partial \mathcal{E}(W)}{\partial S_i} = \sum_{\{m \,:\, u_i \text{ connected to } u_m\}} \frac{\partial \mathcal{E}(W)}{\partial S_m} \frac{\partial S_m}{\partial u_i} \frac{\partial u_i}{\partial S_i} \qquad (11.10)$$

$$= \sum_{m > i} -\delta_m w_{m,i} f'(S_i) \quad \text{by induction and equation (11.9)} \qquad (11.11)$$

$$= -\left(\sum_{m > i} w_{m,i} \delta_m \right) f'(S_i) \qquad (11.12)$$

$$= -\delta_i \qquad (11.13)$$

as desired for equation (11.7) for intermediate cells. Note that in equation (11.11) the weight $w_{m,i}$ is 0 except for cells u_m to which u_i is connected.

Looking at equation (11.8) for intermediate cells:

$$-\frac{\partial \mathcal{E}(W)}{\partial w_{i,j}} = -\frac{\partial \mathcal{E}(W)}{\partial S_i} \frac{\partial S_i}{\partial w_{i,j}}$$

$$= \delta_i u_j \qquad \text{by equation (11.13) and equation (11.9).}$$

$\square$

Equation (11.8) shows that the backpropagation algorithm step 2d performs a gradient descent, where the gradient is estimated from a single training example.

Clearly the fact that the proof sets $\mathcal{E}(W)$ to one-half the squared error only affects the size of the computed gradient vector, not its direction. This is of little concern because there is an arbitrary small positive multiplicative constant ρ for the step size in any case.

11.3   Practical Considerations

11.3.1   Determination of Correct Outputs

A cell always produces an activation strictly greater than 0 and strictly less than 1. Therefore if the desired outputs are 0 or 1 we have to decide when the cell's output is correct. The usual practice for training is to try to get output cells below or above certain thresholds, for example below 0.1 for desired output of 0 and above 0.9 for 1. If cells are below or above correct thresholds (or no more progress is being made) then training stops.

Of course these training thresholds are arbitrary. For faster training we can use 0.2 and 0.8, or if we think more extensive training would produce a better model then we could set the thresholds at 0.05 and 0.95 respectively.

After training, when we present new inputs to the network, we can interpret the outputs as 0 or 1 using the same thresholds used for training. Any value in between thresholds we can define as unknown (or "reject"). Alternatively we can guarantee a response of either 0 or 1 by simply thresholding at 0.5. Setting output thresholds gives a way to tune the fraction of correct responses versus the reject rate. For example we might set the thresholds to minimize rejects while providing performance better than 99 percent correct.

Another important technique for use during training is to define the correct outputs C^k as 0.2 or 0.8 rather than 0 or 1. This keeps the targets in the quasilinear part of the sigmoid where learning is faster. It also prevents weights from growing indefinitely as the top cell strives to produce a 0 or a 1 output.

11.3.2 Initial Weights

Initial weight values should be small, randomly generated positive and negative quantities. For cells with many inputs, the initial weights should be made smaller so that weighted sums S_i are not too far from 0. Otherwise if these sums are too large (positive or negative) it will make $f'(S_i)$ too close to 0 so that learning will be slowed. A practical range for initial weights is to keep them in $[-2/z, 2/z]$ for a cell with z inputs.

11.3.3 Choice of ρ

A larger value of ρ gives bigger step sizes and faster convergence, but only up to a point. When ρ is chosen too large, the algorithm may become unstable and fail to converge at all. Unfortunately the appropriate choice of ρ is problem-specific, but it is probably best to keep it no larger than 0.1.

We can also change ρ during a run. This allows more control, but of course requires manual intervention. A number of researchers have proposed automated methods for adjusting the step size, including Jacobs [105] and Fahlman [51].

11.3.4 Momentum

Another way to speed convergence while avoiding instability is by adding a *momentum* term to the weight adjustment. The idea is to keep weight changes on a faster and more even path by adding fractions of previous weight changes.

Implementing momentum is easy. If $\Delta w_{i,j} = w_{i,j}^* - w_{i,j}$ was the previous weight change in step 2d of the algorithm (figure 11.2), we make the next weight change:

2d. $w_{i,j}^* = w_{i,j} + \alpha \Delta w_{i,j} + \rho \delta_i u_j$

2e. $\Delta w_{i,j} = w_{i,j}^* - w_{i,j}$

Step 2d replaces the corresponding step in the backpropagation algorithm and step 2e keeps track of all previous updates (discounted by α at each iteration). A reasonable value for α is 0.9.

Adding momentum effectively increases step size while filtering out higher-frequency oscillations in the weight changes.

11.3.5 Network Topology

Most applications of backpropagation to free-network problems make use of a 2-layer network (i.e., one layer of hidden nodes). A major reason for this is that intermediate cells not directly connected to output cells will have very small weight changes and will learn very slowly. Another reason for restricting attention to such configurations is that now the only remaining topology decision is how many intermediate cells to use. Finally this topology works well for many practical problems.

On the other hand using two layers of intermediate cells gives better results for some problems where "higher order" functions are important. Unfortunately the only way to determine the number of layers is by trial and error using cross validation or similar tests.

11.3.6 Local Minima

Like all gradient descent algorithms, backpropagation can get trapped in a local minimum. This is an unavoidable fact of life, and the only easy countermeasure is to try starting again with different initial random weights.

In practice local minima do not seem to present severe problems, perhaps because real-world problems tend to have many inputs. Roughly

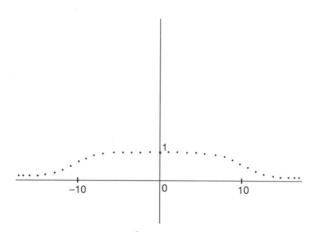

Figure 11.4
Training examples for single-cell backpropagation problem with local minimum.

speaking, a local minimum must be a local minimum in every dimension, so increasing dimensionality seems to help (see also the discussion on Cover's formula, section 8.2.1). In general it can be extremely difficult to determine that a minimum is in fact a global minimum.

Finally it is interesting to note that even a single backpropagation cell with only one input can have a local minimum.[2] Figure 11.4 gives the training examples. Apparently there are two local minima that are close to

$$W = \langle -10 \ +1 \rangle \quad \text{and}$$

$$W = \langle +10 \ -1 \rangle.$$

11.3.7   Activations in $[0, 1]$ versus $[-1, 1]$

Although it is traditional for backpropagation networks to use activations in $[0, 1]$, there is theoretical and experimental evidence that $[-1, 1]$ activations give better results.

Consider the update step

2d. $w_{i,j}{}^* = w_{i,j} + \rho \delta_i u_j.$

If we use $[0, 1]$ activations and input $u_j = 0$ then there is no weight change. On the other hand with $[-1, 1]$ activations u_j would be -1, so $w_{i,j}$ would

2. This example is due to Leemon Baird of Draper Labs.

be changed. Thus $[-1, 1]$ activations promote quicker convergence, and this has been verified by several experimenters.

For activation function

$$f(x) = -1 + \frac{2}{1 + e^{-x}} = \frac{1 - e^{-x}}{1 + e^{-x}}$$

it is easy to verify the following identity (exercise 2):

$$f'(S_i) = \frac{1}{2}(1 - u_i^2). \tag{11.14}$$

It is also straightforward to check that theorem 11.1 goes through with only this change, so the only modification needed in the backpropagation algorithm is to substitute equation (11.14) for computing $f'(S_i)$ in equation (11.4).

11.3.8 Update after Every Training Example

In the backpropagation algorithm we estimate the gradient on the basis of the single training example chosen for the current iteration. Of course it is possible to make a pass through all the training examples to obtain a better gradient estimate, but as noted in section 1.4.2 this usually slows down convergence.

11.3.9 Other Squashing Functions

Note that other squashing functions can be used in place of the usual sigmoid in equation (11.1). For example we could adapt a radial basis function approach and let the intermediate cells compute *distances* from various points. Gradient descent can be used to adjust the locations of such points.

Another possibility is *sigma-pi units* (see Rumelhart et al. [177]). Here pairs of cells with $\{1, 0\}$ activations serve to gate each other by multiplication:

$$S_i = \sum_{m, n} w_{imn} u_m u_n.$$

If $u_m = 0$, then u_n will make no contribution in the w_{imn} term regardless of its value; hence the gating behavior. Gradient descent can also be used to train these cells. For other work on higher-order networks, see Feldman and Ballard [53] and Lee et al. [130].

11.4 NP-Completeness

It is too much to expect that backpropagation or any other algorithm could solve all fixed-network problems in time that grows polynomially in the number of inputs. Judd [109, 110] and Blum and Rivest [24] have provided very strong theoretical evidence to this effect by showing that even very simple networks lead to NP-complete problems.

NP-complete problems (see Garey and Johnson [75] for an overview) form a particular class of problems that can be transformed into each other with effort that is polynomially bounded by some key parameter for each problem (such as number of inputs). These problems have no known polynomial time algorithms, but nobody has proven an exponential lower bound on effort either. Perhaps the most important unsolved problem in the field of computer science theory is whether any (and hence all) NP-complete problems can be solved in polynomial time. Because a large number of very capable people have failed to find polynomial algorithms for NP-complete problems, most theorists tentatively accept that NP-complete problems cannot be solved in polynomial time.

Judd has shown that determining whether a backpropagation network has *any* set of weights that satisfy all training examples is an NP-complete problem. He has even shown that deciding whether a network can correctly classify 2/3 of the training examples is NP-complete, so approximate training of networks can also be hard. Blum and Rivest showed that deciding whether all training examples can be correctly classified for multilayer perceptron networks with only one output cell and two intermediate cells is also NP-complete. Of course it is at least as hard to find out the actual *values* for the weights as it is to determine that they exist. Therefore the fact that fixed-network problems are at least as hard as solving NP-complete problems makes it very unlikely that *all* fixed-network problems can be solved in time polynomial in the number of inputs.

What are the consequences of this fact? First it would be naive to attempt to solve all fixed-network problems in time polynomial in the number of inputs, unless we intend to succeed where many top researchers over the last decade have failed.

Second, we should be on the lookout for ways to restrict or ease the fixed-network problem. One way is to try to convert fixed-network problems to free-network problems whenever possible. Another is to restrict problems by eliminating the "weird" instances that force (presumably) exponential growth, while still being able to handle "real-world" data. (See for example Baum [19] for nonaggressive data.) A third approach is simply to live with the fact that algorithms will not produce optimal results for large networks, yet work to get "good" results for such problems in reasonable time.

11.5   Comments

11.5.1   Overuse

Yann LeCun, one of the independent discoverers of backpropagation, has said that "among all the supervised learning algorithms, backpropagation is probably the most wi(l)dely used" [127]. Currently there seems to be a tendency to use backpropagation without even checking whether the data is separable. Many researchers have been surprised to find that single-cell models were best suited for their complex tasks, for example Qian and Sejnowski [165] in their study of protein folding and Sakata, Hayashi, and Gallant [93] in their experiments with recognition of hand-stamped characters. Therefore a good rule is always to try a single-cell model before trying anything more complicated.

Similarly if we have an algorithm quicker than backpropagation and with about the same generalization capabilities, then we should use it (or at least try it alongside backpropagation and compare the results). This is just common sense.

11.5.2   Interesting Intermediate Cells

A nice property of backpropagation is its ability to generate weights for the intermediate cells. Sometimes the intermediate cells compute features that are interesting in their own right. For example, Sejnowski and Rosenberg [186] studied these cells in their NETtalk model that pronounces English text, and Hinton [98] showed how intermediate cells can correspond to interesting classes when leaving family trees. More frequently, however, these cells become parts of distributed representations and are hard to interpret in simple terms. Interest in what the intermediate cells compute seems to have tapered off over the last few years.

11.5.3   Continuous Outputs

Backpropagation is well suited for problems with outputs not restricted to 0 and 1. We can easily scale (bounded) output values into $[0, 1]$ and run the algorithm without any changes. Note that using discrete models and a thermometer code might harm generalization because extra cells must be added. The corresponding extra weights might cause overfitting if only a small amount of training data is available.

Another way to represent continuous data is with a multicell hump, as described in section 2.4.3.

11.5.4 Probability Outputs

It is interesting to note that backpropagation *automatically* computes probability outputs in some situations.[3]

Consider a continuous model with activation in $[0, 1]$. Suppose there is one output cell, u_i, in a probabilistic environment where input E^k gives output 1 with probability P_k. Then the expected error function for this input is

$$\mathscr{E} = P_k(1 - u_i)^2 + (1 - P_k)u_i^2$$

$$= u_i^2 - 2P_k u_i + P_k.$$

By taking the derivative with respect to u_i it is easy to see that the error is minimized for input E^k when

$$u_i = P_k.$$

Thus the optimal activations that give minimum errors occur when the output cell duplicates the probability that a training example has classification of 1.

11.5.5 Using Backpropagation to Train Multilayer Perceptrons

A fairly common practice is to train with backpropagation, and then to use the weights in a multilayer perceptron. In other words, after training we replace the sigmoid function in a backpropagation network with the threshold function of a $\{1, 0\}$ MLP. This gives good results in some cases, but this technique must be used with care. For example the BPN might rely upon intermediate cell activations at several values between 0 and 1, whereas the corresponding cell in an MLP would be restricted to two values only.

---

3. This was pointed out by Aviv Bergman of SRI.

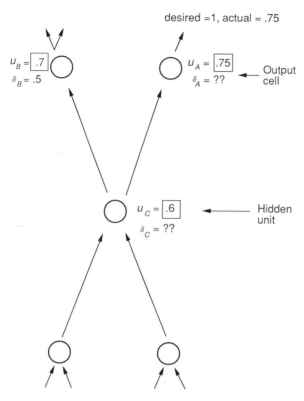

desired =1, actual = .75

Figure 11.5
Part of a backpropagation network.

11.6   Exercises

1. Suppose in the backpropagation algorithm, we have the subnetwork given in figure 11.5. Some cell activations are pictured in squares. (Assume the usual logistic squashing function.)

For output cell A and hidden unit C, what is the value of δ_A and δ_C respectively? (Avoid calculations by giving unsimplified answers such as $(.23)(.98 - .14)(.62)$.)

2. (a) Verify equation (11.14).

(b) Can the multiplicative constant of $1/2$ be ignored for purposes of the backpropagation algorithm?

3. (M. Jordan [107, 106]) Suppose one or more output cells has a range of acceptable values $[a, b]$ where $0 \le a \le b \le 1$. How can we modify backpropagation for this eventuality?

11.7 Programming Projects

1. Add backpropagation to your learning program, and try it on the XOR problem using a network with 1 output cell, 2 intermediate cells, and 2 input cells. Connections run from each input to each intermediate and from each intermediate cell to the output cell. Use 0.2 and 0.8 as cutoffs to interpret the top cell's output as 0 and 1 respectively (to know when to stop iterating). Make your program interactive, prompting for number of iterations to run and ρ. Print out the number of correct training examples and the squared error at the end of each set of iterations.

(a) Add training examples to the *Taxtime!* exercise to make it nonseparable, and then generate a network using backpropagation. Compare training time to nets generated by constructive algorithms.

(b) Compare generalization using cross validation.

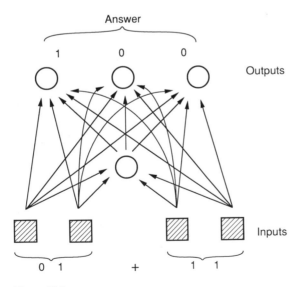

Figure 11.6
An adder network for a backpropagation network.

2. Modify your backpropagation program to accept inputs and produce activations in $[-1, 1]$ rather than $[0, 1]$. Also add a momentum calculation for weight updates. Try it again on XOR (with inputs of $\{+1, -1\}$ rather than $\{1, 0\}$). Was there any improvement for this problem?

3. Experiment to determine sensitivity to the setting for step size ρ and momentum α.

4. Obtain nonartificial data and try to fit it using backpropagation in a 2-layer network with various numbers of intermediate cells.

5. Repeat the previous exercise holding part of the data aside. Then use this data for testing generalization performance.

6. (adder) Try to train a backpropagation network to be a binary adder, as illustrated in figure 11.6. The inputs consist of two 2-bit binary numbers and the output is a 3-bit binary number. One way to do this is if the intermediate cell learns to compute the "carry" of the addition of the two low-order bits.

12 Backpropagation: Variations and Applications

In this chapter we will look at several variations and applications of backpropagation; they show how versatile gradient descent algorithms can be. First we examine NETtalk, a well-known application that helped revive interest in neural networks. Then we will look at a basic recurrent network model called backpropagation through time, followed by applications to control and to character recognition.

12.1   NETtalk

Sejnowski and Rosenberg's NETtalk [186] was an early application of backpropagation to the task of pronouncing written English. For this problem the inputs consisted of strings of text, and the desired outputs were the pronunciation at each letter.

12.1.1   Input and Output Representations

In order to capture most of the effects of surrounding letters, Sejnowski and Rosenberg used a sliding *window* over the input that consisted of 7 characters: 3 before and 3 after the character to be pronounced. See figure 12.1. Each of the 7 positions had 29 input units (for characters, space, and punctuation) for $p = 203$ total inputs. The window is a simple but effective approach for capturing the effects of surrounding characters, though it does have its limitations. For example there is a tradeoff involving window size between context information versus increased storage and complexity requirements.

The output consisted of 26 articulatory features such as *low, tensed, voiced, labial,* etc. Each feature independently could be true or false, and various patterns (most with 3 features true and the rest false) represented about 55 phonemes. The output representation was usable with the phoneme pronouncer part of DECtalk (a Digital Equipment Corporation product), so that speech sounds could be evaluated.

The full DECtalk system also converts text to speech, but by a rule-based expert system. DECtalk is composed of two main stages. The first stage converts text to a feature-based phoneme representation, and the second produces the actual speech. Thus the goal for NETtalk was to learn the functionality of the text-to-phoneme stage.

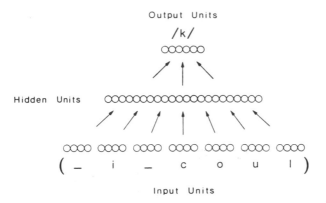

Figure 12.1
Architecture for NETtalk.

12.1.2 Experiments

In a typical test, Sejnowski and Rosenberg chose 1,024 words for training and 439 words for testing. They then used 80 intermediate cells and trained the network for 12 CPU hours on a VAX. All of the output cells were trained independently, so there were two natural measures of performance. Output was judged *perfect* if all output cells had desired activations; output was only *correct* if the vector of output cells was closer (in angle) to the correct phoneme feature vector than to any other phoneme feature vector.

Results for training and testing data were:

	Training	Testing
Correct	95%	78%
Perfect	55%	35%

As another test, the output from NETtalk was combined with the second stage of DECtalk to produce audible speech. For most people the utterances were reasonably understandable. It was also very interesting to hear how the speech progressed during training, from babbling to garbled words to understandable words.[1] The more frequently used characters were learned first.

---

1. The second stage of DECtalk has several settings that control various characteristics of the speech output. Using a "child" voice to play the initial babbling output of NETtalk heightened the impact of NETtalk's learning.

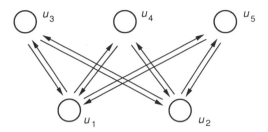

Figure 12.2
Recurrent network.

Sejnowski and Rosenberg [171] also studied the functions learned by the intermediate cells, but found more of a distributed than a local representation. However, this did have the benefit of making the model resistant to damage and noise. Several researchers have used the NETtalk task for other experiments, including Stanfill and Waltz [190] for their case-based reasoning system.

12.1.3   Comments

NETtalk was a milestone for several reasons. First it demonstrated the feasibility of using connectionist learning in place of programming for messy real-world tasks. While the DECtalk first stage outperformed NETtalk, the differences in implementation effort were quite large.

Second, NETtalk used a 2-layer architecture (one layer of intermediate cells) that has become fairly standard for fitting data with backpropagation.

Finally Sejnowski and Rosenberg gave a good demonstration of how to employ effective practical techniques for particular problems. Their use of a window and a feature-based representation made NETtalk's performance possible.

12.2   Backpropagation through Time

Recall that a recurrent network has directed cycles. Ron Williams [178] has developed an important method for training recurrent networks called *backpropagation through time.* (See also Werbos [201].)

Consider, for example, the network in figure 12.2. This model differs from a standard backpropagation network in two respects. First the cells u_1 and u_2 act as both input and output cells. Second the dynamics are different. We initialize activations for cells u_1 and u_2, and then starting with u_3 we compute activations in (cyclic) numerical order for several iterations (ending with u_2). For example, 3 iterations would compute activations in the following order:

$$u_3 u_4 u_5 u_1 u_2 \quad u_3 u_4 u_5 u_1 u_2 \quad u_3 u_4 u_5 u_1 u_2.$$

Our task is to train the network so that for a set of specified inputs we get corresponding specified outputs (in cells u_1 and u_2) after some number (say 3) of iterations. Let us denote the activation of cell u_i at time (iteration) t by $u_i(t)$, where $u_1(0)$ and $u_2(0)$ are the initial values for u_1 and u_2. Then we might want:

$$u_1(3) = u_1(0) \lor u_2(0) \quad \text{and}$$

$$u_2(3) = u_1(0) \,\&\, u_2(0).$$

(There are 4 training examples.)

Williams showed how backpropagation could be used for such problems by "unrolling the network" as in figure 12.3. We duplicate nodes to

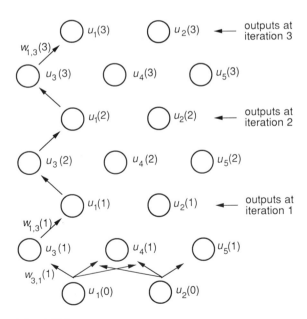

Figure 12.3
An unrolled network for backpropagation through time.

construct a feedforward network that works just like the recurrent network. Then we can use backpropagation, but with one modification: we must be sure that the weight from u_i to u_j is invariant with respect to time. More precisely, let

$w_{i,j}(t) =$ connection to $u_i(t)$ from either $u_j(t)$ or $u_j(t-1)$.

(One or the other connection is present.) Then we require

$$w_{i,j}(1) = w_{i,j}(2) = w_{i,j}(3) \quad \text{for all } i, j. \tag{12.1}$$

If we simply apply backpropagation to the network in figure 12.3, then equation (12.1) will be violated. However, it is easy to fix this problem. We can sum the weight changes computed for $w_{i,j}(1)$, $w_{i,j}(2)$ and $w_{i,j}(3)$ and apply the sum to all 3 (identical) weights. This keeps the weights identical and preserves equation (12.1) as desired.[2] When the algorithm is completed, we get weights $w_{i,j}$ for the original network of figure 12.2 by

$$w_{i,j} = w_{i,j}(1) \quad (= w_{i,j}(2) = w_{i,j}(3)).$$

Exercise 1 explores modifications to this procedure when we

1. "don't care" what values certain outputs have, or

2. want to restrict certain activations at intermediate times, for example $u_1(2) = 1$.

The ability to force weights to be equal in backpropagation is an important idea; we will see it again in the next section. There has been much recent work on training recurrent nets; see Williams and Zipser [206, 207, 208].

12.3   Handwritten Character Recognition

In this section we will look at work by LeCun and associates [128] that applies a backpropagation model to handwritten zip code recognition.

12.3.1   Neocognitron Architecture

Previously Fukushima, Miyake, and Ito [61, 62] tackled a similar problem with their *neocognitron*, a hierarchically structured multilayer network.

---

2. The three weights must also be given the same initial values.

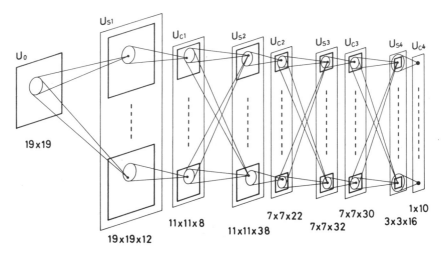

Figure 12.4
Layers and planes of cells in the neocognitron. (© 1988 IEEE.)

The neocognitron consisted of 9 main *layers*, as illustrated in figure 12.4, where each layer contained several square *planes* of cells. All cells in a plane shared the same weights, but each cell viewed slightly shifted cell groups in the planes at the next lower level. Weights for a representative cell in a plane were trained to detect a particular pattern or group of patterns.

The actual model was even more complex than this description; there were several different types of cells and a nonstandard training algorithm. However, the main idea of using a hierarchical fan-in of cells to permit small shifts and deformations of the characters is appealing, and it was adopted by LeCun and associates in their model.

12.3.2   The Network

Figure 12.5 shows the layer and plane arrangement of cells in LeCun and associates' model. Each cell is a backpropagation cell. At the bottom is the picture image, consisting of a 16 × 16 grid of continuous (gray scale) values.

Layer H1 consists of twelve planes, H1.1 through H1.12. Each plane in layer 1 consists of an 8 × 8 square of cells. Each of the 64 cells in a layer 1 plane sees a 5 × 5 grid in the input image; thus each cell has 25 weights and a bias. Neighboring cells see 5 × 5 grids shifted by 2 pixels, so there is

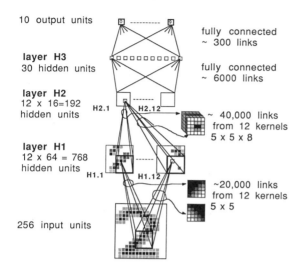

10 output units

fully connected
~ 300 links

layer H3
30 hidden units

fully connected
~ 6000 links

layer H2
12 x 16=192
hidden units
H2.1   H2.12

~ 40,000 links
from 12 kernels
5 x 5 x 8

layer H1
12 x 64 = 768
hidden units
H1.1   H1.12

~20,000 links
from 12 kernels
5 x 5

256 input units

Figure 12.5
Network architecture.

both overlap and data reduction. All cells in a plane share the same weights, but biases are allowed to differ. Thus there are $64 \times (25$ weights $+ 1$ bias) total weights in a layer 1 plane, but only 89 independent weights (64 biases + 25 shared weights).

The main idea here is that each of the planes will learn to be a grid of (identical) feature detectors, and that the same feature will be useful when viewing more than one position on the input grid.

Layer H2 is also composed of 12 planes, H2.1 through H2.12. Each of these planes has 16 cells arranged in a 4×4 grid. Cells in each plane in H2 look at only 8 of the 12 planes in H1, and every cell sees a 5×5 neighborhood in each of those 8 planes. Thus each cell has a bias plus $8 \times 5 \times 5 = 200$ weights. There are $4 \times 4 \times (1$ bias $+ 200)$ weights in a layer H2 plane, but because all cells in a plane share weights (but not biases) there are only 4×4 biases and 200 weights in the plane. Layer H2 has planes that respond to more complex features than planes in layer H1.

Layer H3 has 30 cells, each of which sees all layer H2 cells; layer H4 has 10 output cells, each of which sees all 30 H3 cells. All weights and biases in these last two layers are allowed to vary independently. The total network has 1,256 units, 64,660 weights, and 9,760 independent weights and biases.

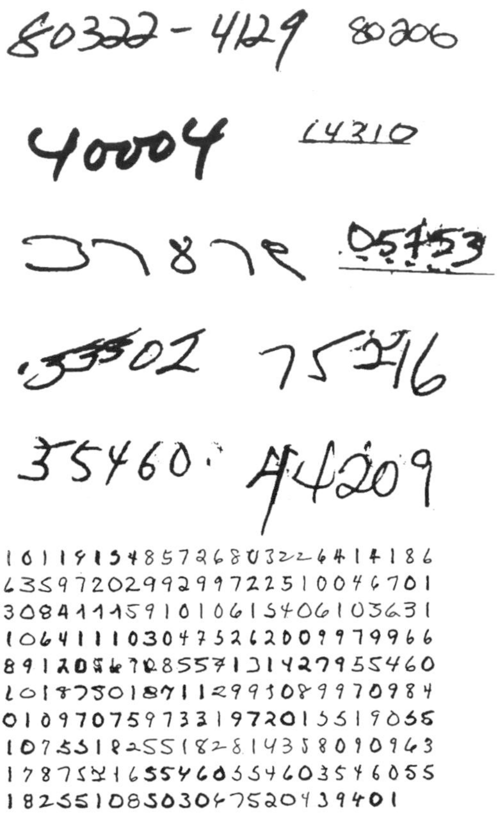

Figure 12.6
Examples of original zip codes (top) and normalized digits from the testing set (bottom).

12.3.3 Experiments

LeCun and associates experimented with handwritten zip codes provided by the United States Postal Service. Figure 12.6 shows how noisy and poorly formed this data could be. All digits were segmented and normalized before presentation to the network. 7,291 digits were used for training and 2,007 were used for testing. Training consisted of 23 passes over the entire training set (168,000 iterations), consuming 3 days on a Sun workstation. At this point the classification performance and the MSE averaged over patterns and output units were:

	Training data	Test data
Percent correct	99.86	95.0
MSE	2.5×10^{-3}	1.8×10^{-2}

They also determined how many patterns would have to be rejected so that the remaining test patterns were 99 percent correct. Rejections were made when the output cell with the second highest activation was within a certain range of the highest output. They determined that rejecting 12.1 percent led to 99 percent correct classification of the remainder.

It is interesting to note that other networks with fewer feature maps produced worse results, and that various fully connected, unconstrained networks generalized poorly. For example a fully connected net with one layer of 40 units (10,690 weights) trained to 98.4 percent but generalized to only 91.9 percent.

12.3.4 Comments

As with backpropagation through time, the digit recognizer shows the usefulness of backpropagation with constraints on the weights. Reducing the number of free parameters seems necessary in this example to prevent overfitting of the data. This is an important technique to remember.

It is worth remarking on the simplicity of LeCun and associates' model as compared to the neocognitron. There is only one type of cell, and it is a simple backpropagation cell. Moreover there is no need to predefine features for the planes in layers H1 and H2 nor to train them separately; all this was done by the learning algorithm. The fixed trained network is a state-of-the-art digit recognizer produced by connectionist learning.

12.4 Robot Manipulator with Excess Degrees of Freedom

Mike Jordan [108] has shown how to apply backpropagation to inverse kinematic problems commonly encountered in robot control.[3] Often such problems are characterized by excess degrees of freedom, which are balanced by added constraints such as smooth motion through a sequence of positions. Here we will consider a modified version of Jordan's model that emphasizes the inverse kinematic problem.

---

3. See Barto [17] for an excellent overview of neural networks and control.

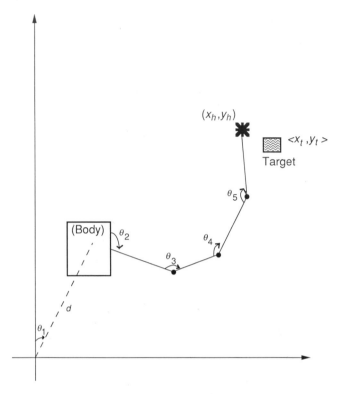

Figure 12.7
Robot body and arm showing 6 degrees of freedom. (Modified from Jordan [108].)

12.4.1   The Problem

Consider the robot body and arm in figure 12.7. The hand position is determined by 6 parameters: (d, θ_1) gives the position of the robot body in polar coordinates,[4] and $\theta_2 - \theta_5$ are angles for the joints. Our goal is to move the hand from its starting position to the target. Clearly this task is underconstrained because we do not need to modify all 6 parameters. However, if we seek smooth motion to the target, it would be desirable to make small changes in all 6 control variables.

---

4. Jordan used rectangular coordinates $(\hat{x}, \hat{y})$ rather than polar coordinates, but to make things a little harder for illustrative purposes we position the target and hand in rectangular coordinates and the body in polar coordinates.

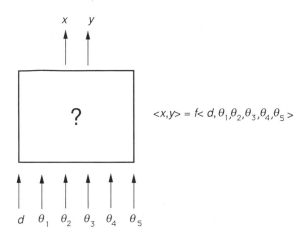

Figure 12.8
The abstract control problem.

From a control point of view the situation is as pictured in figure 12.8. We can specify $\langle d, \theta_1, \ldots, \theta_5 \rangle$ and easily obtain $\langle x, y \rangle$, but we want to solve the *inverse* problem of producing $\langle d, \theta_1, \ldots, \theta_5 \rangle$ given $\langle x, y \rangle$.

12.4.2 Training the Inverse Network

Jordan's approach is to build a rough neural network forward model using backpropagation, and then to use backpropagation again with this model to construct a network for the inverse problem. Figure 12.9 shows the two networks involved: one for the forward model and the other for the inverse model.

To train the forward model we simply generate random control values and compute their corresponding positions:

$$E^k = \langle d, \theta_1, \ldots, \theta_5 \rangle; \quad C^k = \langle x, y \rangle = f(E^k).$$

We then train a 2-layer network using backpropagation to (approximately) compute $\langle x, y \rangle$ given $\langle d, \theta_1, \ldots, \theta_5 \rangle$.

Now we want to train the inverse model so that when the inputs have a certain "plan number," say $\langle 1\ 0\ 0\ 1 \rangle$, then the 6 control units will produce outputs that cause the arm to touch the square.

If we try to use backpropagation directly with just the 2-layer inverse model we run into a problem. We can certainly set input units to $\langle 1\ 0\ 0\ 1 \rangle$ and use the current network weights to compute values for

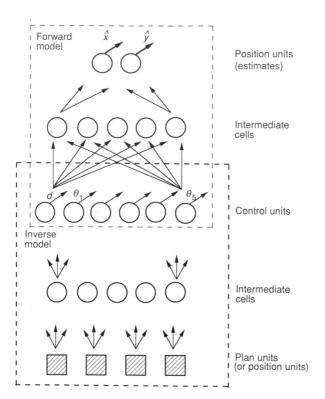

Figure 12.9
Networks for inverse kinematics.

control units, $\langle d, \theta_1, \ldots, \theta_5 \rangle$. We can then directly compute the actual hand position $\langle x_h, y_h \rangle = f(\langle d, \theta_1, \ldots, \theta_5 \rangle)$ (without using the network forward model) and compute the error:

$$\mathscr{E}_x = x_t - x_h$$

$$\mathscr{E}_y = y_t - y_h.$$

But for backpropagation learning in the inverse model we need an error for $\langle d, \theta_1, \ldots, \theta_5 \rangle$. How can this be obtained?

Here's where the forward mode comes in. We concatenate the networks as in figure 12.9 and continuing from $\langle d, \theta_1, \ldots, \theta_5 \rangle$ we forward-propagate to compute $\langle \hat{x}, \hat{y} \rangle$. These outputs will be an approximation to $\langle x_h, y_h \rangle$, but we do not care too much about that. What we are really interested in is applying the error $\mathscr{E}_x$ and $\mathscr{E}_y$ to the output and backpropagating through the combined network so that we can find weight changes $\Delta w_{i,j}$ for the *inverse* model. (We ignore the weight changes computed for the forward model.) We then modify inverse model weights in the normal way. Note that the δ_i's for control units give the directions and magnitudes that these units must change to decrease error in the hand position; this is just what we needed.

This method of training also allows us to increase or decrease the contributions of the various control units by multiplying their δ_i's by appropriate positive values. For example to minimize robot body movement we could simply multiply δ_d and δ_{θ_1} by 1/2 in the backpropagation step.

12.4.3 Plan Units

Jordan did a number of interesting experiments involving the plan (input) units. For example he taught the model to smoothly touch a set of 4 different points in order. For this experiment he made 2 plan units go through the sequence

$$\langle 0\ 0 \rangle, \langle 0\ 1 \rangle, \langle 1\ 1 \rangle, \langle 1\ 0 \rangle, \langle 0\ 0 \rangle, \ldots.$$

These units determined which of the 4 targets was to be touched. Other plan units copied the estimated positions $\langle \hat{x}, \hat{y} \rangle$ from position units. This gave an idea of where the hand was starting from in its motion from the current target to the next target. Still other plan units signaled that a different set of 4 targets was to be touched in order.

Of course we could also use the plan units to specify only the position of the target $\langle x_t, y_t \rangle$ (a thermometer encoding would be helpful here.) In this case the inverse network would actually compute an inverse of the forward function.

12.4.4 Comments

Jordan's work opened the door to using neural networks for control, a potentially important application. It also showed that backpropagation allows us to compute "input errors," i.e., δ_i for *input* cells. Normally this information is not needed, but we have seen it can be quite handy with forward models used for training inverse models.

12.5   Exercises

1. For backpropagation through time,

(a) How can "don't care" values be handled in learning? (For example suppose any value of $u_2(3)$ is acceptable.)

(b) How can we make restrictions on certain activations at intermediate times?

2. For the robotics problem in section 12.4, suppose it was easy to compute partial derivatives for the forward problem

$$\left\{ \frac{\partial a}{\partial b} \middle| a = x, y; b = d, \theta_1, \ldots, \theta_5 \right\}.$$

How could this information be used to train a network for the inverse problem?

*3. (generalized radial basis functions) Develop a modification to the radial basis function algorithm where the basis functions are trained using gradient descent.

12.6   Programming Projects

*1. Modify your backpropagation program to perform backpropagation through time, and try it on the example mentioned on page 234 with the network of figure 12.2. Was the algorithm able to find appropriate weights? If so, what do the intermediate cells compute; if not, could more intermediate cells be of help?

*2. Design and program a robotics experiment similar to that in section 12.4.

3. *Image compression:* One way to perform data compression is to use a strictly layered backpropagation network with the same number of input and output cells, and with one layer of intermediate cells. The network is trained to reproduce its inputs so that the layer of (fewer) intermediate cells gives a compressed representation of the inputs. (See Cottrell et al. [40] and Saund [184].) Obtain digital images and try this method for data compression. Research: compare with other standard methods.

4. (research) Obtain the NETtalk database and compare various learning algorithms for it.

*13 Simulated Annealing and Boltzmann Machines

In this chapter we will explore simulated annealing, which is a general approach to finding a global minimum for a continuous function (even though local minima may exist). An important neural network application of simulated annealing is to learn weights for Boltzmann neural network models, commonly referred to as *Boltzmann machines*.[1] Historically the work on Boltzmann machines and Hopfield's model (section 5.3) were key to reviving interest in neural networks. Nevertheless, the current versions of Boltzmann learning are significantly slower than backpropagation, and for that reason this chapter is marked as optional.

13.1 Simulated Annealing

The goal of *simulated annealing* is to find a global minimum in the presence of local minimum. To see how this works, suppose we have a sealed box that contains an unknown landscape surface inside, as illustrated in figure 13.1. Suppose also that the box contains a marble, and that our goal is to move the marble into the deepest well. Of course we are not allowed to peek inside the box!

One way to do this is by shaking the box vigorously for a time, then shaking it slightly less vigorously for another period, and so on until we barely shake it at all. The basic idea is that during one of the shaking periods there will be just enough energy to shake the marble out of any well except for the deepest well. If shaking at this critical level is continued long enough, then with high probability the marble will enter and remain in the deepest primary well (there may be subwells, as in the figure). As shaking further decreases, it will not be powerful enough to dislodge the marble from the primary well, only form subwells within the primary well. Therefore at the end of our box shaking the marble will (with high probability) come to rest in the deepest well.

This kind of model is very familiar to physicists, and they represent the "vigor" of the shaking as a *temperature T*. (At higher temperatures there is more molecular activity in physical systems.) *Annealing* refers to a way of tempering certain alloys of metal by heating and then gradually colling them. Hence the name *simulated annealing*.

Our next task is to apply simulated annealing to a neural network model.

---

1. Geoff Hinton has remarked that calling the model a *machine* gave it a certain air that helped spark interest.

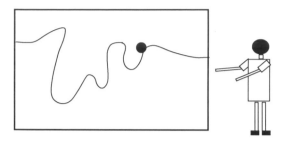

Figure 13.1
Sealed box containing landscape surface and a marble.

13.2 Boltzmann Machines

Boltzmann machines are neural network models based upon systems commonly studied in physics. Similar systems were explored independently by a number of researchers, including Ackley, Hinton, and Sejnowski [1, 177], Geman and Geman [76], and Smolensky [187]. We will examine the Boltzmann machine model proposed by Ackley et al. and then look at its learning algorithm.

13.2.1 The Boltzmann Model

With respect to *network properties*, Boltzmann machines consist of input, output, and intermediate cells. All weights are *symmetric weights* where

$$w_{i,j} = w_{j,i} \quad \text{for } i \neq j.$$

Thus Boltzmann networks are highly recurrent, and this recurrence eliminates any basic difference between input and output cells; cells can be considered as either inputs or outputs as convenient.

As for *cell properties*, activations take on discrete $\{1, 0\}$ values.[2] Activations are computed *probabilistically* and depend upon T, a temperature variable:

$$S_i = \sum_{j=0}^{n} w_{i,j} u_j \tag{13.1}$$

---

2. The Hopfield model was presented with $\{+1, -1\}$ activations for ease of exposition. However, Boltzmann machines are based upon an equivalent model with $\{1, 0\}$ activations.

$$u_i = \begin{cases} 1 & \text{with probability } p_i = \dfrac{1}{1 + e^{-S_i/T}} \\[2mm] 0 & \text{with probability } 1 - p_i. \end{cases} \tag{13.2}$$

Several things are apparent from equation (13.2). First, the new value of u_i will be either 1 or 0 *with equal probability* if either $S_i = 0$ or T is very large. Second, for very small T the new activation is computed deterministically and the cell behaves like a familiar discrete $\{1,0\}$ cell.

Input and output cells can be either *clamped* or *free-running*. If they are clamped, then their activations, u_i, are fixed and do not change. If they are free-running, then they change according to equation (13.2). Intermediate cells are always free-running.

The dynamic properties of Boltzmann machines are as follows. We begin with a high temperature T and follow a simulated annealing schedule where T is gradually reduced as iterations proceed. At each iteration we select a cell u_i at random and, if it is not clamped, compute u_i's new activation according to equation (13.2). When T becomes sufficiently small, we let the system reach equilibrium (no further cell changes), and read off the activations.

For Boltzmann machines, we can compute an energy by the same formula Hopfield used:

$$\mathscr{E}(t) = -\sum_{i<j} u_i(t)u_j(t)w_{i,j}. \tag{13.3}$$

Using essentially the same calculation as in section 5.3.1, with $T = 0$ every change in activation to 0 decreases the energy and every change in activation to 1 does not increase energy. Hence the system must reach equilibrium if $T = 0$. This equilibrium will be a local minimum. However, if we perform simulated annealing while gradually lowering the temperature, we can theoretically guarantee that a global minimum will be reached with high probability. Unfortunately in practice the huge computational demands that are involved make it less than certain that we will actually reach a global minimum.

13.2.2 Boltzmann Learning

Energy plays a key role in learning the weights. Here some nice physics enters the picture.

Let α and β represent two *states*, i.e., sets of cell activations. For example we might have

$$\alpha = \langle 1\ \ 0\ \ 1\ \ 1\ \ 0 \rangle$$

$$\beta = \langle 0\ \ 1\ \ 1\ \ 0\ \ 0 \rangle.$$

Also let $P(\alpha)$ be the probability at equilibrium that the system is in state α, and similarly for $P(\beta)$. Finally we define $\mathscr{E}(\alpha)$ as the energy of state α and similarly for $\mathscr{E}(\beta)$. Then it can be shown that $P(\ )$ satisfies the Boltzmann distribution:

$$\frac{P(\alpha)}{P(\beta)} = e^{-(\mathscr{E}(\alpha) - \mathscr{E}(\beta))/T}. \tag{13.4}$$

At temperature $T = 1$, this means the difference in the log probabilities of two states is just (the negative of) their energy difference, a pretty relation.

The goal for Boltzmann machines is to model their environment. We want the probability of any pattern over the input and output cells (only) to match the distribution of input/output cell patterns in the training examples.

One way to quantify how closely two distributions match up is Kullback's asymmetric divergence [124]. Letting $P(\alpha)$ be the probability of state α given by the training examples, and $P'(\alpha)$ be the probability of state α when a network is running freely at equilibrium, then we define the asymmetric divergence, G, by

$$G = \sum_{\alpha} P(\alpha) \ln \frac{P(\alpha)}{P'(\alpha)}. \tag{13.5}$$

It can be shown that G is 0 if and only if the two distributions are identical, and that otherwise G is positive.

This suggests doing gradient descent with respect to G, i.e., treating G as an error function. Following Ackley, Hinton, and Sejnowski, we can define p_{ij} as the probability that $u_i = u_j = 1$ when measured over the training examples, and p'_{ij} as the probability that $u_i = u_j = 1$ when the network is freely running at equilibrium. Then they show

$$\frac{\partial G}{\partial w_{i,j}} = -\frac{1}{T}(p_{ij} - p'_{ij}).$$

Therefore a weight update learning rule is given by

---

1. Estimate p_{ij}:

    1a. Clamp the input vectors.

    1b. Let the network reach equilibrium twice:

        1ba. Set all unclamped activations to 0 or 1 at random (approximates $T = \infty$).

        1bb. Perform 8 iterations at $T = 20$:

            1bba. Choose a cell at random.

            1bbb. Update activations by equation (13.2).

        1bc. Perform 8 iterations at $T = 15$.

        1bd. Perform 8 iterations at $T = 12$.

        1be. Perform 16 iterations at $T = 10$.

        1bf. Gather statistics during 40 iterations at $T = 10$.

2. Estimate p'_{ij} as was done with p_{ij}, except the network is completely unclamped.

3. Update weights. Increase or decrease all weights by 2, with sign determined by the sign of $p_{ij} - p'_{ij}$.

Figure 13.2
A typical Boltzmann machine learning algorithm for the 4–2–4 encoder problem. Typically 200 learning cycles are used to compute weights.

$$\rho(p_{ij} - p'_{ij})$$

where ρ is the learning rate.

13.2.3 The Boltzmann Algorithm and Noise Clamping

Figure 13.2 gives a typical version of a Boltzmann learning algorithm. It is glacially slow.

An important modification to the basic algorithm is useful when the training examples contain only a small subset of the possible states. (This is almost always the case, because a noncontradictory set of training examples can contain at most 1/2 of the possible states.) The modification fixes a problem involving states that occur with probability 0. The only way a Boltzmann machine running at nonzero temperature can prevent a state from occurring is if that state has infinitely high energy, thereby requiring infinitely large weights. A practical solution to this problem is to add noise to the training examples so that all states have nonzero probability of occurring. For example if training examples are generated dynamically, then each activation u_i could be inverted with some small probability. Adding noise prevents the weights from becoming too large.

13.2.4 Example: The 4–2–4 Encoder Problem

Ackley, Hinton, and Sejnowski demonstrated Boltzmann learning with a 4–2–4 encoder problem, as illustrated in figure 13.3. Here there are 4 inputs, 2 intermediate cells, and 4 outputs. Each training example has exactly one of its 4 inputs on and the others off, and the desired output is for the 4 output units to duplicate the 4 input units.

The connectivity of the net is as follows. All inputs see all other inputs plus intermediate cells, all outputs see all other outputs plus the intermedi-

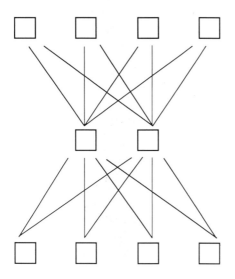

Figure 13.3
4–2–4 encoder. All connections are symmetric.

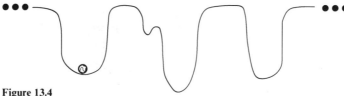

Figure 13.4
Marble and landscape.

ate cells, and all intermediate cells see all inputs and outputs. Note that *outputs do not see inputs directly*; they must communicate via the intermediate cells. Of course the only way the network can learn this task is by having the 2 intermediate cells develop a base-2 code to represent the 4 input states. Ackley et al. successfully trained the net to do just this in 250 consecutive tests.

13.3   Remarks

Boltzmann machines are very important historically because of their role in sparking renewed interest in neural networks. They showed that it was possible to train intermediate cells in interesting ways, and to find global error minima for simple tasks. Unfortunately Boltzmann machines are too slow to be used for practical problems.

There is current research under way to speed up Boltzmann learning, for example Szu [192]. If this and similar research is successful, then Boltzmann learning would become very important from a computational perspective. Until such time, however, it is advisable to seek other algorithms for practical problems.

13.4   Exercises

1. Consider the marble shaking experiment where the landscape is as in figure 13.4. Can we shake the box at some *constant* rate so that after a very long time we could be *arbitrarily certain* that the marble would be in the deepest, center well? Give a heuristic argument to justify your answer.

2. At temperature $T = 0$, how much does the energy (equation (13.3)) change when a cell changes its activation?

3. Prove the asymmetric divergence of two identical distributions is 0.

*4. For the 4–2–4 encoder problem, could p_{ij} have been computed directly, or was simulation necessary? Does the addition of noise make a difference?

13.5   Programming Project

*1. Program a Boltzmann machine, and try it on the binary adder exercise (project 6 of chapter 11). (Use stand-alone code.)

IV NEURAL NETWORK EXPERT SYSTEMS

14 Expert Systems and Neural Networks

Our goal for part IV is to develop expert system models that have neural network knowledge bases. There are several reasons for this.

First we want to solve (or at least ameliorate) the problem of constructing knowledge bases for expert systems. Generating and debugging a knowledge base is the most difficult, time-consuming, and expensive task involved in creating an expert system. We would like to use the learning algorithms from previous parts to generate expert systems *automatically* from training data. This would be especially helpful where there is a large amount of noisy data, because humans are notoriously bad at making decisions in such cases, and because methods that are more statistical in nature tend to do a better job with noisy data. If we can fully automate the process of knowledge base generation, then we will open the door to cheap (even "throwaway") expert systems for short-term or personal use.

Another motivation is the challenge of using a neural network as an expert system knowledge base. Can a network make inferences from partial information, suggest useful pieces of information that are not yet known, and justify inferences by producing If-Then rules (even though there are no If-Then rules explicitly in the knowledge base)? We shall see that the answer to all these questions is yes.

This chapter will first review some expert system basics, then give an overview of neural network decision systems and expert systems, and finally look at some basic representation issues. Following chapters will give details of the MACIE model for neural network expert systems, examine a case study that involves noise and redundancy, and look at the problem of extracting If-Then rules from neural networks. Much of this material is extracted from Gallant [67, 68, 66, 69, 70] and Gallant and Hayashi [73].

14.1 Expert Systems

Expert systems are the biggest success story for artificial intelligence. Many—perhaps thousands—of companies use them for complex tasks such as configuring computers and for simpler tasks such as routing telephone requests. Other applications include process control, stock trading, scheduling, tax preparation, prediction, medical diagnosis, and military uses.

Although a thorough exposition of expert systems is beyond the scope of this book, a brief overview of conventional expert systems is clearly in order. For more on standard expert system methods see Duda and Shortliffe [49] and Jackson [104].

14.1.1 What Is an Expert System?

Definition by Usage

There is no general agreement as to exactly what constitutes an *expert system*. One simple definition is *"a computer program that performs a task normally done by a human expert."* Firebaugh [54] gives a more lengthy definition:

Expert systems are a class of computer programs that can advise, analyze, categorize, communicate, consult, design, diagnose, explain, explore, forecast, form concepts, identify, interpret, justify, learn, manage, monitor, plan, present, retrieve, schedule, test, and tutor. They address problems normally thought to require human specialists for their solution.

Definition by Functionality

To give a more detailed definition that emphasizes functionality, expert systems also can be characterized as programs designed to solve (or help solve) problems in a particular narrow domain, where the following features are important:

1. *Inferencing:* The program should be able to draw conclusions without seeing all possible information. For example a medical system cannot require all potentially available tests prior to reaching a conclusion.

2. *Interactive acquisition of data:* The program should direct the acquisition of new information in an efficient manner. For a medical system, this means seeking out highly relevant information through questions, and ignoring possible tests that would not be relevant to the case at hand.

3. *Justification of conclusions:* The expert system should be able to tell how a conclusion was reached. This provides a check on the internal logic of the system and might give a novice user insights into the problem at hand.

4. *Modular structure:* An expert system usually contains three major parts (figure 14.1):

• The *knowledge base* is a problem-specific module containing information that controls inferencing. Traditional expert systems generally employ

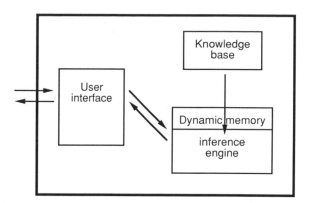

Figure 14.1
Expert system structure.

If-Then rules to represent this information, for example:

Rule 37:

> **If blood-pressure ≤ 5**
> **and skin-color = ashen**
> **Conclude vivacious = false.**
> **(Confidence = 0.95)**

Here the "confidence" measurements are intended to capture the probabilistic nature of rules, and confidences for variables are usually propagated around the system in a manner inspired by fuzzy logic (Zadeh [217]). It can be very difficult creating a set of consistent If-Then rules and appropriate confidence measurements so that a system functions as intended.

Other classical expert systems use different representations. Prospector (Duda and Reboh [48]) made use of network models (that are not neural networks), and Internist-I (Miller et. al. [143]) used tables of probability-related information. In all of these cases the knowledge bases were constructed by "knowledge engineers" working with human experts, some devoting tens of person-years to the effort. Recall that one of our goals is to (partially) automate the construction of such knowledge bases.

• The *inference engine* is the "driver program" for the expert system. Ideally it is problem-independent so that it does not vary from one expert system to another.

• The *user interface* is the third major element in an expert system. This component links the inference engine to the external environment using standard programming techniques.

For this book we will adopt the functional definition of expert systems, as given by the above four features.

14.1.2 Why Expert Systems?

Expert systems allow us *to preserve expertise*. For example NASA faces a problem of having to replace many key personnel who are reaching retirement age. If part of the experience known to these people can be captured in a program, it will greatly help.

Another benefit of expert systems is that they are easily *replicable*. It is much easier to copy a program than to train a person. Therefore a domain with too few human experts becomes especially attractive for expert system development.

For some applications the key consideration is *quick action*. For example stock trading or arbitrage by computer places great emphasis upon speed. Approving credit card purchases must be done by computer; an army of people could not do as good a job.

In general, any task that can be done by a computer is a strong candidate for such automation. Expert systems constitute an important group of programs for automation.

14.1.3 Historically Important Expert Systems

Probably the four most important expert systems from a historical perspective are MYCIN, Prospector, Internist-I, and R1/XCON. Each had a significant impact on the field.

MYCIN and Backward Chaining
MYCIN (Buchanan and Shortliffe [31]), an expert system for diagnosing microbial diseases of the blood, is the most famous expert system. It employed a knowledge base of If-Then rules and is *the* classic backward chaining system.

In a *backward chaining* system a subset of rules are examined, and any rule that has its conditions satisfied will "fire" (execute associated actions). In order to determine whether conditions are satisfied, backward chaining must be done recursively using those rules whose actions affect the conditions of the current rules being checked. Consider for example the following rule:

Rule 37:

> **If blood-pressure = extremely-low**
> **and skin-color = ashen**
> **Conclude vivacious = false.**
> **(Confidence = 0.95)**

If the conditions are already known then the rule can be evaluated immediately to determine whether it fires or not. Suppose, however, that the blood pressure is not yet known. Then we can recursively perform backward chaining *using only those rules having conclusions that set the variable* **blood-pressure**. If this recursive step still fails to determine the blood pressure, we could then ask the user for this information.

Note that the recursive calls affect the order in which rules are examined. In fact, the recursive calls control the expert system. For example the entire expert system might begin with a rule such as:

Rule 0:

> **If initial-info-asked**
> **and diagnosis-found**
> **and treatment-found**
> **Conclude done = true.**
> **(Confidence 1.00)**

This rule "calls" the phases of the expert system corresponding to the variables **initial-info-asked, diagnosis-found, treatment-found** in the given order. After each phase the corresponding variable will be set to true. The checking of conditions for Rule 0 will then "call" the next phase.

The *confidence measurements* are intended to help handle the imprecision involved with diagnosis (and many other processes). For example the presence or absence of a symptom may not be clear-cut, and a rule's conclusion usually will not hold 100 percent of the time. A typical way of handling confidence measurements is given in figure 14.2.

Confidence manipulations are based upon fuzzy logic (Zadeh [217]) and, make no mistake, they are somewhat ad hoc in nature. They may differ from classical probability theory, although fuzzy logic proponents cite this as an advantage, claiming practical results *better* than those given

1. A rule fires only if the minimum confidence of its conditions is greater than a certain threshold (typically 0.5).

2. When a rule fires, the confidence for conclusions are the minimum confidence for rule conditions, multiplied by the confidence specified for the rule as a whole.

   For example with Rule 37, if confidence for blood pressure being extremely low is (0.9), and for skin color being ashen is (0.8), then the rule fires and the confidence that the patient is not vivacious is

   $$\min(0.9, 0.8) \times 0.95 = 0.76.$$

3. If two or more rules conclude a variable to be TRUE (or FALSE), each with certain confidences, than the "evidence is combined" to establish an overall confidence for the variable. For example if one rule fires to conclude *heart-problem* $= TRUE$ with confidence (0.7), and a second rule reaches the same conclusion with confidence (0.6), then the overall confidence is typically computed as

   $$0.7 + 0.6 - (0.7)(0.6) = 0.88.$$

Figure 14.2
Typical procedures for manipulating confidence measurements.

by Bayesian probability. Clearly, fuzzy logic can provide useful engineering tools to help with building conventional expert systems, and these tools are frequently good enough for the particular task at hand. The Japanese have had good success in applying fuzzy logic to actual products, including subway brakes, washing machine controllers, and automatic-focusing cameras.

For work that combines fuzzy logic with neural network expert systems, see Gallant and Frydenberg [59], Gallant and Hayashi [73], Hayashi [89, 91, 92, 90], and Kosko [123]. See also exercise 21 of chapter 2.

Prospector and Inference Networks
Prospector (Duda and Reboh [48]) was an expert system for geological exploration. This system actually helped make a mineral discovery, an accomplishment that is particularly notable when we consider that an average geologist does not make such a discovery in his or her lifetime. Unfortunately the knowledge base was never fully completed, nor was it used on a regular basis.

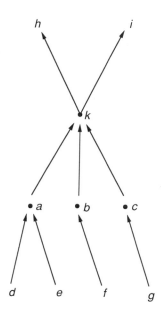

Figure 14.3
Inference network: if probabilities for a, b, and c are known, then knowing d, e, f, and g gives no additional information for computing the probability of k.

An important contribution of the Prospector system was the use of inference networks, which will also be employed with the MACIE neural network expert system. An *inference network* is a tree where the nodes correspond to assertions. Inference networks have the following important property. If we know the probability for those assertion nodes directly connected to a given node u_i, then knowing any other values will not help us for computing the probability for u_i. See figure 14.3. Prospector worked by estimating the probability of important nodes in such networks.[1]

Prospector had nodes that computed probability values from their inputs in three ways: AND nodes, OR nodes, and "weighted combination" nodes. The AND and OR nodes were calculated using the fuzzy logic approach of substituting MAX and MIN functions respectively. The weighted combination nodes involved more complex calculations, and were motivated by Bayesian probability theory.

1. For later work on inference nets, see Spiegelhalter [189], Lauritzen and Spiegelhalter [126], Kim and Pearl [115], and Pearl [153, 157, 155, 154].

Internist-I

Internist-I is a large medical diagnosis system created by Miller, Pople, and Myers [143]. The original version could diagnose any of 500 diseases based upon 3,550 symptoms. It took 15 person-years to build. In a clinical comparison it performed on a par with a competing group of physicians.

Internist-I is a table-driven system that uses a heuristic strategy for deciding which diseases are present. The key tables it uses are:

- *evoking strength:* How strongly does a symptom *s* suggest a diagnosis *d*?

- *frequency:* How often do patients with diagnosis *d* have symptom *s*?

- *import:* How important is it to account for symptom *s* by some diagnosis?

All tables were entered by experts.

Internist-I operates by first scoring every disease in terms of initially known symptoms, and then applying a heuristic to find additional symptom information to request from the user. Various strategies attempt to establish leading disease candidates or weed out competitors. A particular focus of Internist-I is the difficult problem of diagnosing multiple diseases, even though diseases frequently share many of the same symptoms.

Internist-I is very similar in spirit to a neural network expert system, because possible diagnoses are scored (much like a winner-take-all group) to determine which to select. Research using Internist-I is still in progress.

R1/XCON

The first major success story for commercial expert systems was Digital Equipment Corporation's R1/XCON system,[2] created by John McDermott and colleagues [140, 11]. R1/XCON configures computers, a difficult and complex task that used to be performed by a very few overworked people. The R1/XCON system has grown even more complex over the years as new hardware has been introduced. The system is currently in daily use by DEC, and a team of programmers maintain it and continue to enhance it as new hardware becomes available.

R1/XCON is a classic *forward chaining* system programmed in the language OPS-5 (Forgy [56]). The program begins with a set of values for initially known variables, and then repetitively performs *recognize-act*

---

2. The system was originally called R1 and is now referred to as XCON.

cycles:

1. Find all rules whose conditions are satisfied.

2. Pick one of these rules (*conflict resolution*) to "fire" based upon how recently its conditions changed and on its length.

3. Execute the actions specified for the rule that fires.

Sometimes the action of a rule is to prompt the user for additional information. It is interesting to note that OPS-5 programs are essentially invariant with respect to the order of statements. Roughly speaking, we could shuffle a deck of statements and come up with the same program! For more details on OPS-5 see Brownston et al. [30].

14.1.4 Critique of Conventional Expert Systems

The main practical problem in building a conventional expert system is constructing and debugging its knowledge base. It can be difficult and expensive to get a human expert to express his or her knowledge in terms of If-Then rules and confidence factors.[3] Once extracted, a set of rules is almost certain to be incomplete, inconsistent, and require tuning of confidence factors.

Another problem with conventional expert systems occurs with statistical or pattern recognition domains. For example it would be somewhat difficult to construct an expert system for recognizing whether a pixel pattern in a large grid was a 0, 1, ..., or 9. This is partly a problem with representation; If-Then rules are not well suited for such tasks.

The neural network approach is appealing for expert systems because it can take advantage of learning algorithms to construct knowledge bases, and because neural network representations seem better suited for more numerical or statistical tasks.

On the other hand, if a task is more naturally and conveniently specified by a collection of If-Then rules, for example directing incoming calls at a switchboard, then no advantage would be gained by using neural network methods. Similarly if the output is significantly more complex than arriving at a decision or sequence of decisions, then once again it would be better for a conventional expert system to play the main role.

---

3. Apparently many human experts are not aware that they use such If-Then rules for reasoning, as mandated by conventional AI "wisdom."

14.2   Neural Network Decision Systems

If we are primarily interested in making decisions, then most of the learning algorithms from earlier sections are directly applicable. For example suppose we want a system to approve or reject credit card purchases, based upon the limited information available (amount of charge, type of purchase, past history of charges and payments, etc.). We will need to make hundreds of thousands of such decisions every day, and each decision must be taken quickly, or else customer inconvenience will lose us business. Clearly an automated system is necessary.

We can approach such a problem by first deciding upon an appropriate set of features. For example good features might include current credit status, size of charge relative to previous charges (expressed in standard deviations), recent large charges, etc. Designing good features requires both creativity and knowledge of the specific problem. Once the features have been determined, we can look up past records of good and bad charges for all customers and compute the values of the features for all of this training data. Now we must decide upon an appropriate learning algorithm based upon problem specifics such as size, speed requirements, Boolean or real-valued features, etc. The next important task is to generate, evaluate, and tune the network. The network can then be deployed for our decision task, after which the focus will shift to performance monitoring, enhancements, and retraining based upon recently acquired data.

Most of the above tasks require some technical or domain knowledge; rarely can we simply throw in the data and immediately produce a system that works well. On the other hand the requirements from our human expert have changed considerably. For example the decision of which features of the data to consider would seem more appropriate for our human expert than the production of If-Then rules and confidence factors.

We have seen several cases of neural network decision systems in previous chapters. Chapter 3 contained a weather prediction example, and the exercises in chapter 5 showed how to construct a simple decision system using an autoassociative model. Then in section 6.6 we saw how to determine the next input value by using a tapped delay line to filter noisy inputs, and chapter 8 gave an example of a neural network decision system for Hepatobiliary data. The RCE networks we briefly examined in section 10.5 can be adapted to give some expert system functionality. Finally we can include NETtalk (and even the character recognition system) in chapter 12 as other examples of neural network decision systems.

Several more examples are given in the following sections.

14.2.1 Example: Diagnosis of Acute Coronary Occlusion

A typical and nice example of a neural network decision system was implemented by William Baxt of the San Diego Medical Center [21]. He studied the problem of diagnosing acute coronary occlusion (myocardial infarction) using a backpropagation network. Baxt first split 356 cases randomly into training and testing groups. Then he tried various subsets of inputs, numbers of intermediate cells, and network architectures on the training data. He settled on a network with 20 inputs (out of 40 that were available) and 2 layers of 10 intermediate cells each. After training the network he evaluated its performance on the test cases. He concluded that the network performed at a level substantially better than that reported for either physicians or other analytical approaches. If these results hold up in further testing, then this approach could help reduce health care costs. Moreover it is clear that this technique can also be used for other diagnostic problems.

Note that Baxt's domain knowledge and engineering skills entered into the choice of inputs, network architecture, and training.

For another example of a medical diagnostic system that handles multiple disorders based upon spreading network activations, see Wald et al. [198].

14.2.2 Example: Autonomous Navigation

Driving a vehicle by computer on the basis of visual sensors is quite difficult. However, Pomerleau and associates [163] are achieving good success at this task using a backpropagation decision system. The ALVINN Project (Autonomous Land Vehicle In a Neural Network) uses a 32×32 retina of inputs, a single layer of 5 intermediate cells, and 30 continuous output cells. The output cells code the steering wheel position using a "hump" representation as described in section 2.4.3.

The network is trained by observing a driver's reaction in response to the current visual inputs. To make the network more robust, each visual input and correct steering wheel position are used to generate 14 additional inputs and wheel positions. This helps prevent problems due to the human always steering down the center of the lane. Training takes 5 minutes with a Sun 4, during which time a person drives at 4 miles per hour. After training, the car can drive at the vehicle's limiting speed of 20 mph. Pomerleau reports success in training the vehicle to drive in a variety of conditions, including single-lane paved and unpaved roads and multilane lined and unlined roads. Currently this is a wider variety of driving situations than can be handled by any other autonomous vehicle.

A new vehicle is under construction that should allow ALVINN to drive considerably faster. Software simulations suggest that speeds in excess of 100 mph may be possible.

14.2.3 Other Examples

There are many other examples of neural networks applied to practical problems. To give a flavor for the diversity of applications, consider the following projects that were presented in papers or demonstrated by vendors at one typical conference, IJCNN-91 in Seattle:

- Vision-based system to sort apples
- Lightning prediction
- Diagnosing heart attacks
- Recognition of glass defects
- Data compression
- Nonlinear adaptive filtering
- Fault detection
- Handwritten digit recognition
- Handwritten Kanji recognition
- Sound localization
- Valve diagnosis
- Multiple object recognition
- Industrial inspection
- Signal processing
- Commodity trading
- Time series prediction
- Economic forecasting
- Chemical plant modeling.

14.2.4 Decision Systems versus Expert Systems

Note that the above *decision systems* do not require some of the capabilities of *expert systems*, namely:

- ability to make inferences based upon partial input data
- ability to interactively direct input in an efficient manner
- ability to justify inferences by means of If-Then rules.

These capabilities can be important. For example in a more general medical diagnostic system it would be ludicrous to require that all possible symptoms and all possible test results be entered prior to reaching a diagnosis. As another example, a bank or insurance company may be required to give an If-Then rule as justification for any loan or insurance application that is denied. The next section and following chapters show how to incorporate these features.

Note, however, that we are adopting a definition of expert systems that is on the narrow side. Others use *expert systems* to include what we have called *decision systems*. Also, there are models that do not fit cleanly into either class. For example Hall and Romaniuk's *FUZZNET* [85] is a decision system with some consultation and explanation facilities and some use of fuzzy logic. Hayashi's *FNES (fuzzy neural expert system)* [89] also tries to unite fuzzy and neural expert systems within a MACIE-like architecture. It will be interesting to see how these systems develop.

14.3 MACIE, and an Example Problem

Much of the discussion in part IV will center around the neural network expert system *MACIE*. The name comes from MAtrix Controlled Inference Engine, and this approach was developed during the mid-1980s (Gallant [63, 67, 68]). It is amusing to note that MACIE got its name because it was thought that "matrix controlled" would sound less objectionable than a name involving "perceptron" or "neural network"; the early 80s were not hospitable times for such terms.

However, times change, and more recently HNC Inc. of San Diego, California, has brought out *KnowledgeNet*, a product based upon MACIE. Thus much of what we have to say about MACIE will also apply to *KnowledgeNet*.

14.3.1   Diagnosis and Treatment of Acute Sarcophagal Disease

We will consider an artificial example to illustrate MACIE's operation, before turning to algorithmic details in the following chapters. The example deals with acute theoretical diseases of the sarcophagus.[4]

Our model consists of symptoms, diseases, and treatments. There are 6 symptoms, 2 diseases whose diagnoses are based upon (subsets of) the symptoms, and 3 possible treatments. Each training example is a patient's case history that lists:

• Symptoms present, symptoms absent, and symptoms for which there was no information

• Diseases present, diseases absent, and diseases for which there was no information

• Treatments performed and treatments not performed.

This information is used to generate a multilayer perceptron as in figure 14.4. The network then serves as a knowledge base for a connectionist expert system. We put off discussion of how the network was created until the following section.

Figure 14.4 shows all connections and their associated weights $w_{i,j}$. The numbers within the nodes are bias values, $w_{i,0}$.

By giving names to nodes of the network we can specify a semantic interpretation for the activation of any cell. Thus if we set each input cell to either true ($+1$), false (-1), or unknown (0) and make one iteration over the intermediate and output cells, the network will compute which diseases are present and which drugs to prescribe from corresponding cell activations. For example if the patient has swollen feet ($u_1 = +1$) but neither red ears ($u_2 = -1$) nor hair loss ($u_3 = -1$) then we can conclude that supercilliosis is present ($u_7 = +1$) because

$$0 + (2)(1) + (-2)(-1) + (3)(-1) > 0.$$

If other symptoms are false ($u_4, u_5, u_6 = -1$) then we can similarly conclude that namastosis is absent ($u_8 = -1$), placibin should not be prescribed ($u_9 = -1$), and biramibio should be prescribed ($u_{10} = +1$). Cells

---

4. Although this is a simple example, it nevertheless captures over 85 percent of what is currently known in this highly specialized domain.

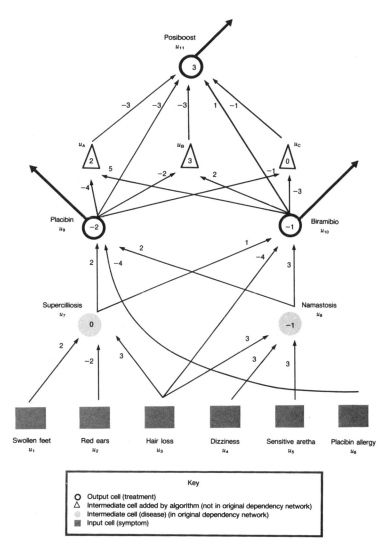

Figure 14.4
Final multilayer perceptron network for sarcophagal disease. Biases are pictured within
cells. The triangular cells were added to the original dependency network by the learning
algorithm. (© Association for Computing Machinery; used with permission.)

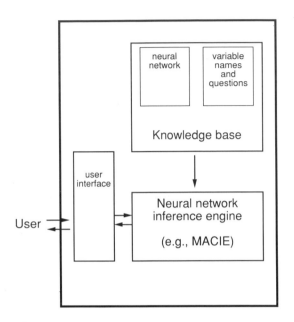

Figure 14.5
A connectionist expert system.

u_A, u_B, and u_C are intermediate cells added to help with the computation of u_{11} (posiboost). Their activations are seen to be $u_A = +1$, $u_B = +1$, and $u_C = -1$. The addition of intermediate cells is necessary because without such cells no assignment of weights to u_{11} would work for all training examples. Finally we compute that posiboost should also be prescribed ($u_{11} = +1$).

This example illustrates a very weak type of inference since it requires information on all input variables. Later we will see how to make more useful deductions based upon partial information.

The network with weights in figure 14.4 serves as the knowledge base for a connectionist expert system that uses a special inference engine as in figure 14.5.

14.3.2 Network Generation

Inputs
To generate the connectionist knowledge base we must specify the following information (see the sample input file in figure 14.6):

```
6  2  3
NAMES  AND  QUESTIONS:
 swollen feet
 Does the patient have swollen feet?
 red ears
 Does the patient have red ears?
 hair loss
 Is the patient suffering from hair loss?
 dizziness
 Is the patient dizzy?
 sensitive aretha
 Is the aretha sensitive?
 placibin allergy
 Is the patient allergic to placibin?
 Supercilliosis
 Namastosis
 Placibin
 Biramibio
 Posiboost
```

DEPENDENCY:	U1	U2	U3	U4	U5	U6	U7	U8	U9	U10	U11
	1	1	1	0	0	0	0	0	0	0	0 → U7
	0	0	1	1	1	0	0	0	0	0	0 → U8
	0	0	0	0	0	1	1	1	0	0	0 → U9
	0	0	1	0	0	0	1	1	0	0	0 → U10
	0	0	0	0	0	0	0	0	1	1	0 → U11

EXAMPLES:

1	1	1	−1	0	−1	1	−1	1	−1	1	TE#1
−1	−1	−1	1	1	−1	−1	1	1	1	−1	TE#2
−1	−1	1	1	−1	1	1	1	−1	−1	−1	TE#3
1	1	−1	−1	1	−1	−1	−1	−1	−1	−1	TE#4
1	−1	0	1	1	1	1	1	−1	1	1	TE#5
1	−1	−1	1	1	−1	1	1	1	1	−1	TE#6
1	1	1	−1	−1	1	1	−1	−1	−1	−1	TE#7
−1	1	1	−1	1	1	−1	1	−1	−1	−1	TE#8

Figure 14.6
Input file.

1. The name of each cell corresponding to variables of interest (symptoms, diseases, treatments). Each variable will correspond to a cell u_i. For figure 14.4 the correspondence is as follows:

Symptoms
u_1: swollen feet
u_2: red ears
u_3: hair loss
u_4: dizziness
u_5: sensitive aretha
u_6: placibin allergy

Diseases
u_7: supercilliosis
u_8: namastosis

Treatments
u_9: placibin
u_{10}: biramibio
u_{11}: posiboost

2. A question for each input variable to elicit the value of that variable from the user (*"Does the patient have swollen feet?"*).

3. Dependency information for intermediate variables (diseases) and output variables (treatments). Each of these variables has a list of other variables whose values suffice for computing it. For example when deciding whether to prescribe placibin, it suffices to know which diseases the patient has and whether the patient is allergic to this drug. Symptoms such as "swollen feet" are *not* included in the placibin dependency list even though they indirectly influence whether placibin is prescribed. It is much easier to extract such qualitative information about "immediate causes" from a domain expert than it is to extract a specific function relating inputs to outputs. (See [154, 156] for a discussion of this point).

The dependency information is optional because every output cell may be specified as dependent upon every input cell as in figure 14.7. This figure

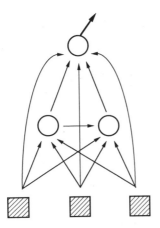

Figure 14.7
Default network with no dependency information.

shows a default dependency that is useful for some applications. However, if more precise dependency information is available then dependency lists improve network generation algorithms since accidental correlations between unrelated variables are prevented from influencing the final network weights.

For the sarcophagal problem, suppose the dependency information is as follows:

u_7 directly depends upon u_1, u_2, u_3
u_8 directly depends upon u_3, u_4, u_5
u_9 directly depends upon u_7, u_8, u_6
u_{10} directly depends upon u_7, u_8
u_{11} directly depends upon u_9, u_{10}.

The dependency information specifies a *dependency network* consisting of an arc from u_j to u_i for every node u_j on the dependency list for u_i. This is the same network topology as in figure 14.4, except Δ cells are not present. In figure 14.6 this network is represented as an adjacency matrix.

Another way to think of dependency networks is from the point of view of connections not present. If u_j is not connected to u_i then this means we can always compute u_i without directly considering u_j, even though u_j might affect other variables that we do look at for u_i's computation. Eliminating a connection from u_j makes it easier to learn u_i's function because it reduces the number of inputs to u_i, thereby reducing the complexity of the learning problem. Therefore we should expect better generalization to new data from our learned model of u_i, given that the same set examples is used for training with or without the connection.

Some caution may be required to prevent directed loops from occurring in the dependency network when, for example, two cells could logically depend upon each other. This situation is handled by eliminating arcs and letting the training examples implicitly specify any mutual dependency, or by the use of choice variables.

4. The final information supplied to the learning program is the set of training examples. For the Sarcophagal problem each example is a particular case and specifies which symptoms and diseases were present and which treatments were appropriate. This is illustrated in the input data where variables take on values of $+1$, -1, or 0 for true, false, or unknown respectively. (See chapter 2 for ways to represent non-Boolean variables.)

Generating the Final Network

If training examples are labeled with correct values of intermediate cells then we are in luck. We have an easy learning problem that we can decompose into independent single-cell learning problems as in section 10.6. More precisely we have an *expandable network problem* (section 10.6.2) because we are free to add intermediate cells in order to improve performance of any particular cell. For this example the distributed method of chapter 8 was used to improve cell u_{11}'s fit of training data. This was necessary because u_{11} needed to compute a (nonseparable) XOR function. The added distributed cells (marked by Δ's) allow u_{11} to correctly classify all inputs. Of course in practice it is best to try to fit the data using only cells in the dependency network first, before experimenting with multilayer free-network (or fixed-network) methods. Thus in the sarcophagal example the pocket algorithm with ratchet was first used for all cells, indicating that all but cell u_{11} were separable. Then the distributed method with three intermediate cells was used to recompute weights for u_{11} so that all training examples were correctly classified.

If our problem has intermediate cells for which most of the training data do not contain correct activations, then we are forced to use fixed-network methods such as backpropagation.

In practice we are most often presented with nonseparable problems where there are no prespecified intermediate cells. In such cases the most important issue is getting a model that generalizes well without requiring too much training time, so we can use any of the free- or fixed-network methods from part III.

No matter what learning algorithm we use, if dependency information is available then we can expect to generate a better fitting model more quickly and from fewer training examples. This is because the dependency information reduces the number of inputs at each cell, so we can work with smaller-dimensional problems.

Note that in the sarcophagal example we did not really need to add all three cells in figure 14.4; either one of the first two cells (u_A or u_B) would have permitted us to compute weights for u_{11} that worked for all examples. The third randomly generated cell, u_C, duplicated an input and was therefore of no help whatsoever; it could have been eliminated and different but equivalent weights computed for u_{11}. In practice there is little point in testing for and eliminating such useless cells, because the increase in speed would be negligible.

In some cases the original dependency network can be used unchanged for the final network if it can capture the behavior specified by the training examples. Also it is sometimes better to dispense with the addition of extra cells, even though original cells cannot correctly model all of the examples (i.e., the training examples are nonseparable). Forgoing extra cells can prevent "overfitting the data" with a model that is accurate on the training examples but does not properly generalize to new inputs.

The network, weights, and names and questions for variables constitute the knowledge base for a connectionist expert system as diagramed in figure 14.5. The actual knowledge base for the sarcophagal example is given in figure 14.8. In this file the connectionist network of figure 14.4 is represented in matrix form, with one row being used for each intermediate or output cell in the final network. There is one column for each cell, including input cells and the bias terms.

```
  6    5    3
swollen feet
Does the patient have swollen feet?
red ears
Does the patient have red ears?
hair loss
Is the patient suffering from hair loss?
dizziness
Is the patient dizzy?
sensitive aretha
Is the aretha sensitive?
placibin allergy
Is the patient allergic to placibin?
I/ Supercilliosis
    0    2   -2    3    0    0    0    0    0    0    0    0    0    0    0    0
I/ Namastosis
   -1    0    0    3    3    3    0    0    0    0    0    0    0    0    0    0
O/ Placibin
   -2    0    0    0    0    0   -4    2    2    0    0    0    0    0    0    0
O/ Biramibio
   -1    0    0   -4    0    0    0    1    3    0    0    0    0    0    0    0
I/ Intermediate Var. 1 for Posiboost
    2    0    0    0    0    0    0    0    0   -4    5    0    0    0    0    0
I/ Intermediate Var. 2 for Posiboost
    3    0    0    0    0    0    0    0    0   -2    2    0    0    0    0    0
I/ Intermediate Var. 3 for Posiboost
    0    0    0    0    0    0    0    0    0   -1   -3    0    0    0    0    0
O/ Posiboost
    3    0    0    0    0    0    0    0    0   -3    1   -3   -3   -1    0
   BIAS swol red hair dizz sens plac Supe Nama Plac Bira Int1 Int2 Int3 Posi
```

Figure 14.8
Knowledge base for the sarcophagal example (edited).

14.3.3   Sample Run of MACIE

Figure 14.9 and figure 14.10 illustrate the runtime behavior of MACIE.[5] We'll look at some important highlights here, but implementation details will be saved for following chapters.

Initialization
The first thing to notice is that MACIE gives the user the option of entering initial values for any variables. This is very important for large systems, because we want to focus the operation of the expert system without having to enter massive amounts of data. Consider medical diagnosis system with thousands of possible symptoms. If we tried a decision tree approach for such a problem then the first group of questions would likely be irrelevant to the case at hand. This is because the first question would always be the same, and its answer would always determine the second question to be asked, etc. By contrast MACIE makes good use of any initial information.

Backward Chaining for More Information
In the example, the initial information is not sufficient for MACIE to draw any conclusions, so it performs backward chaining to determine a useful variable that is not yet known. MACIE then asks the user for the variable's value:

Is the patient allergic to placibin?

The goal is to gather enough important information to make an inference as quickly as possible. Another way to look at this process is to view it as guided (or "smart") data acquisition.

Unavailable Information and Graceful Defaults
Notice that the user always has the option of answering "unknown" to any question. "Unknown" means that the correct value for the variable being asked will not be available for the entire run.

Being able to deal with missing data is important for real-world problems, but missing data can present difficulties for any method. For example if any of the p inputs might independently be unavailable, then we are faced with 2^p possible subsets of available information. Even for medium-sized p this is much too large a set of possibilities to deal with directly. The only

5. HNC's commercially available version has a much better user interface.

```
MACIE Version 2.4
Numbers and names of variables:
             1:  swollen feet
             2:  red ears
             3:  hair loss
             4:  dizziness
             5:  sensitive aretha
             6:  placibin allergy
             7:  Supercilliosis
             8:  Namastosis
             9:  Placibin
            10:  Biramibio
            11:  Intermediate Var. 1 for Posiboost
            12:  Intermediate Var. 2 for Posiboost
            13:  Intermediate Var. 3 for Posiboost
            14:  Posiboost

Enter initial values for Input variables.

Format:  Variable number, value, ...
  2t   4f

PURSUING Posiboost
PURSUING Intermediate Var. 2 for Posiboost
PURSUING Placibin

 Is the patient allergic to placibin?
 --> y)es, n)o, u)nknown, ?)explain, i)nformation on vars.

n

PURSUING Posiboost
PURSUING Intermediate Var. 2 for Posiboost
PURSUING Biramibio

 Is the patient suffering from hair loss?
 --> y)es, n)o, u)nknown, ?)explain, i)nformation on vars.

?

Enter '0' for explanation of the last question
      '#' for explanation of variable number # (E.g. '3')

0

 hair loss is a factor
    which gives negative support for Biramibio
    which gives positive support for Intermediate Var. 2 for Posiboost
    which gives negative support for Posiboost
    which is the Goal Variable with highest Likelihood.

PURSUING Posiboost
PURSUING Intermediate Var. 2 for Posiboost
PURSUING Biramibio

 Is the patient suffering from hair loss?
 --> y)es, n)o, u)nknown, ?)explain, i)nformation on vars.

y

CONCLUDE:  (10) Biramibio FALSE.

CONCLUDE:  (13) Intermediate Var. 3 for Posiboost TRUE.

PURSUING Placibin
PURSUING Supercilliosis
```

Figure 14.9
Sample run of MACIE (edited), part 1.

```
Does the patient have swollen feet?
--> y)es, n)o, u)nknown, ?)explain, i)nformation on vars.

?

Enter '0' for explanation of the last question
        '#' for explanation of variable number # (E.g. '3')

10

Biramibio is  FALSE  due to the following rule:

    IF hair loss is  TRUE

    THEN CONCLUDE Biramibio is  FALSE


Does the patient have swollen feet?
--> y)es, n)o, u)nknown, ?)explain, i)nformation on vars.

y

CONCLUDE:  (7) Supercilliosis TRUE.

CONCLUDE:  (9) Placibin TRUE.

CONCLUDE:  (11) Intermediate Var. 1 for Posiboost FALSE.

CONCLUDE:  (12) Intermediate Var. 2 for Posiboost FALSE.

CONCLUDE:  (14) Posiboost TRUE.


Would you like to try a new case?
--> y)es, n)o, ?)explain, i)nformation on vars.

?

        '#' for explanation of variable number # (E.g. '3')

9

Placibin is  TRUE   due to the following rule:

    IF placibin allergy is  FALSE
        AND Supercilliosis is  TRUE

    THEN CONCLUDE Placibin is  TRUE


Would you like to try a new case?
--> y)es, n)o, ?)explain, i)nformation on vars.

?

        '#' for explanation of variable number # (E.g. '3')

14

Posiboost is  TRUE   due to the following rule:

    IF Intermediate Var. 1 for Posiboost is  FALSE
        AND Intermediate Var. 2 for Posiboost is  FALSE

    THEN CONCLUDE Posiboost is  TRUE


Would you like to try a new case?
--> y)es, n)o, ?)explain, i)nformation on vars.

n
```

Figure 14.10
Sample run of MACIE (edited), part 2.

alternative is to have a built-in *graceful default* for dealing with unavailable information. In the next chapter we will see that neural networks have a natural way of handling such unavailable information.

Explanations of Questions

As illustrated in figure 14.9, MACIE can give explanations as to why it asked for a particular value. For example, its reason for asking about hair loss was:

```
hair loss is a factor
  which gives negative support for Biramibio
which gives positive support for Intermediate
  Var. 2 for Posiboost
which gives negative support for Posiboost
which is the Goal Variable with highest Likelihood.
```

Admittedly this is not a very satisfying explanation for why the question was posed, but on the other hand we got it for free. No such explanation was entered when building the network knowledge base.

Inferences from Partial Information

Near the bottom of figure 14.9, MACIE starts giving inferences based upon what is currently known. Such inferences also trigger additional inferences by nodes higher up in the network. This *forward chaining* occurs with u_{10} and u_{13} in the figure, and in other cases in figure 14.10.

Clearly the ability to make inferences from partial information is important for expert system applications. Without it all data would have to be entered for every run of the system.

Note that inferencing really involves two separate decisions:

1. Is *enough information known* to make an inference?

2. If so, *what is that inference?*

We will see that the MACIE model gives very simple criteria for deciding these questions.

Explanations by If-Then rules

MACIE is able to justify its conclusions by giving out If-Then rules. Any such rules should satisfy several constraints:

validity: The rule must be valid for any future run of the expert system, whenever its conditions are met.

applicability: The rule's conditions must be satisfied by the current run of the expert system.

maximal generality: The rule should be as short as possible, without sacrificing validity. In other words, any condition that is removed should result in an invalid rule.

For example, consider the explanation MACIE gave for concluding that placibin should be prescribed:

If Placibin allergy is false
        and Supercilliosis is true
Then Conclude Placibin is true.

This rule is valid, because for *any* run of the expert system where the two conditions are satisfied the same conclusion will be deduced. It is applicable because the two conditions were in fact satisfied by the particular example. It is also maximally general because no condition could be safely removed. For example a rule

If Placibin allergy is false
Then Conclude Placibin is true

would be violated by some runs of the expert system.

In chapter 17 we will see that it is possible for MACIE to produce rules that are not as short as possible, but that validity and applicability constraints are always met for justifications of inferences. We will also look at the problem of generating a *set of rules* (that are not tied to any particular run of the expert system) from a neural network knowledge base.

It is worth emphasizing that MACIE produces If-Then rules as justifications, even though there are no If-Then rules in its knowledge base. Of course a network contains many implicit If-Then rules, and chapter 17 gives several ways to get them out.

This completes our quick look at a run of MACIE. Before leaving this chapter, however, we will examine some important representation issues.

14.3.4   Real-Valued Variables and Winner-Take-All Groups

In the previous section our sarcophagal example showed only Boolean variables, but the MACIE model can easily accommodate continuous variables or winner-take-all groups of variables.

For continuous *input* variables we have several choices. We can either:

1. Use a discrete network model directly with continuous inputs,

2. Use a group of discrete variables and a thermometer code as described in section 2.4.1, or

3. Use a continuous network model, such as a backpropagation network.

From the user's perspective the representation will be invisible. All he or she will see will be a question such as:

```
Please enter the patient's blood pressure.
```

For continuous *output* (or *intermediate*) variables, only options 2 and 3 can be used.

Winner-take-all groups of variables (chapter 4) present no special representation problems. We can use them directly as input, intermediate, or output units.

14.3.5   Not-Yet-Known versus Unavailable Variables

It is important to make a distinction between not-yet-known variables and unavailable variables.

Not-yet-known variables have values that may be asked for and obtained (at a later time) during a run of MACIE. For example at the start of a run, all variables fall into this category.

By contrast *unavailable variables* have been identified by the user as being unknowable for the remainder of the current run. These might correspond to tests that cannot be performed for a particular patient. Whenever the user enters "Unknown" in a run of MACIE then the variable whose value is being asked is marked as unavailable. Assuming that we must make decisions in the presence of unavailable variables, we are forced to rely on some default procedure.

14.4   Applicability of Neural Network Expert Systems

Not all expert system problems are suitable for a neural network approach. The most suitable problems are those that seek to classify inputs into a small number of groups. For example medical diagnosis in specialized domains, fault detection, process control, and credit and loan decisions make good candidates.

By contrast, expert system problems that require something close to a conventional computer program can be unsuitable for neural network approaches. Digital Equipment Corporation's R1/XCON system for configuring VAX computers would fall into this category. However, even this type of application is likely to have subproblems that are ideal classification tasks for neural network expert systems. For example with R1/XCON it might be important to predict peak usage or average power load based upon a large number of factors. This subtask would be a natural for neural network expert systems.

Another important factor in determining the applicability of a neural network expert system approach is the availability of training examples; the more the available training examples the better. Also, note that training examples may be typical cases given by a human expert. If there is noise in the training examples and/or redundancy is present, then this usually leads to better comparative performance with respect to human experts. People find masses of noisy data difficult to deal with.

In section 17.5.1 we will see ways to combine a human expert with automated techniques.

14.5   Exercise

1. Consider the problem of allowing or rejecting a credit card charge. Construct an example where the decision is based upon 5–10 characteristics. Cast the problem as a neural network decision problem, and make up 10 training examples for it.

14.6   Programming Projects

1. Using the data from exercise 1, generate a neural network for making credit card decisions.

2. Improve the interface for your neural network learning algorithm program to allow

(a) specification of cell names, and

(b) appropriate questions for input variables.

This information must also be included in the output from the program (see figure 14.8) to allow a neural network expert system shell (like MACIE) to access this information.

15 Details of the MACIE System

In this chapter we will examine the algorithms that MACIE uses for inferencing (forward chaining), confidence estimation, and information acquisition (backward chaining). The subject of justification of inferences using If-Then rules will be saved until chapter 17.

15.1 Inferencing and Forward Chaining

How can we tell whether we have enough information to make an inference and, if so, what that inference should be? We will need to answer these questions for several different neural network models.

15.1.1 Discrete Multilayer Perceptron Models

Consider figure 15.1. Here we are focusing in on a single cell in a multilayer perceptron network, and we are partway through an expert system consultation. This cell may be either an intermediate cell or an output cell. Currently we know that inputs u_0 and u_2 are true,[1] inputs u_4 and u_6 are false, and input u_5 is not available for this run. Inputs u_1 and u_3 are currently unknown, but their values are potentially available based upon additional information from the user.

Our first task is to see whether we already have enough information to make an inference. We compute:

$$\textbf{CURRENT}_i = \sum_{u_j \notin \{\text{unknown}\}} w_{i,j} u_j$$

$$\textbf{UNKNOWN}_i = \sum_{u_j \in \{\text{unknown}\}} |w_{i,j}|.$$

Notice that we include unavailable variables in the **CURRENT** summation, even though all of their corresponding terms are 0. The bias is always true, and is also included. For our example we have:

$$\textbf{CURRENT} = (-3)(+1) + (2)(+1) + (-3)(-1) + (-4)(0)$$
$$+ (-2)(-1)$$
$$= 4$$

$$\textbf{UNKNOWN} = |-1| + |-2|$$
$$= 3.$$

---

1. The bias is always true.

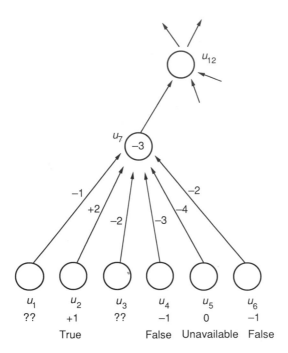

Figure 15.1
A single cell, partway through a run of MACIE.

CURRENT gives the current weighted sum, and **UNKNOWN** gives how much this weighted sum might possibly change in either direction based upon any possible combination of unknown information. For example if we should find u_3 to be true (or false), then this would change the weighted sum by -2 (or $+2$) respectively. In our example the weighted sum can change by no more than ± 3.

Because the final weighted sum will be greater than 0 regardless of eventual values for any unknown variables, we can now make the inference that u_7 must be true.

More generally, whenever

$$|\textbf{CURRENT}_i| > \textbf{UNKNOWN}_i$$

then we can make an inference for u_i, namely that u_i is true or false according to whether **CURRENT**$_i$ is positive or negative respectively. MACIE's inferencing method is *conservative*, because the inference can

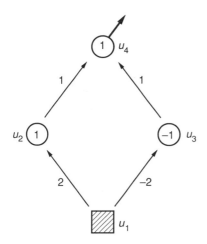

Figure 15.2
Cell u_4 will be true, regardless of the values for the input cell u_1.

never be changed by finding out more information (i.e., values for unknown variables).

Note that once we infer a value for a cell, this might trigger other
inferences higher up in the network. This is a type of forward chaining in
expert systems.

MACIE's inferencing is also fairly powerful, in that most valid inferences
will be made. However, we can construct cases where a valid inference can
be made, yet MACIE's inferencing mechanism misses it until additional
information becomes known. Figure 15.2 gives one simple example. Either
cell u_2 or cell u_3 will be true, regardless of the value for the input cell u_1.
Therefore u_4 will *always* be true. However, MACIE's inferencing method
would not catch this inference for u_4. To catch all such inferences in general
would require work that (presumably)[2] grows exponentially with the size
of the network, something best avoided.

15.1.2 Continuous Variables

We can also do inferencing for continuous models, such as backpropagation networks. However, we must make several arbitrary decisions, and
the overall model is not quite as "clean" as with a discrete multilayer

2. This is an NP-complete problem.

perceptron model. On the other hand a backpropagation network is better suited to continuous data, and the backpropagation algorithm is very popular.

The first decision we must make is to determine a threshold for true and false. For example if we take .5 as a threshold for both true and false, then this has the advantage of allowing us to use the same simple inferencing procedure we used for discrete multilayer perceptrons in section 15.1.1.

Another possibility would be to use other values, say .10 and .90, as thresholds. Now whenever we can be sure that a cell will ultimately be true or false, we can still make an inference. More precisely, we can define

$$S_i^+ = \textbf{CURRENT}_i - \textbf{UNKNOWN}_i$$

$$S_i^- = \textbf{CURRENT}_i + \textbf{UNKNOWN}_i$$

$$f(x) = \frac{1}{1 + 1/e^x}$$

Now we conclude u_i to be true if

$$f(S_i^+) \geq .9$$

and false if

$$f(S_i^-) \leq .1.$$

When neither of these inferencing conditions is satisfied, we can treat the variable as unattainable and pass either its activation or 0.5 up the network.

No matter where we draw the threshold, we must also decide whether a unit u_i that is inferred to be true will pass $+1$ along the network or will pass u_i's activation ($u_i < 1$). Similarly for units inferred to be false.

15.1.3   Winner-Take-All Groups

Inferencing is slightly more complicated for winner-take-all groups. Let us return to the discrete multilayer perceptron model, and assume the situation is as pictured in figure 15.3. Here only u_2 is known and the other two inputs are unknown. Presently u_6 has the highest weighted sum among the output variables, with u_4 in second place. What inferences, if any, can we make?

Consider the pair of variables u_5 and u_6. Their weighted sums currently differ by 7. How much can this *relative* difference change?

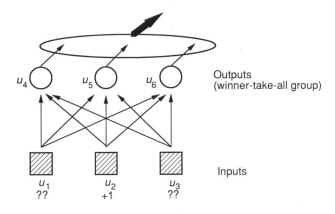

| $w_{i,j}$ | | | | | |
i	$j = 0$	1	2	3	CURRENT$_i$
4	-1	2	2	5	1
5	-2	2	-1	-5	-3
6	1	3	3	4	4

Figure 15.3
Inferencing in a winner-take-all group.

Knowing u_1 could change the relative differences by $|2 - 3| = 1$ in either direction, and knowing u_3 could change relative sums by $|(-5) - (+4)| = 9$ in either direction. Therefore we cannot conclude that u_6 will ultimately have a higher weighted sum than u_5 because $7 \le 1 + 9$.

However, if we consider u_4 and u_6, the situation is different. Although u_6 is only 3 ahead of u_4, the relative weighted sums can change by at most $|2 - 3| + |5 - 4| = 2$. Therefore we can infer that u_4 is false, i.e., that it will not have the highest weighted sum, and eliminate u_4 from further consideration.

In general, as more information comes in we continue inferring variables to be false until only one remains; this will be the single unit with an output of true ($+1$).

For continuous models, inferencing with winner-take-all groups goes exactly the same; passing weighted sums through any monotonic increasing squashing function will not change their relative order.

*15.1.4   Using Prior Probabilities for More Aggressive Inferencing

More aggressive inferencing is possible if a probability distribution or prior probabilities are available, and if we are willing to be less than certain that our inference will remain valid when more inputs become known. Consider the network in figure 15.4. This is the same network as in figure 15.1, except we do not know the value of input u_2. It is easy to check that we do not yet know enough information to make a standard MACIE inference. However, given the prior probability information in the diagram (and assuming inputs are independently distributed), we can see that u_7 will be true with probability

$$P(\overline{u_3}) + P(u_3 u_2 \overline{u_1}) = .9 + (.1)(.8)(.8) = .964.$$

Therefore we can be fairly sure that the model will eventually conclude that u_7 is true.

More generally we can establish a threshold for inferences, say probability $> .9$, and make inferences whenever we have at least this certainty. However, we must now be prepared to occasionally revise inferences that have already been made in light of new, unexpected data.

Note that the assumption of independence we used in the example was not critical; it merely made computations simpler. We could have

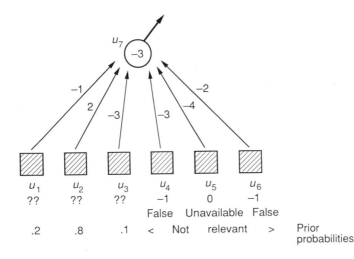

Figure 15.4
Network, known variables, and prior probabilities.

worked from the conditional probability distribution for $\{u_1, u_2, u_3\}$ given $\{u_4, u_5, u_6\}$.

15.2 Confidence Estimation

15.2.1 A Confidence Heuristic Prior to Inference

At any time during a run we can compute $\text{Conf}(u_i)$, an estimate of the likelihood that an unknown variable u_i will eventually be deduced to be true or false. $\text{Conf}(u_i)$ is useful for comparing two unknown variables, but it cannot be interpreted as the probability that u_i will eventually be found true.

Several heuristics are available for computing $\text{Conf}(u_i)$. One of the simplest is the following:

• For a known cell,

$\text{Conf}(u_i) = u_i$.

• For an unknown *input* cell,

$\text{Conf}(u_i) = 0$.

• For other unknown cells we compute $\text{Conf}(u_i)$ in index order by

$$\text{Conf}(u_i) = \frac{\sum\limits_{j=0}^{i-1} w_{i,j} \, \text{Conf}(u_j)}{\sum\limits_{j:u_j \text{unknown}} |w_{i,j}|}.$$

We can compute likelihoods for all cells with one bottom-up pass through the network. It is easy to check that $-1 \le \text{Conf}(u_i) \le +1$.

15.2.2 Confidence in Inferences

There is a second and perhaps more useful way to get confidence information. The key observation is that MACIE's inferencing method for partial information is conservative, in that an inference based upon partial information is never violated by additional information (more variables) becoming known. More specifically, MACIE makes an inference only when the currently known partial information is sufficient to guarantee the ultimate positivity or negativity of a cell's weighted sum, and hence determine the output (± 1) for that cell.

Now suppose we have tested a network with data drawn from some population and have determined probability estimates of how well the network performs with *full* samples, i.e., samples with all inputs specified. Say we have 99 percent confidence that the network is correct at least 85 percent of the time. Then this estimate will also apply to inferences based upon *partial* information (where some inputs are unknown), provided the partial information comes from full samples drawn from the same population used in testing. Thus if we make an inference having seen only 5 out of the 25 inputs, we could still have 99 percent confidence that the inference would be correct with probability $\geq .85$. The reason is that this is our confidence in the full 25-input sample and MACIE is guaranteed to make the same inference with the full sample.

Similarly any statistical test of the performance of the network using full samples applies to partial inferences. In particular, we have seen in chapter 9 how to derive Valiant-style distribution-free generalization bounds for various neural network models. These same bounds also apply to inferences.

Thus if we train a single-cell model having 10 inputs on 3,626 training examples, and the resulting network correctly classifies 95 percent of the *training* data, then we have at least 90 percent confidence that the network will correctly classify at least 90 percent of new test data drawn from the same population (see figure 9.6). The data may contain noise, provided that training examples are independently noisy.

15.3   Information Acquisition and Backward Chaining

If the system has not yet reached conclusions for enough of the output cells to complete the session, it must find an input cell with unknown activation and ask the user for its value. Again there are several possible heuristics for this task. Perhaps the simplest is the following:

1. Select the unknown output variable u_i such that $|\text{Conf}(u_i)|$ is maximum. (This strategy starts with an output cell close to having its value set.) We say u_i is the cell being *pursued.*

2. If pursuing cell u_i, find the unknown cell u_j with the greatest absolute influence on u_i. In other words, find a j yielding

$$\max_{j:\, u_j \text{ unknown}} |w_{i,j}|.$$

If u_j is an input variable, ask the user for its value (employing the character string question for u_j in the knowledge base). Otherwise pursue u_j and repeat 2.

Since we have been careful to prevent directed loops in the connectionist network, no variable can be pursued more than once without a question being asked. Therefore this method of backward chaining quickly chooses an unknown variable to ask the user with no need for backtracking.

Other heuristics are also possible. For example in step 1 we might look for $\max \text{Conf}(u_i)$ rather than $\max |\text{Conf}(u_i)|$ to emphasize output variables with values of true. Or for step 2 we might choose u_j by

$$\max_{u_j \text{ unknown}} |w_{i,j}| \left(|\text{Conf}(u_j)| + \frac{1}{\text{level}(u_j)} \right)$$

to take into account confidence estimates and how far removed nodes are from the input nodes. Here we define

$\text{level}(u_j) \equiv 1 + \text{distance to closest input cell.}$

For confidence estimates and for backward chaining the choice of heuristics does not appear to affect the practical performance of the inference engine very much.

15.4   Concluding Comment

One of the most appealing—and important—aspects of the MACIE model is its *simplicity*. Inferencing, backward chaining, and (as we shall see) justifications are all performed by very simple algorithms. By keeping things simple we can derive and apply analytic results, such as those in chapter 9 and chapter 16. Also, as a rule, *simplicity promotes generalization*. Therefore when considering modifications and extensions to MACIE, or other approaches, it is good to ask ourselves whether added complexity is justified in terms of basic capabilities: inferencing, learning, ease of use, domains of applicability, resistance to noise, and so on.

15.5   Exercises

1. In a run of MACIE, suppose there is one goal (output) variable, G, and 5 input variables, A, B, C, D, and E. Suppose also that the weights for G are:

Bias	A	B	C	D	E
-2	-3	4	-5	6	7

and that we know:

B *is false*, C and D are both *true*.

(a) Tell what happens from now until the end of the run. (Note that any of the remaining variables might be *unavailable*.)

(b) Give a short If–Then rule that justifies each conclusion reached in part (a).

2. For the variable pictured in figure 15.5 in a MACIE-style expert system,

(a) give the shortest rule for u_5 to be concluded true

(b) give the shortest rule for u_5 to be concluded false.

3. Suppose we have a single-cell network with bias of $+2$ and 8 inputs having the following weights and input values:

Weight	$+1$	-3	$+4$	-4	-1	$+5$	$+3$	$+3$	-17
Value	$+1$	-1	$+1$	??	??	-1	-1	$+1$	U

where

$+1 =$ True

$-1 =$ False

 U $=$ Unavailable for this run

 ?? $=$ Not yet known, possibly will be determined later in the run.

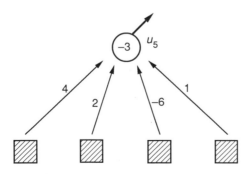

Figure 15.5
A variable in a MACIE expert system model.

(a) What inference can be made?

(b) Give an If-Then rule that contains a minimum number of terms to justify this inference.

15.6 Programming Projects

1. Extend your neural network simulator to a neural network expert system shell. Assume discrete multilayer perceptron networks and no winner-take-all groups. Implement inferences based upon partial information, and implement a backward chaining algorithm to obtain additional information from the user. Use your expert system shell on one or more *Taxtime!* networks generated in previous chapters. Be sure to try some new inputs and to comment on performance.

2. Extend your program to cover the case where all output cells form a winner-take-all group.

3. (research) Implement a system similar to the Internist-I system using neural networks.

16 Noise, Redundancy, Fault Detection, and Bayesian Decision Theory

We will look at a case study in this chapter, High Tech Lemonade Corporation's (HTLC) fault detection problem. This problem illustrates the potential for neural network expert systems in noisy domains, especially where there is redundancy in the data. Humans are notoriously bad with this kind of problem,[1] so it is not surprising when an automated analytic method does better than a human.

After seeing how to generate the neural network expert system using neural network learning algorithms and MACIE, we will compare the resulting system with an optimal system constructed by a Bayesian analysis of the same problem. When calculating the optimal Bayes decision rule, we have the luxury of knowing the underlying process that generates data for the HTLC example. (This knowledge is not used by the neural network learning algorithm.) It would be much more difficult to analyze a more complex problem, or a problem where we did not know exactly how the data was generated.

Finally we examine a class of fault detection problems, called NSB fault detection problems, that generalize the HTLC fault detection problem.

We can prove some analytic results for NSB problems. The most important result is that the pocket algorithm produces a network that, with arbitrarily high probability, implements the (optimal) Bayes rule for the class of NSB fault detection problems.

Knowing how to use neural network expert systems for noisy problems and for fault detection is more important for most people than a knowledge of the theoretical results in this chapter. Therefore the theory parts are marked optional.

But, now, time for a drink!

16.1 The High Tech Lemonade Corporation's Problem

High Tech Lemonade Corp. produces ice cold lemonade from three ingredients: hydrogen, oxygen, and lemons (see figure 16.1). A fuel cell combines the gases to produce electricity and water. The water goes into the lemonade while the electricity powers a lemon squeezer and a refrigeration unit to cool the resulting drink.

There are a number of failure modes for this somewhat dangerous process (figure 16.2) and a variety of measurements that are used to diag-

---

1. Especially if they're thirsty.

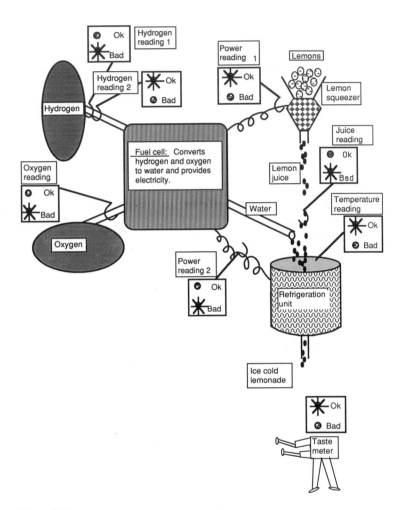

Figure 16.1
High Tech Lemonade Corporation's process for producing ice cold lemonade from
hydrogen, oxygen, and lemons.

G1: Hydrogen gas problem
G2: Oxygen gas problem
G3: Fuel cell not working
G4: Water line from fuel cell clogged
G5: Short in power line 1 to lemon squeezer
G6: Short in power line 2 to refrigeration unit
G7: Lemon squeezer malfunction
G8: Refrigeration unit malfunction
G9: All systems operating correctly

Figure 16.2
Failure modes for lemonade process. Each mode corresponds to an output variable G1–G9.

Variable	Noise
V1: Hydrogen reading 1	15%
V2: Hydrogen reading 2	25%
V3: Oxygen reading	20%
V4: Power reading 1 (to lemon squeezer)	15%
V5: Lemon juice reading	10%
V6: Power reading 2 (to refrigeration unit)	20%
V7: Temperature reading	10%
V8: Taste reading (ignoring temperature)	5%

Figure 16.3
Measurements used for diagnosing problems (variables V1–V8). A value of true indicates a problem.

nose problems (figure 16.3). Measurements are noisy and redundant and not always available (since the people who monitor the gauges sometimes take several hours off to sit and drink ice cold lemonade).

Suppose we estimate that for 80 percent of the times that the system is examined it will be operating correctly, and when it doesn't work there will be a single failure mode. Suppose also that the lemon squeezer (G7) and refrigeration unit (G8) are twice as likely to fail as other failure modes. Finally let us assume that it is 20 times as important to detect a hydrogen gas problem (G1), and 2 times as important to detect other failures (G2–G8), as it is to detect correct operation of the system (G9).

Our objective is to build an expert system that determines whether any part is not functioning normally based upon whatever data is at hand. For example, our operator might know that hydrogen reading 2 indicates a problem and the temperature reading is too low but that the lemonade tastes OK. What can he or she conclude? What additional information would be useful? What if that information were not available?

It would be tedious and somewhat difficult to tackle this particular case analytically. To produce a decision tree analysis for all sets of initial information would compare with cleaning the Augean stables.

Building an expert system using a conventional rule-based approach is possible, but it would be difficult to build a nonbrittle system. For example, there would be a tendency to generate a rule for hydrogen failure of the form:

If one (or both??) hydrogen readings indicate a problem
Then Conclude there is a hydrogen problem (with certainty factor ???).

Such a rule would be tricky to construct and debug. It would also be brittle, because it would fail to take into account the other readings that are affected by hydrogen problems. These other readings might indicate that there was no hydrogen problem after all, just noisy hydrogen instrument readings.

It is also not clear how a hand-crafted rule should take into account frequency information and relative importance. For example if the importance of diagnosing a hydrogen problem is raised high enough, the system should *always* conclude that such a problem exists. (Even if all readings are normal, there is a small chance that there is a hydrogen problem and all readings are noisy.)

High Tech Lemonade Corporation truly has a problem on its hands.

16.2   The Deep Model and the Noise Model

We tackle this problem by first constructing a deep (or "structural") model for the system that captures all information except for noise. For each failure mode, we list the corresponding meter measurements (assuming no noise) as in figure 16.4.

For example, a failure in power to the refrigeration unit (G6) would show up on power reading 2 (V6) and cause the temperature to rise (V7). Other readings would be normal.

				A matrix							
				Noise-free instrument readings							
Failure mode	Frequency	Importance	Final ratio	V1	V2	V3	V4	V5	V6	V7	V8
G1:	1	20	20	1	1	−1	1	1	1	1	1
G2:	1	2	2	−1	−1	1	1	1	1	1	1
G3:	1	2	2	−1	−1	−1	1	1	1	1	1
G4:	1	2	2	−1	−1	−1	−1	−1	−1	−1	1
G5:	1	2	2	−1	−1	−1	1	1	−1	−1	1
G6:	1	2	2	−1	−1	−1	−1	−1	1	1	−1
G7:	2	2	4	−1	−1	−1	−1	1	−1	−1	1
G8:	2	2	4	−1	−1	−1	−1	−1	−1	1	−1
G9:	40	1	40	−1	−1	−1	−1	−1	−1	−1	−1
Total examples:			78	15%	25%	20%	15%	10%	20%	10%	5%

← Noise →

Figure 16.4
Frequency data, importance data, and effects of failure modes on instrument readings (in the absence of noise). The final ratio column is the product of frequency and importance.

The next step is to construct a set of training examples from figure 16.4 where entries are duplicated to reflect their relative frequencies. For example we use two copies of failure mode examples for the squeezer (G7) and refrigeration unit (G8) and 40 copies of the example of correct functioning (G9). Thus a randomly selected example would correspond to a failure mode $10/50 = 20$ percent of the time and would correspond to a correctly functioning system 80 percent of the time, as desired.

We now make one last change to the set of training examples. We make additional duplicates to represent increased priority of any training examples. For our case, we use a total of 20 copies of the training example for hydrogen supply failure (G1), because we judged this to be 20 times as important as detecting no failure (G9). Similarly we double the copies for other failure modes. The final ratios of training examples are given in figure 16.4 as the product of frequency and importance.

The reason for duplicating examples is that the pocket algorithm that we use to generate the knowledge base seeks to minimize the probability that a randomly selected training example will be misclassified. By duplicating training examples, we effectively adjust the frequency of selection of each particular training example so that the learning program will solve the problem at hand. (Of course the examples do not have to be physically duplicated; they only have to be chosen in accordance with the final ratio column in figure 16.4.)

The set of training examples we have collected represents the deep model for the problem in the absence of noise. This collection specifies all of the information concerning failure modes, frequencies, and importance.

The noise model has already been given in figure 16.4. It is the probability that any particular measurement will be incorrect, independently of other measurements. Together these two models allow us to generate noisy training examples that are representative of the problem.

16.3 Generating the Expert System

Because the problem calls for exactly one fault (possibly the "normal operations" fault) to be produced at any time, a winner-take-all group model is appropriate for the output cells. We can train the network using training examples selected according to the final ratio numbers in figure 16.4. Each training example has noise dynamically added to it, as in figure 3.13. The modified training example is then presented to the pocket algorithm with ratchet for winner-take-all groups. This algorithm was given in figures 4.4 and 4.5, except that the ratchet cannot be used due to the dynamic generation of the training examples. Note that dynamic generation of training examples is necessary because too many examples would be needed in a static representative set of noisy training examples. Thus each iteration proceeds as follows:

1. Pick one of the 78 noise-free training examples at random. It will have exactly one failure mode variable (G1–G9) that is true.

2. Change the value of each *input* variable (V1–V8) from true to false or vice versa, with probability given in figure 16.3. Output variables corresponding to the correct responses (G1–G9) are not changed.

3. Present the modified example to the pocket algorithm.

Using this procedure, the network illustrated in figure 16.5 was produced. The connection weights are given in figure 16.6 in matrix format. There were 8 input nodes and 9 trainable output cells. The output cells form a winner-take-all group where the only cell to fire is the one with the highest weighted combination of its inputs. 10,000 iterations were used to generate the network knowledge base, taking about one minute elapsed

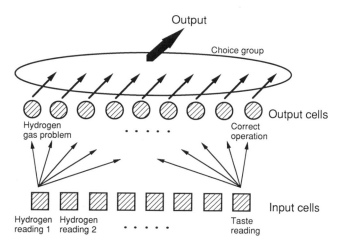

Figure 16.5
A network for the lemonade fault detection problem.

```
G/ Problem with Hydrogen supply
    9      9    5   -3    3    5    3    3    5
G/ Problem with Oxygen supply
   -4     -2   -2    8    2    2    0    2    2
G/ Fuel cell malfunction: not working
   -2      0    0    4    4    4    2    0
G/ Fuel cell malfunction: water clogged
   -3     -1    1   -1   -5   -7   -1   -3    1
G/ Short in power line to lemon squeezer
   -3     -3   -1   -1    3    1   -3    1    5
G/ Short in power line to refrigeration unit
    0      0    0   -2   -4   -4    4    2   -6
G/ Lemon squeezer malfunction
   -3      1   -1   -3   -5    5    1   -5    5
G/ Refrigeration unit malfunction
   -1     -1    1    1    1   -5   -5    5   -5
G/ System functions correctly
    7     -3   -3   -3    1   -1   -3   -7   -7
  bias   V1   V2   V3   V4   V5   V6   V7   V8
```

NOTE: The first column is a bias constant to be added to the corresponding
cell's sum.

Figure 16.6
Weights for the HTLC network.

time on a Sun 3/50. Additional intermediate cells were not needed for this problem.

Notice that the resulting system will diagnose a hydrogen problem whenever both of the hydrogen gauges have normal readings and other readings follow the pattern for a hydrogen problem. This is an example of how redundancy can be used to overcome noise, in this case the independent failure of both hydrogen gauges.

It is possible to compute a *figure of merit*[2] for the generated system by checking its performance on groups of 1,000 noisy training examples randomly selected in accordance with the final ratios of figure 16.4. The figure of merit averaged approximately 810 out of a possible 1,000 points. This might be compared with random selection of an output ($1/9 \times 1,000 = 111$ points) or with always choosing the most frequently seen output ($40/78 \times 1,000 = 513$ points).

A system was also generated without adding noise. This system produced a figure of merit of about 750, significantly worse performance than the model generated with noise. It is interesting to note that the model generated without noise works on every noise-free training example, while the model generated with noise works on only 90 percent, again evidence that the addition of noise makes a significant difference in the model that is generated.

Notice that this was a rather noisy problem; a completely noise-free training example is generated only about one time in four. It seems unlikely that a hand-built expert system would do as well as the automatically generated system; in fact, we shall see that the neural network model has close to optimal performance. Moreover it is easy to make changes to the resulting system, because regenerating the knowledge base is relatively fast.

For inferencing in an expert system, we can use MACIE's winner-take-all group algorithm from section 15.1.3.

16.4 Probabilistic Analysis

Because this problem is a fairly simple artificial problem (if we know how the training examples are generated), it is straightforward to find the

---

2. The figure of merit is merely the sample estimate of the expected utility, multiplied by 1,000; see next section.

optimum decision rule by analysis. First we restate the fault detection problem with more formality and generality.

A Boolean fault detection problem uses a set of Boolean instrument readings

$$V = \langle V_1, \ldots, V_n \rangle,$$

where each $V_j = \pm 1$ corresponding to *true* or *false*. For now we assume all readings are known; later we relax this assumption to allow unknown readings ($V_j = 0$). The possible failure modes are $\{G_1, \ldots, G_m\}$ with corresponding priors $\{P(G_i)\}$. We assume that the utility function has previously been folded into $P(G)$ as was done with the lemonade problem so that our goal is to maximize correct classifications based upon $P(G)$ as a prior.[3]

By Bayes's rule, the most likely failure mode G^V given a set of instrument readings V and taking importance into account is given by the $i \in [1 \ldots m]$ that maximizes

$$P(G_i | V) = \frac{1}{P(V)} \{ P(V | G_i) P(G_i) \}. \tag{16.1}$$

Therefore an optimal Bayesian decision rule for selecting G_i given V is to select the fault G_i that maximizes

$$P(V | G_i) P(G_i) \tag{16.2}$$

with ties in the maximum broken arbitrarily.[4]

This will give us an expected utility of

$$\text{mean}(P(G^V | V))$$

where

$$\text{mean}(P(G^V | V)) = \sum_V P(G^V | V) P(V)$$

$$= \sum_V \frac{1}{P(V)} \max_i \{ P(V | G_i) P(G_i) \} P(V) \quad \text{from (16.1)}$$

$$= \sum_V \max_i \{ P(V | G_i) P(G_i) \}. \tag{16.3}$$

---

3. This is possible only if the penalty for an incorrect diagnosis is independent of which fault was mistakenly selected.
4. We could refer to *the* optimal Bayes rule if there were no ties for maximum.

Note that the "figure of merit" used in section 16.3 is this expected utility multiplied by 1,000.

To compute $P(V|G_i)$ we first define noise-free patterns by:

$A_{i,j} = \pm 1$ according to the entry for G_i and V_j given in figure 16.4
                (these are *actual* readings before noise is applied)

and define noise by:

$\mathcal{N}_{i,j} = P(V_j \neq A_{i,j}|G_i).$

Then the probability that instrument reading j will take on value V_j when fault G_i occurs is given by

$$P(V_j|G_i) = \begin{cases} 1 - \mathcal{N}_{i,j} & \text{if } A_{i,j} = V_j \\ \mathcal{N}_{i,j} & \text{otherwise.} \end{cases} \tag{16.4}$$

Finally we can compute

$$P(V|G_i) = \prod_j P(V_j|G_i) \tag{16.5}$$

because the V_j's are conditionally independent given G_i according to the noise generation model. Note that for the lemonade problem noise does not depend upon the underlying fault so that

$\mathcal{N}_{1,j} = \mathcal{N}_{2,j} = \mathcal{N}_{m,j} = \text{noise}_j$

where noise_j is listed in figure 16.4. For example,

$P(V = \langle 1, -1, 1, 1, 1, 1, 1, 1 \rangle | G_1)$

$\qquad = (.85)(.25)(.20)(.85)(.90)(.80)(.90)(.95).$

The optimal expected utility was computed from equation (16.3) for the lemonade problem, a calculation involving 256 maximizations of 9 computed quantities. The resulting optimal expected utility was .8278.

Calculations were checked and some additional statistics were also gathered as follows: 5,000 additional noisy training examples were produced (using a different random seed) and the most likely G_i was computed by the connectionist network and by the optimal Bayesian rule (16.2). The Bayesian rule was correct for 4,119 cases, giving an average utility of .8238. This was in close agreement with the theoretical .8278. In 4,511 cases (90 percent) both methods gave the same answer. The comparison matrix was:

	Bayes correct	Bayes wrong
Network correct	3830	200
Network wrong	289	681

For these runs the network model was correct for 4,030 cases, giving an average utility of .806. The optimal Bayes figure is clearly better than the network's but the difference is small. The ratio of performance is about $.806/.8278 = 97$ percent. Thus the neural network does almost as well as the optimal Bayes approach.

Note, however, that the neural network was generated solely from training examples *without any information about the underlying process*, whereas the optimal Bayesian decision rule was constructed using this knowledge. Thus a standard probabilistic approach based solely upon the examples that were used for network generation might easily do worse than the network (and almost certainly *would* do worse if its prior selection of underlying models was poorly matched to the problem at hand).

Although it may seem surprising that the neural network's performance was so close to optimal Bayes performance, the following theorems give an explanation.

*16.5   Noisy Single-Pattern Boolean Fault Detection Problems

We first formalize and generalize the lemonade problem.

Define a *noisy single-pattern Boolean (NSB) fault detection problem* $\chi = \{G, V, P, A, \mathcal{N}\}$ as

• a set of faults $G = \{G_i, i = 1, \ldots, m\}$ with priors $P(G_i)$. (The priors may subsume importance information as with the lemonade problem.)

• instrument readings consisting of Boolean n-vectors, $V = \langle V_j \rangle$, where $V_j = \pm 1, j = 1, \ldots, n$.

• a set of m n-dimensional pattern vectors $A_{i,*}$ where $A_{i,j} = \pm 1$. $A_{i,*}$ is the single pattern that corresponds to fault G_i in the absence of noise.

• noise probabilities $0 \le \mathcal{N}_{i,j} \le 1/2$ where $\mathcal{N}_{i,j}$ is the probability that V_j differs from $A_{i,j}$ for fault G_i. Note that instrument noise is considered to be independent for any given fault.

Equivalently we could view NSB fault detection problems as multi-valued classification problems involving probabilistic Boolean features, where the features are conditionally independent given a particular classification. Then we could define

$$A_{i,j} = \begin{cases} +1 & \text{if } P(V_j = +1 \mid G_i) \geq 1/2 \\ -1 & \text{otherwise,} \end{cases}$$

$$\mathcal{N}_{i,j} = 1 - P(V_j = A_{i,j} \mid G_i).$$

Clearly NSB fault detection problems can also be viewed as a class of pattern recognition problems. For example we might consider the problem of deciding which of m images is present upon a retina of binary points where noise is present. Similarly we may be interested in diagnosing which of m diseases is present given a set of n possible symptoms, where each disease is associated with a subset of symptoms and noise is present in the symptoms.[5]

Finally we let $\mathscr{C}_n^m$ represent the class of *multilayer perceptron models with n inputs, no intermediate cells, and m output cells where the output cells form a winner-take-all group.* (See chapter 4 for details.)

The following theorem says that any NSB fault detection problem has an optimal Bayesian decision rule that is representable by a $\mathscr{C}_n^m$ network. Nilsson [149] credits J. W. Jones for the essential idea, but Minsky and Selfridge [146, 144] first published it. Nilsson and Duda and Hart [47] also presented versions. The theorem given here incorporates the noise-free case where $\mathcal{N}_{i,j}$ is allowed to be 0. The notation $|\{\cdots\}|$ denotes the size of the set within brackets.

THEOREM 16.1   *Given an NSB fault detection problem* $\chi = \{G, V, P, A, \mathcal{N}\}$ *and any numbers* α, β *where* $\alpha > 0$, *then there exists a* $\mathscr{C}_n^m$ *network,* $C(\alpha, \beta)$, *that computes the optimal Bayesian decision rule for* χ *where weights and biases for* $C(\alpha, \beta)$ *are given by:*

for $j > 0$:

$$w_{i,j} = \begin{cases} \alpha A_{i,j} \log\left(\dfrac{1 - \mathcal{N}_{i,j}}{\mathcal{N}_{i,j}}\right) & \text{if } \mathcal{N}_{i,j} > 0 \\[2em] \alpha A_{i,j} K & \text{if } \mathcal{N}_{i,j} = 0 \end{cases}$$

bias:

---

5. Conditional independence of symptoms given a disease is not realistic in general. However, if we consider associated symptom *groups* rather than lower-level symptoms then conditional independence of groups given a disease seems more plausible.

$$w_{i,0} = \beta + \alpha \left\{ 2 \log P(G_i) + \log \left(\prod_{j: \mathcal{N}_{i,j}>0} (1 - \mathcal{N}_{i,j})(\mathcal{N}_{i,j}) \right) \right.$$

$$\left. - K|\{j: \mathcal{N}_{i,j} = 0\}| \right\} \tag{16.6}$$

and K is any constant greater than

$$\max_i \left\{ 2|\log P(G_i)| + \sum_{j: \mathcal{N}_{i,j}>0} |\log((1 - \mathcal{N}_{i,j})(\mathcal{N}_{i,j}))| \right.$$

$$\left. + \sum_{j: \mathcal{N}_{i,j}>0} \left| A_{i,j} \log \left(\frac{1 - \mathcal{N}_{i,j}}{\mathcal{N}_{i,j}} \right) \right| \right\}$$

Proof: For any $V = \langle V_1, \ldots, V_n \rangle$ the connectionist model chooses G_i to maximize

$$S_i = w_{i,0} + \sum_j w_{i,j} V_j$$

with ties broken arbitrarily. Clearly the maximum G_i is not affected by multiplying all weights by positive α and then adding β to all sums. Therefore without loss of generality we assume $\alpha = 1/2$ and $\beta = 0$.

We first consider the case where all $\mathcal{N}_{i,j} > 0$. Then

$$S_i = \log P(G_i) + \sum_j \frac{1}{2} \log((1 - \mathcal{N}_{i,j})(\mathcal{N}_{i,j})) + \sum_j \frac{1}{2} A_{i,j} \log \left(\frac{1 - \mathcal{N}_{i,j}}{\mathcal{N}_{i,j}} \right) V_j$$

$$= \log P(G_i) + \sum_j \frac{1}{2} \{ A_{i,j} V_j [\log(1 - \mathcal{N}_{i,j}) - \log(\mathcal{N}_{i,j})]$$

$$+ [\log(1 - \mathcal{N}_{i,j}) + \log(\mathcal{N}_{i,j})] \}$$

$$= \log P(G_i) + \sum_j \frac{1}{2} \{ 2 \log P(V_j|G_i) \} \quad \text{by equation (16.4) since } (A_{i,j} V_j) = \pm 1$$
$$\text{according to whether } A_{i,j}$$
$$\text{agrees with } V_j$$

$$= \log \left[P(G_i) \prod_j P(V_j|G_i) \right]$$

$$= \log[P(G_i)P(V|G_i)] \quad \text{from equation (16.5)}$$

Then S_i is a maximum weighted sum iff $P(G_i)P(V|G_i)$ is maximized since the log function is monotonic increasing. But this is exactly the optimal Bayesian choice given by (16.2).

In the case where noise-free readings exist, S_i will take on the same value as computed above if $V_j = A_{i,j}$ for all $\{j: \mathcal{N}_{i,j} = 0\}$. Otherwise S_i will be decreased by $2K$ for every $V_j \neq A_{i,j}$. Thus any mismatch of a noise-free reading would prevent fault i from having the maximum S_i. This is also the way the Bayesian rule works with noise-free parameters.   □

Note that for the lemonade problem we can simplify the bias weights to:

$$w_{i,0} = \beta + 2\alpha \log P(G_i)$$

since $\mathcal{N}_{i,j} = \text{noise}_j > 0$.

The above weights agree with our intuitions about NSB problems in several respects. First $A_{i,j}$ agrees in sign with $w_{i,j}$, which is reasonable if we interpret the input as a noisy version of $A_{i,j}$. If $\mathcal{N}_{i,j} = 1/2$ then $w_{i,j} = 0$; in other words we ignore an input that adds no information due to noise. Similarly if $\mathcal{N}_{i,j}$ is small then $|w_{i,j}|$ is large; we pay heed to reliable inputs.

For the remainder of this chapter we assume all probabilities and noise parameters are rational numbers.

*16.6   Convergence Theorem

The pocket algorithm used for network generation was given in section 4.3. The main theorem of this chapter states that for NSB fault detection problems, the pocket algorithm converges in probability to a $\mathscr{C}_n^m$ network that computes the optimal Bayesian decision rule.

THEOREM 16.2   *Given an NSB fault detection problem χ and given $\varepsilon > 0$, there exists N_0 such that after $N > N_0$ iterations with probability $P > (1 - \varepsilon)$ the pocket algorithm will have produced weights for a $\mathscr{C}_n^m$ network that computes an optimal Bayesian fault classification for χ.*

Proof: In theory we can generate a finite set of training examples $\mathbf{E} = \{\langle V, G_i \rangle\}$ that reflects $P(G)$, $\mathcal{N}_{i,j}$, and $P(V|G)$ since all probabilities are assumed rational. For the lemonade problem, $78(20)^8$ is a loose upper bound on $|\mathbf{E}|$. (In practice $\mathbf{E}$ is often too large to actually create.) Then generating training examples according to probabilities $P(G)$ and then adding noise to instrument readings is exactly equivalent to picking training examples at random from $\mathbf{E}$. Theorem 16.1 asserts the existence of a set of weights giving optimal Bayesian performance. By the pocket convergence theorem (theorem 3.7), the pocket algorithm will produce a set of weights with at least equal performance to any set of weights, with probability approaching 1 as the number of iterations grows large. Therefore these weights must give optimal Bayesian performance since it is impossible to do better.   □

Recall that large problems require too many iterations of the pocket algorithm to actually produce an optimal solution, but simulations indicate that the solutions that are generated are reasonably good (as was the case in the lemonade problem). Several classes of NSB problems were tried to see how low the relative performance could be made. The worst performance involved problems with 10 inputs and 20 possible faults where prior fault probabilities were constrained to be approximately equal. In this case the neural network model did 85 percent as well as a theoretically optimal Bayesian model. (Note, however, that a Bayesian model generated from available training examples would not achieve the theoretical optimum performance.)

An interesting way of looking at the proof for theorem 16.2 is to consider a black box generator of training examples for an arbitrary fault detection problem. If we use these training examples to generate a $\mathscr{C}_n^m$ network, then (in the limit) that model would fit at least as well as the NSB fault detection model that *best* fits the given data.

The converse to theorem 16.1 also holds:

THEOREM 16.3   *Given a $\mathscr{C}_n^m$ network C, there exists an NSB fault detection problem χ satisfying*

1. $\mathscr{N}_{i,j} = 1/2$ *only where* $w_{i,j} = 0$

2. $A_{i,j}$ *is* $+1$ $\{-1\}$ *if* $w_{i,j}$ *is positive* $\{negative\}$

3. *an optimal Bayesian decision rule for χ is given by the network C.*

The first two items prevent trivial solutions consisting of NSB fault detection problems where all faults are equally likely for every set of instrument readings.

Proof: The formulas for the weights given in theorem 16.1 are invertible. We set $\alpha = 1$, then solve for $A_{i,j}$ and $0 < \mathscr{N}_{i,j} \leq 1/2$ for $j > 0$, and then solve for β and $P(G_i)$ to satisfy equation (16.6) and $\sum P(G_i) = 1$. Details omitted.   □

We have now seen that there is a one-to-one correspondence between all NSB fault detection problems and all $\mathscr{C}_n^m$ networks. Each fault detection problem is solved optimally by a network and for each network there exists an NSB problem for which it gives an optimal Bayesian decision rule. This correspondence can help our intuition in both domains.

16.7 Comments

The Lemonade problem shows the importance of "wide-angle" algorithms that simultaneously consider a large number of inputs. The redundancy and noise make it imperative to consider the effects of all the sensor readings when determining which fault is present; a list of conventional expert system If-Then rules with few clauses would not do as well.[6] Also note that decision trees and DNF representations have a difficult time with "wide-angle" functions because of a tendency toward combinatorial explosion (see the appendix).

We have seen how to construct a neural network expert system for a noisy problem based solely upon (noisy) training examples. We also saw that for a class of fault detection problems the pocket algorithm for winner-take-all groups produces networks that with arbitrarily high probability implement the optimum Bayes decision rule.

It is interesting that NSB fault detection problems present a large class of nonseparable problems for which we can compute optimal solutions for the corresponding linear discriminant problems (for $n \leq 20$). Therefore this class might serve as convenient test data to evaluate the actual performance of the pocket algorithm or other algorithms.

Finally it would be interesting to obtain analytical or empirical results on convergence speed of the pocket algorithm for this class of fault detection problems.

16.8 Exercises

1. Could the essential functionality of High Tech Lemonade (MACIE) be easily implemented by a conventional expert system? Why or why not?

2. Suppose we have a fault diagram illustrated in figure 16.7. Also suppose the relative likelihoods of faults are:

6. It would be an interesting experiment to present a human with a large set of noisy training examples from the Lemonade problem and to ask for a list of expert system If-Then rules and confidence factors. We could then evaluate the resulting expert system using a new set of training examples, and compare its performance with the neural network.

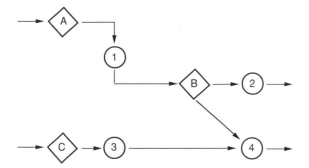

Figure 16.7
A fault detection problem. Diamonds give possible faults that cause negative values for all succeeding instrument readings (in circles). Fault D corresponds to error-free performance.

A:3, B:1, C:2, D:1

and all instruments are incorrect 15 percent of the time.

(a) Give a set of (noise-free) training examples that could be used with the pocket algorithm for generating a neural network expert system.

(b) What would happen if the unreliability of the instruments increased from 15 percent to a value close to 50 percent?

(c) What would happen if we changed the relative likelihood of fault A from 3 to 1,000,000 (unreliability remains at 15 percent)?

(d) What would happen if we changed the relative likelihood of fault A from 3 to 1,000,000 and dropped the unreliability to 0 percent (i.e., no noise)?

3. (research) Perform the human-generated expert system versus neural network expert system comparison experiment suggested in section 16.7. It would also be interesting to keep track of the human's improvement over time, to make some estimate of how well a human *expert* could generate If-Then rules. (Another interesting comparison would be the human's performance versus the expert system generated by that person.)

16.9 Programming Projects

1. Modify the *Taxtime!* data by adding noise to features. Regenerate the network and expert system and experiment with its performance.

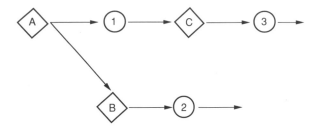

Figure 16.8
Another fault detection problem. Diamonds give possible faults that cause negative values
for all succeeding instrument readings (in circles). Fault D corresponds to error-free
performance.

2. Suppose for the process in figure 16.8 there are 4 possible modes of
operation (failure A, failure B, failure C, normal) that must be diagnosed
by Boolean instruments numbered 1–4. The process is cumulative in the
sense that in the absence of noise instrument 3 would indicate a problem
for either failure A or failure C. Suppose instruments give incorrect readings due to noise 10 percent of the time, and suppose the relative likelihood
of faults is

failure A:1, failure B:2, failure C:1, normal:4.

Also assume we are trying to correctly diagnose the system as often as
possible.

Create an appropriate set of training examples and generate a neural
network knowledge base using your pocket algorithm program for
winner-take-all groups from chapter 4.

3. Suppose for the process in figure 16.7 there are 4 possible modes of
operation (failure A, failure B, failure C, normal) that must be diagnosed
by Boolean instruments numbered 1–4.

The following table gives prior probabilities and costs for failure to
detect a fault.

Fault	Priors	Costs
A	1/4	2
B	1/4	3
C	1/8	4
Normal	3/8	1

Suppose instruments give incorrect readings due to noise 10 percent of the time.

Create an appropriate set of training examples, and generate a neural network knowledge base.

17 Extracting Rules from Networks

17.1 Why Rules?

In this chapter[1] we will see how to produce If-Then rules from neural networks. There are several reasons for doing this. First, neural networks have been criticized for "not being able to explain their conclusions." Justifications are especially important for banks and insurance companies, which must be able to give their customers and regulators reasons for their decisions. We will see how to justify an expert system inference by producing an appropriate If-Then rule, i.e., a rule that is valid, applicable, and (usually) maximally general as discussed in section 14.3.3.

A second use for If-Then rules occurs when constructing a neural network expert system with the aid of a human expert. We can take rules that are implicitly encoded in the network, and ask for *comments* from our human expert. Whenever the expert disagrees, he or she will likely remark:

Rule 23 is not right because in the case where ... I would conclude the opposite.

This comment gives us a new training example that we can use to regenerate the network knowledge base. Presumably it is easier for experts to comment upon rules than it is to create consistent collections of If-Then rules (with confidence measurements) as in conventional expert systems. More on this in section 17.5.1.

Finally we might consider using the rules that are implicitly encoded in a neural network in a conventional expert system. However, this approach has some difficulties, as we shall see in section 17.2.2.

17.2 What Kind of Rules?

17.2.1 Criteria

We seek rules that satisfy two main criteria:

• *Validity:* Rules must hold regardless of the values that unmentioned variables take on. For example, suppose we have the rule:

---

1. Some of this research was performed while visiting the Institute for Scientific Interchange, Turin, Italy.

Rule 1:
If u_3 is true
      and u_5 is false
Then Conclude u_8 is true.

Then this rule must hold regardless of the values for u_1, u_2, u_4, u_6, u_7.

• *Maximal generality:* We want the rule to be maximally general in the sense that if we remove any of the conditions, then the rule will no longer be valid. For example if rule 1 is valid, then the following is also a valid rule:

Rule 2:
If u_3 is true
      and u_5 is false
      and u_7 is false
Then Conclude u_8 is true.

However, rule 2 applies to fewer cases than rule 1. Moreover we can remove the third condition and still have a valid rule. Therefore rule 2 is not maximally general, and we prefer rule 1 (provided it is valid), because shorter rules apply to more situations.

17.2.2 Inference Justifications versus Rule Sets

When running a neural network expert system and an inference is made, we desire a *single rule* to justify that inference. For other tasks we might desire a *rule set* that approximates the collection of If-Then rules that are implicitly encoded in a neural network. We can produce an inference justification very efficiently, but rule sets are another matter. The basic problem is that a neural network can implicitly encode exponentially many If-Then rules, as compared to the number of weights in the network. (The plurality and majority functions give good examples of this; see also the appendix.) Thus for a reasonable-sized network we have to make some compromise rather than trying to produce all of its If-Then rules.

We will examine inference justifications and rule sets in greater detail in the next two sections.

17.2.3 Which Variables in Conditions

Another choice to be made is whether to express rule conditions in terms of *cells directly connected* to the cell whose value is being inferred, or to

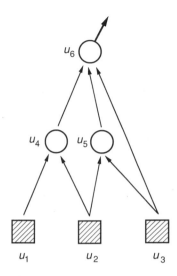

Figure 17.1
Which cells should appear in rules for u_6?

limit ourselves to *input variables* only. For example in figure 17.1 we can use either a subset of $\{u_4, u_5, u_3\}$ or a subset of $\{u_1, u_2, u_3\}$ for rule conditions. If we express rules in terms of directly connected cells, then we have a single-cell problem that generally eases our work. On the other hand, the directly connected cells might be distributed cells (section 8.2) that are not meaningful for the user. In this case a rule involving input variables might be better.

17.3 Inference Justifications

In this section we will examine several methods for extracting a single rule that justifies an inference. We assume that some inference has already been made based upon partial (or complete) input values. Consider, for example, figure 17.2. Note that the value for u_4 might be determined in the future, but that the value for u_6 is not available for the entire run. We have sufficient information to conclude that u_7 is true, and now we want to give a rule that justifies this inference.

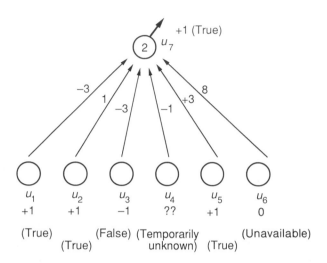

Figure 17.2
Justifying the inference that u_7 is true.

17.3.1 MACIE's Algorithm

We first look at the inference justification implemented in the MACIE system (Gallant [67, 68]). This algorithm produces a rule that uses the cells that are directly connected to the cell in question. For example in figure 17.2 the rule could involve cells u_1-u_6, even though these cells may be intermediate cells.

To understand the algorithm, we must first define a *contributing variable*. Roughly speaking, a contributing variable is one that does not move the weighted sum in the wrong direction. If we are trying to explain an inference C^i for cell u_i, then cell u_j is contributing if

$$C^i w_{i,j} u_j \geq 0.$$

For example in figure 17.2, the contributing variables are $\{u_2, u_3, u_5, u_6\}$. We also define the *size of the contribution* by $|w_{i,j}|$. Thus u_3 contributes 3. Now the basic idea of the algorithm is to add clauses to a rule that contributed to its inference, in order of size of contribution, until there are enough clauses to form a valid rule.

Figure 17.3 gives the algorithm, and several comments are in order. First note that if the bias is big enough then it is possible to have a cell that is

---

Given: Cell u_i inferred to have value $C^i = \pm 1$.

1. Set CURRENT $= w_{i,0}$ (the bias for u_i).

   Set VARS_UNUSED $= \{ j \mid w_{i,j} \neq 0 \text{ and } j \neq 0 \}$

   $=$ set of nonbias cells connected to u_i that are not used in the rule.

   Set UNKNOWN $= \sum_{j \in \text{VARS\_UNUSED}} |w_{i,j}|$

   $=$ max value that CURRENT can change by.

2. If $|\text{CURRENT}| > \text{UNKNOWN}$ then stop; clauses generated so far give a valid justification that is (usually) maximally general.

3. Find an input $j \in \text{VARS\_UNUSED}$ such that

   $C^i w_{i,j} u_j \geq 0$

   and $|w_{i,j}|$ is maximized. (Ties are broken arbitrarily.)

4. Output a rule condition using cell u_j and its value (possibly "unavailable").

5. Set

   CURRENT $=$ CURRENT $+ w_{i,j} u_j$

   UNKNOWN $=$ UNKNOWN $- |w_{i,j}|$

   VARS_UNUSED $=$ VARS_UNUSED $- \{ j \}$.

6. Go to step 2.

Figure 17.3
MACIE's algorithm for justifying inferences.

always true (or false), regardless of its inputs. Thus the cell in figure 17.2 would always assume activation $+1$ (true) if the bias were 200 rather than 2 (other weights being equal). In this case the justification is merely "u_7 is always true."

Second, the test in step 3 is to find contributing variables with maximum size contribution. These are variables that are either known or unavailable (but not temporarily unknown), and that participate in, or are necessary for, the inference. Thus u_1 adds a negative amount to a weighted sum that is ultimately positive, so it would not appear in a maximally general rule.

Also note that it is possible for unavailable inputs to participate in rules, and this occurs with our example.

The rule that MACIE eventually produces is:

If u_6 = Unknown
      and u_3 = False
      and u_5 = True
Then Conclude u_7 = True.

MACIE's algorithm produces valid justifications that are usually maximally general, and it runs quickly (exercise 1). Note that justifications need not be unique (exercise 2).

17.3.2   The Removal Algorithm

Another simple method for generating maximally general and valid rules is given in figure 17.4. We merely examine each variable (in any order) and see whether it can be removed from the set of known or unavailable variables while still leaving a valid inference.

Like MACIE's justification algorithm, the *removal algorithm* can be used for justifications involving directly connected cells, but it can also be used for justifications involving input variables only.

Note that in step 4 of the algorithm, we determine validity using MACIE's inferencing algorithm to avoid testing all possible settings of

---

1. Set VARS_USED = {all variables that may appear in conditions for a rule that are either known or unavailable variables (exclude temporarily unknown variables)}.

   Initially no variables have been EXAMINED.

2. If all $j \in$ VARS_USED have been EXAMINED, then form a rule using variables in VARS_USED and quit.

3. Pick $j \in$ VARS_USED that has not yet been EXAMINED.

4. Mark j EXAMINED, and if the rule formed from VARS_USED $- \{j\}$ is valid (using MACIE's inferencing algorithm) then remove j from VARS_USED.

5. Go to step 2.

Figure 17.4
Removal algorithm for generating justifications.

unknown variables. This means that if the removal method produces rules involving input variables for multilayer networks, then it might produce a rule that is valid and applicable, but not maximally general. Also, note that we can easily adapt the removal algorithm for winner-take-all groups of cells.

17.3.3   Key Factor Justifications

An insurance company that turns down an applicant may prefer to justify its action by giving a *key factor* that influenced its decision, for example:

If SALARY had been above \$15,000 rather than below \$15,000 then application would have been granted.

Usually key factors are restricted to input variables and there are few (if any) unavailable variables to contend with. Murry Smith of Adaptive Decision Systems has noted[2] that in many cases it is easy to produce such key factor justifications. We merely reverse the value of each input in turn, seeing if the inference is reversed. If so, we have found a key factor. If not, then we must try reversing pairs of inputs (there are $\frac{1}{2}p(p-1)$ of them). If this fails, then try reversing triples, etc. In practice we might simply quit and admit failure rather than try quadruples at great computational expense.

17.3.4   Justifications for Continuous Models

All of the previous justification methods have straightforward extensions for most continuous models. For example consider a backpropagation cell u_i that gives true or false if its output is greater than .9 or less than .1 respectively. This gives lower and upper bounds on the weighted sum, S_i, using

$$u_i = \frac{1}{1 + e^{-S_i}}$$

$$\Rightarrow S_i = \ln\left(\frac{u_i}{1 - u_i}\right).$$

For the MACIE justification algorithm we can now modify the test in step 2 to be:

2. Personal communication.

$$\text{CURRENT} - \text{UNKNOWN} \geq \ln\left(\frac{.9}{1 - .9}\right) \quad \text{if } C^i = \text{true}$$

$$\text{CURRENT} - \text{UNKNOWN} \leq \ln\left(\frac{.1}{1 - .1}\right) \quad \text{if } C^i = \text{false.}$$

There are many other variations that can be treated in a similar way using the MACIE or removal algorithms.

17.4   Rule Sets

In this section we examine the problem of producing a set of rules from a neural network. As previously mentioned we have to make some compromise, because the task is inherently impossible. We are not going to generate all $C(101, 50)$ rules[3] from a single cell with 101 inputs! We will look at the two main approaches to the problem, limiting the number of conditions in a rule and giving approximate rules.

17.4.1   Limiting the Number of Conditions

The first approach (Gallant [67, 70, 68]) is to limit the number of conditions in the rules to be generated in order to limit the number of possible rules. For example suppose we seek rules with at most 3 out of p Boolean input variables, where each variable in a condition is either true or false (but not unavailable). Then we can check all rules for 0, 1, 2, and 3 terms, giving at most

$$\sum_{t=0}^{3} C(p, t) 2^t$$

cases. (This scales by p^3.)

When determining whether a particular setting of 3 out of p variables constitutes a valid rule, we have to avoid checking the 2^{p-3} settings of other variables or we will be in big trouble. The easy way to handle this problem is with MACIE inferencing; this allows a check in time that is linear in the number of weights in the network. Any rule that passes

---

3. $C(r, s)$, the number of combinations of r objects taken s at a time, is defined to be $\dfrac{r!}{s!(r - s)!}$.

Let T = maximum number of terms allowed in a rule.
1. RULES_SET = $\varnothing$.
2. For number of terms $t = 0, 1, \ldots, T$:
    2a. For each choice of t variables, and for each setting of these variables to true ($+1$) or false (-1):
    2aa. If MACIE's inferencing indicates a valid rule, and if no subset of $t - 1$ out of the t variables gives a valid rule, then add this rule to RULES_SET.
3. Output RULES_SET.

Figure 17.5
Producing rule sets with a limited number of conditions using enumeration and MACIE's inferencing.

MACIE's inference test will be valid. However, for multilayer networks we might miss valid inferences in some cases, resulting in overlooked rules or rules that are not maximally general.

Figure 17.5 gives the algorithm. The basic algorithm can be speeded up by pruning away some of the cases (in step 2a) whenever valid inferences are made. For example if u_3 = true and u_5 = false gives an inference, there is no use in looking at anything involving variables $\{u_1, u_3,$ and $u_5\}$.

There is another speedup for single-cell models (or when producing rule sets involving directly connected cells). In the enumeration in step 2a we should choose variables in order of the absolute magnitude of their weights. This allows us to prune away cases that do not involve enough large-weight variables. We omit the details of this technique.

Context
Limiting the number of variables that can appear in conditions is not as severe a limitation as might appear at first glance. We can always specify a subset of variables with particular values, for example:

$$u_3 = \text{true}, \quad u_5 = \text{false}, \quad u_8 = \text{true}, \quad u_{10} = \text{true},$$

and then ask for a rule set involving at most 3 *additional* variables in its conditions. This allows us to explore rules in a given context or "corner" of the input space. It is easy to modify the algorithm in figure 17.5 accordingly.

Continuous Variables
Algorithms for networks with continuous activations are straightforward extensions of previous algorithms. (See section 15.1.) Note, however, that for continuous variables represented by a thermometer code, we can reduce the number of cases to be tried. For example if 4 cells are used to represent a continuous value, there are only 5 settings for this set of cells (rather than 2^4).

17.4.2   Approximating Rules

Kazumi Saito and Ryohei Nakano [181] have developed a different approach for extracting rules from networks that takes advantage of the set of training examples that were originally used to train the network. Their *RN method* generates a small set of rules that *approximate* the rules implicitly encoded in the network, with effort that grows by about the square of the number of training examples.

Rule Representation
The RN method works with either continuous or discrete network models and represents rules by modified Boolean conditions, such as:

$(u_1 \in [.2, .8]$ And $u_3 \in [.3, .7])$ Or Not $(u_5 \in [.2, .3]$ And $u_3 \in [.6, .8])$.

Figure 17.6 gives a modified version of the algorithm. The basic idea is to "grow" a region containing a training example that the network correctly classifies as $+1$ by changing one dimension at a time until the region bumps up against a $+1/-1$ network boundary for that dimension. Next we take the resulting hyperrectangle and subtract out misclassified negative examples by growing regions for them.

For example if $p = 2$ is the number of inputs and we first pick $E^k = \langle .3 \ .5 \rangle$ with $C^k = +1$, then varying just the first dimension we might find that the network classifies $u_1 \in [.1, .6]$ and $u_2 = .5$ as $+1$. Similarly we might find that $u_1 = .3$ and $u_2 = [.4, .7]$ is also classified as $+1$. Then

$u_1 \in [.1, .6]$ AND $u_2 \in [.4, .7]$

is the starting hypercube for our first term.

Next we look for a training example E^l with $C^l = -1$ that is misclassified by this approximation, say $E^k = \langle .5 \ .6 \rangle$. We then grow another region (changing each dimension independently) for negative classifications, say

Given: a neural network, $\mathcal{N}$, and a set of training examples, $\{E^k\}$.

1. Pick a positive training example E^k not yet covered by any term.

2. For each input variable j:

    2a. Find a range around E_j^k that $\mathcal{N}$ classifies as positive (with other components of E^k unchanged).

3. Intersect (AND together) all such ranges to produce a new term, $\mathcal{T}$, corresponding to a hyperrectangle.

4. For each negative training example, E^l, misclassified by $\mathcal{T}$:

    4a. Find ranges for E^l as in step 2a and subtract ranges from $\mathcal{T}$, modifying $\mathcal{T}$ so that it classifies fewer inputs as true. Do not let the subtracted hyperrectangle extend to E^k in any coordinate.

5. If some positive example is not covered by any term, go to step 1.

6. Join all terms by OR's to form the final rule.

Figure 17.6
An algorithm for extracting approximate rules from neural networks.

$u_1 \in [.4, .55]$ AND $u_2 \in [.55, .65]$

and subtract out this region from the current term, leaving

$u_1 \in [.1, .6]$ AND $u_2 \in [.4, .7]$ AND NOT $(u_1 \in [.4, .55]$ AND

$u_2 \in [.55, .65])$.

We repeat for all negative training examples covered by the term until there are no more. Then we pick a positive training example not yet correctly classified and repeat the process to generate a second term, continuing until all positive training examples are correctly classified by some term. Finally we join all terms by OR's to produce the rule.

Figure 17.7 shows the regions generated for a 2-layer network with 30 intermediate cells.

17.5   Conventional + Neural Network Expert Systems

We have seen that there is a problem in taking implicitly represented rules from a neural network and plugging them into a conventional expert system: there are too many such rules. A better approach would be to take

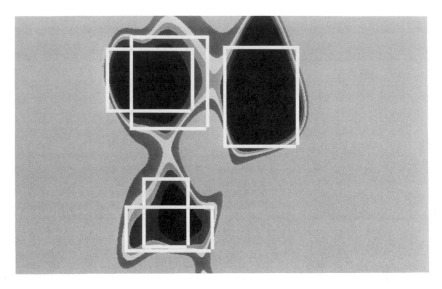

Figure 17.7
The RN method applied to a 2-dimensional problem.

a conventional expert system and implement calls to a neural network expert system for inferring values of key variables (and for generating the network from data). Such combinations are just beginning to enter the market, and it will be interesting to see their effect.

17.5.1 Debugging an Expert System Knowledge Base

We now turn to the problem of debugging an expert system knowledge base with the aid of a human expert. Rules can be helpful here, as we shall see.

For conventional expert systems, debugging the knowledge base can be difficult. Whenever we add or change a rule, we run the risk of introducing subtle bugs due to the complex interrelationship of rules and confidence factors. Debugging a neural network expert system knowledge base can also be difficult, but at least in this case we have several automated tools that can help with the task.

The most important automated tool is the learning algorithm itself. Whenever we add or modify training examples the learning algorithm assures us that *a newly created neural network knowledge base will remain consistent with the collection of training examples*. (In some cases the algo-

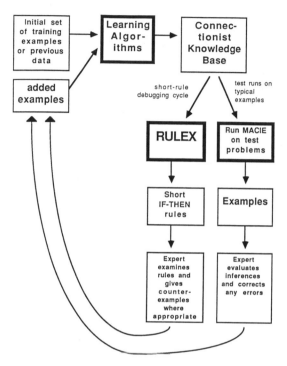

Figure 17.8
Example-based knowledge engineering: generating and debugging a neural network expert system using automated tools (boxes with heavy borders) in conjunction with a human expert.

rithm will indicate that the revised set of examples has become contradictory or that a more complex network model should be considered.)

This raises the question of how to produce such "perfecting" training examples in an efficient manner. The old (yet valuable!) way of gathering additional examples is to run the current knowledge base on a group of typical new cases, and whenever incorrect results are produced (as judged by our human expert) to add such perfecting counterexamples to the original set of training examples. This procedure is illustrated in figure 17.8 by the right descending branch labeled "test runs on typical examples."

17.5.2 The Short-Rule Debugging Cycle

The new way of gathering perfecting training examples, called the *short-rule debugging cycle*, is illustrated by the left descending branch in figure

17.8. Here we check that all short If-Then rules implicitly represented in the knowledge base are correct. This can be done with RULEX, a program that extracts such rules from a neural network knowledge base using the algorithm in figure 17.5.

After generating the list of short rules, we present them to our human expert. He or she then either approves each rule or suggests a specific case where that rule would not hold; i.e., a *counterexample*.

Such a list of perfecting counterexamples is just what we are looking for. We can add them to our previous set of examples, regenerate the knowledge base, extract the list of short implicit rules, and present the revised list (or just the changes) to our human expert. This is called the *short-rule debugging cycle*.

Because there are only a finite number of possible examples, and because each cycle adds to our set of examples, we will arrive at an acceptable set of short rules after a finite number of short-rule debugging cycles. Moreover this process should be reasonably efficient, since for p Boolean inputs the number of possible rules involving 3 terms is at most

$$2^3 C(p,3) < 4/3 p^3.$$

Thus if we only examine rules that have at most 3 terms then the computation should be manageable. Note that counterexamples usually cause the elimination of short rules without creating any additional implicit short rules. Thus we would expect one or two short-rule debugging cycles to suffice in most cases.

The short-rule debugging cycle guarantees that we have collected enough training examples so that an overly simple neural network model could not account for them all. This methodology is also appealing because it gives a systematic way of soliciting perfecting counterexamples from our human expert.

17.6   Concluding Remarks

We have surveyed a number of ways for extracting either single-rule justifications or rule sets from neural networks. Such If-Then rules are easier for most humans to understand, but seem to offer no computational advantage over the neural network model from which they were extracted.

We have also looked at how a human expert can work with MACIE in debugging a neural network expert system knowledge base. This technique also gives a way to develop or modify an expert system while automatically checking that changes do not compromise previous versions. We simply base all development on a (growing) set of training examples. The practical usefulness of such *example-based knowledge engineering* should become apparent over the next few years.

17.7 Exercises

*1. How can we make MACIE's justification algorithm (section 17.3.1) run in time n where n is the number of connections to the cell in question?

2. Give an example where there is more than one maximally general and valid rule that justifies an inference.

3. (a) Is MACIE's justification algorithm (section 17.3.1) guaranteed to produce a *shortest* valid rule, i.e., one with fewest conditions that applies to the particular set of inputs at hand? If not, give a counterexample.

(b) Is the removal method (section 17.3.2) guaranteed to produce a *shortest* valid rule, i.e., one with fewest conditions that applies to the particular set of inputs at hand? If not, give a counterexample.

*4. For justifications involving a thermometer-coded variable u, we want to give a condition of the form

AND LOWER $\leq u \leq$ UPPER.

How can we produce such a rule with LOWER as small as possible and UPPER as large as possible?

5. In the RN algorithm for extracting rules from networks, give a 2-dimensional example where the range for a negative training example (step 4a) can include a positive training example (not the one for this item). Does this invalidate the algorithm?

17.8 Programming Projects

1. Augment your neural network expert system shell to give If-Then rule justifications of inferences.

2. Generate several justifications for *Taxtime!* expert system inferences.

3. Implement MACIE's rule-extraction algorithm for multilayer perceptron networks. Try your program on a 3-layer network.

4. Obtain a set of simple If-Then rules for the *Taxtime!* data.

5. Implement the RN algorithm for backpropagation networks. Try your
program on a 3-layer network.

Appendix   Representation Comparisons

This appendix examines the ability of neural network models to represent functions. It then compares representational power of neural networks and other representations, such as disjunctive normal form representations and decision trees.

Some form of representation is obviously necessary for any kind of learning, because we have to be able to express whatever has been learned. The question of *which* representation to employ is often ignored or glossed over, particularly in the machine learning literature. For example if we are interested in learning Boolean functions there are a number of methods that are capable of representing any Boolean function. But this is of little practical use if the number of bits a representation requires to express a simple function is greater than the number of atoms in the universe. Therefore *space* considerations are very important when comparing different representations.

A second important consideration is evaluation *speed*. Representing a function in a highly coded form might make it impractical to actually evaluate that function. For example, consider specifying a function by using colloquial natural language in paragraph form. This could be a relatively compact representation, but it would be useless for computers, because computers cannot interpret such paragraphs with high accuracy.

Other considerations can also be important when comparing representations, such as robustness, error resistance, and parallelism.

This appendix will first define some common representations, then formalize representation comparisons, and conclude by comparing a number of representations using this formalism.

A.1   DNF Expressions and Polynomial Representability

A.1.1   DNF Expressions

Disjunctive normal form (DNF) expressions are an important way of representing Boolean functions. To define DNF expressions we first define a *term* as the ANDing together of a finite number of Boolean variables, any of which may be negated.

For example

- A

- A AND B AND NOT D AND NOT E

are both terms. Now a DNF expression is defined to be the ORing together of a finite number of terms, such as

• (A) OR (NOT A AND NOT B AND C) OR (NOT C).

We can also employ the standard shorthand of $\bar{x}$ for NOT x, $\vee$ for OR, and adjacency of symbols for AND. This allows us to write the previous expression compactly as $A \vee \bar{A}\bar{B}C \vee \bar{C}$.

It is easy to show that any Boolean function of Boolean variables can be represented as a DNF expression.

Conjunctive normal form (CNF) expressions are the duals of DNF expressions. They are formed by interchanging AND with OR in the definitions of term and DNF expression above. Like DNF expressions, CNF expressions also are able to represent any Boolean function. Both formalisms are used extensively in symbolic machine learning.

How do DNF expressions compare with MLP's for knowledge representation? To answer this we must first give a more precise way of comparing representations.

A.1.2   Polynomial Representability

To compare space requirements of representations R_1 and R_2 we must consider the number of symbols R_1 and R_2 require for representing a fixed set Q of objects. For example R_1 and R_2 might be MLP and DNF representations respectively and Q might be the set of Boolean functions (an infinite set). We always assume that R_1 and R_2 have only a finite number of symbols in their respective alphabets; otherwise we could have all-powerful yet trivial representations that attach a single symbol to each object.

We let $|R_1(x)|$ denote the number of symbols that representation R_1 uses in representing object $x \in Q$.

For MLP's the symbols must describe the topology of the network and the weights. One efficient way to do this would be to list for each intermediate or output cell u_i the indices (j) and corresponding weights $(w_{i,j})$ for every cell u_j connected to u_i. For example we could represent the network in figure 2.6 as follows:

{*number of input cells (p)*}	2
{*list for cell u_3*}	$(0, -1)$ $(1, +1)$ $(2, -1)$
$\vdots$	$(0, -1)$ $(1, -1)$ $(2, +1)$
{*list for cell u_5*}	$(0, +1)$ $(3, +1)$ $(4, +1)$.

This way of representing multilayer perceptrons will be called an MLP_{list} *representation*.

Another way of specifying an MLP would be to use an incidence matrix representation as in section 1.7. However, this MLP_{matrix} *representation* is inefficient for sparsely connected networks (exercise 1 below).

Notice that we cannot ignore the number of bits (or other symbols) that are needed to represent individual weights. If we could represent weights of any magnitude by one symbol we could always encode the entire network description (including weights) into one big "weight" symbol.

Furthermore, we would prefer that our method of comparing representations not depend upon trivial choices as to the symbol alphabet or representation. For example we do *not* want to distinguish between representing weights using base 16 notation rather than base 2, and we do not care if we can change the list representation to save a few '(' and ')' symbols.

The following definitions nicely capture the desired granularity of comparison. They follow upon work by Valiant [194], Haussler [87], and others on computational learning theory. (See chapter 9.)

DEFINITION A.1 *Representation R_2 is polynomially representable (π-representable) by representation R_1 over a class of objects Q if there exists a finite polynomial P such that $|R_1(x)| \le P(|R_2(x)|)$ for all $x \in Q$.*

In other words, anything R_2 can represent, R_1 can also represent using a polynomial function of the number of symbols required by R_2.

A stronger notion of representability occurs if we stipulate that R_1 be restricted to a multiple of the number of symbols R_2 uses, for example $|R_1(x)| \le 2|R_2(x)| + 4$.

DEFINITION A.2 *Representation R_2 is linearly representable (λ-representable) by representation R_1 over a class of objects Q if there exists a first order polynomial P such that $|R_1(x)| \le P(|R_2(x)|)$ for all $x \in Q$.*

Clearly:

• λ-representable implies π-representable

• R is always λ-representable {π-representable} by R

• If R_2 is λ-representable {π-representable} by R_1 and if R_3 is λ-representable {π-representable} by R_2 then R_3 is λ-representable {π-representable} by R_1.

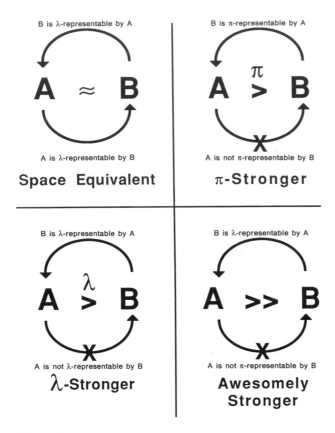

Figure A.1
$\overset{\pi}{>}$, $\overset{\lambda}{>}$, and $\gg$ comparisons.

It is also easy to see that both of these definitions are impervious to trivial changes in representation, such as going from base 2 to base 16 symbols.

Now we can sharpen our comparison tools (see figure A.1):

DEFINITION A.3   *Representation R_1 is polynomially stronger than representation R_2 (over a class of objects Q) if R_2 is π-representable by R_1 but R_1 is not π-representable by R_2. Notation: $R_1 \overset{\pi}{>} R_2$.*

DEFINITION A.4   *Representation R_1 is linearly stronger than representation R_2 (over a class of objects Q) if R_2 is λ-representable by R_1 but R_1 is not λ-representable by R_2. Notation: $R_1 \overset{\lambda}{>} R_2$.*

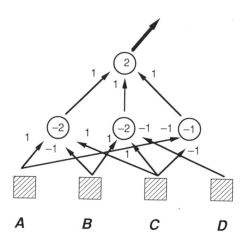

Figure A.2
MLP representation of $A\bar{B}C \vee BC\bar{D} \vee \bar{A}\bar{C}$.

And for younger researchers:

DEFINITION A.5   *Representation R_1 is awesomely stronger than representation R_2 (over a class of objects Q) if R_2 is λ-representable by R_1 but R_1 is not even π-representable by R_2. Notation: $R_1 \gg R_2$.*

Note that

- $\overset{\lambda}{\geq}$ and $\overset{\pi}{\geq}$ do not imply each other (exercise 4)
- $\gg$ is equivalent to the combination of both $\overset{\lambda}{\geq}$ and $\overset{\pi}{\geq}$.

A.1.3   Space Comparison of MLP and DNF Representations

We can now state a main result.

THEOREM A.6 $MLP_{list} \gg DNF$.

Proof: This result is fairly well known, but it is instructive to examine a proof from first principles. First we will see that DNF is linearly representable by MLP_{list}.

Given any DNF expression we can construct a corresponding flat MLP consisting of a selector cell in layer L_1 for every term in the expression and a single OR cell at the top. Here the selector cells have their inputs restricted to elements that appear in the corresponding term of the DNF expression. Figure A.2 illustrates this *restricted selector cell construction.*

The number of noninput cells required is the number of terms plus 1. The number of connections is bounded by the sum of the number of elements in each term plus the number of terms plus one,[1] and the magnitude of each weight is bounded by the larger of (1) the maximum number of elements in a term and (2) the number of terms. Therefore DNF is λ-representable by MLP_{list}.

Next, to show that MLP_{list} is not even polynomially representable by DNF, consider the plurality (or majority) function on k inputs. MLP_{list} represents such functions using $O(k)$ symbols. DNF expressions, however, require $C\left(k, \left\lceil \dfrac{k+1}{2} \right\rceil\right)$ terms.[2] For example the DNF expression for the plurality function on 5 inputs $(A, \ldots, E)$ requires $C(5,3) = \dfrac{5!}{3!2!} = 10$ terms:

$$ABC \lor ABD \lor ABE \lor ACD \lor ACE \lor ADE \lor BCD \lor BCE \lor BDE$$

$$\lor \; CDE.$$

Therefore the number of terms for the DNF representation of the plurality function grows *exponentially* in k. This implies that MLP_{list} is not π-representable by DNF. $\square$

The restricted selector construction for DNF expressions in figure A.2 is worth remembering. Often it gives a much more efficient way of representing Boolean functions than the selector method given in section 2.1.4, even though both methods employ flat networks.

We might wonder whether any representation could be stronger than MLP_{list}. Exercise 9 shows there is an infinite sequence of representations, $\{R_1, R_2, \ldots\}$, (starting from any representation) where $R_j \gg R_{j+1}$.

A.1.4   Speed Comparison of MLP and DNF Representations

To compare the speed of two different representations R_1 and R_2 over a common set of objects Q we must take into account the corresponding

---

1. This factor also counts biases.
2. $C(r, s)$, the number of combinations of r objects taken s at a time, is defined to be $\dfrac{r!}{s!(r-s)!}$. Thus $C\left(k, \left\lceil \dfrac{k+1}{2} \right\rceil\right) \approx C(k, k/2) \approx 2^k/\sqrt{\pi k}$ by Stirling's approximation for factorials. Notice that we are not concerned with values of *unknown* here since we are considering strictly Boolean functions.

algorithms that evaluate the various representations. Furthermore these algorithms may be serial or parallel in nature, and this further complicates comparisons. Therefore we will compare MLP and DNF less formally for speed than for space.

It is important to note that relations for sequential processors also hold for parallel processors if we are limited to a fixed number of processors, because we ignore speedups by a constant multiplier.

The algorithms involved are straightforward. For DNF the serial algorithm evaluates the expression term by term (stopping if any term is found true). If there are t terms and p is the number of inputs then tp is the sequential time bound for evaluating an expression.

The parallel DNF algorithm has a group of processors tackle each term simultaneously, with the final ORing result then computed by another group of processors. The parallel time required to evaluate a function is roughly $\log t + \log p \approx \log t$ using roughly tp processors.

For the MLP_{list} representation the evaluation time is linearly proportional to the DNF time if the restricted selector construction is used to represent the DNF. This is true for corresponding sequential and parallel algorithms.

However, for the plurality function with p inputs, the MLP times are roughly p for sequential and $\log p$ for parallel algorithms using $\log p$ processors. The corresponding DNF times are $C\left(p, \left\lceil \dfrac{p+1}{2} \right\rceil\right)$ for sequential and $\log p$ for parallel processors (but requiring $C\left(p, \left\lceil \dfrac{p+1}{2} \right\rceil\right) \log p$ processors). Recall that $C\left(p, \left\lceil \dfrac{p+1}{2} \right\rceil\right)$ is exponential in p.

Thus we conclude that MLP_{list} representation is at least as fast to evaluate as DNF representation, and can be exponentially faster for sequential algorithms. For parallel algorithms DNF representations can match the evaluation speed of MLP representations, but DNF requires exponentially more processors to do so.

A.1.5 MLP versus DNF Representations

The previous two sections demonstrate clear advantages of MLP_{list} representations over DNF representations for computation.

One arguable disadvantage of MLP representations compared to DNF representations would be in terms of understandability by humans. Cer-

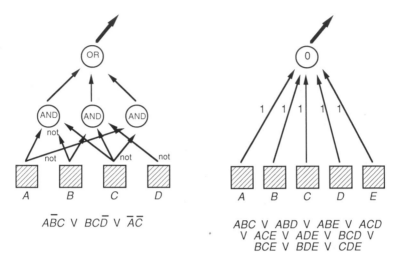

Figure A.3
Which is easier to understand?

tainly the simplest DNF expressions (such as $A \vee B\overline{C}$) are easier to comprehend than the corresponding networks.

However, several points are worth noting. If we are concerned with understandability by humans then we are allowed to draw pictures of networks that are easier to understand than MLP$_{list}$ format. For example we could redraw figure A.2 as in the left half of figure A.3. Looking at the figure, it is no longer clear that DNF is really easier to understand than MLP when we get to slightly complicated expressions.

Moreover it is very difficult for humans to understand complex DNF expressions. For such expressions there is no apparent advantage of DNF over MLP in terms of understandability.

Finally most of us are very much used to seeing DNF expressions and not so used to seeing networks. Networks become much easier to understand as familiarity increases.

A.2 Decision Trees

Decision trees are also widely used for representing Boolean and more general functions (e.g., Breiman et al. [29], Quinlan [167]).

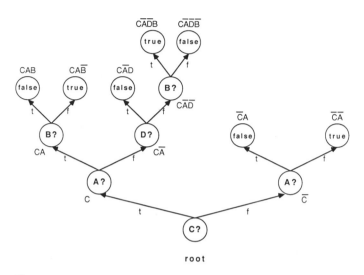

Figure A.4
One possible decision tree for $A\bar{B}C \lor \bar{A}BC\bar{D} \lor \bar{A}\bar{C}$.

We define a (Boolean) *decision tree* as a rooted tree where each node is either

(a) a leaf node that contains an output value (e.g., true) for the function, or

(b) an internal node that contains an input index i between 1 and p. Only internal nodes have connections to other nodes and every such connection is labeled with a possible input value for u_i.

Figure A.4 illustrates a typical decision tree (using $\{A, B, C, D\}$ in place of $\{u_1, u_2, u_3, u_4\}$). To evaluate it we first look at input C and then follow the arrows according to whether C is true or false.

A.2.1 Representing Decision Trees by MLP's

We can define an MLP that represents a decision tree in several ways. Perhaps the best way is the *embedded tree construction* illustrated in figure A.5, where the tree from figure A.4 is represented as an MLP. This construction involves creating a selector internal node in the MLP corresponding to every internal node of the decision tree. The connection topology among internal nodes is exactly the same in the MLP as in the decision tree, with weights of -1 on connections that correspond to *false* branches in the tree. Finally, an OR node is joined to the external nodes of the decision tree that are *true*.

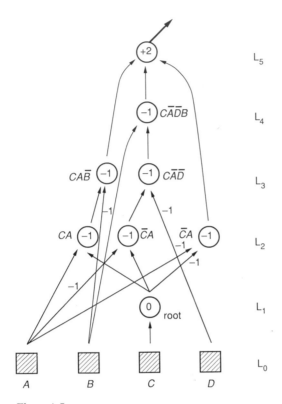

Figure A.5
The MLP representation of the decision tree in figure A.4. All unlabeled connections have
weights of +1.

Note that the MLP is organized into layers and that internal node u_i
is in layer L_k if and only if the corresponding node in the decision tree is
linked to the root by a path that visits k nodes. Thus node CA is in L_3 since
the path $\langle \text{root} \to C \to CA \rangle$ visits 3 nodes in the decision tree.

We can now compare MLP_{list} and decision trees for Boolean functions.

THEOREM A.7 $\text{MLP}_{list} \gg$ *decision trees.*

Proof: The tree-to-MLP construction just presented makes it clear that
decision trees are λ-representable by MLP_{list}.

If we now consider the plurality or majority functions on p inputs,
decision trees require at least $C\left(p, \left\lceil \dfrac{p+1}{2} \right\rceil\right)$ leaf nodes while MLP_{list}

can represent these functions in $O(p)$ symbols. Thus MLP_{list} is not π-representable by decision trees.   □

Notice here that if we consider more general decision *networks* (where nodes are allowed more than one parent) rather than decision *trees*, then plurality no longer requires an exponential number of nodes.

Finally it is interesting that DNF $\overset{\pi}{>}$ decision trees (see exercise 7).

A.2.2 Speed Comparison

Decision trees are very fast. For a problem with p inputs we never need to examine more than p internal nodes to compute an output. Therefore if we make an MLP from a decision tree using the embedded tree construction, the resulting network might take $O(2^p)$ times as long to evaluate as the original decision tree on a sequential computer.

However, there is a more efficient way of evaluating embedded tree networks. First we change the dynamic properties of the MLP so that we evaluate only one cell in any layer, namely that cell determined by the output from the single cell that was evaluated in the previous layer. For example in figure A.5 if cell C was the cell that was evaluated in layer L_2 and its output was false then we would evaluate only cell $C\bar{A}$ in layer L_3.

Second, we change the top cell to have bias 0. This cell will now receive *unknown* values from unevaluated cells and either $+1$ or -1 from the single cell that gets evaluated in layer L_p.

Thus it is possible to evaluate an embedded tree network in roughly the same time as the original decision tree using sequential computers.

For parallel systems, the embedded tree construction clearly takes time linearly proportional to the original decision tree since we can evaluate simultaneously all cells in layer L_1, then all cells in layer L_2, and so on.

A.2.3 Decision Trees versus MLP's

In summary:

• MLP's have clear space advantages over decision trees.

• For sequential processors, decision trees have a speed advantage over MLP's when using the standard order of node evaluations. If we modify the network as in the last section, then MLP's are as fast as decision trees.

• For parallel processors, decision trees and MLP's are about equally fast.

With respect to human understandability, the comparison of MLP's with decision trees is similar to the comparison of MLP's with DNF expressions. For the simplest functions decision trees are easier to understand. For functions like the plurality function on 80 inputs the decision tree is perhaps easy to understand—it just takes a warehouse to store it! Other complex functions are difficult to understand with either representation.

A.3 π-λ Diagrams

We can concisely summarize π-λ relationships with diagrams such as figure A.6. This shows relations between previously examined representations, plus the following additional ones:

enumeration: Number with consecutive integers every Boolean function with 0 inputs, then every Boolean function with 1 input, 2 inputs, etc. (Order is fixed but arbitrary for functions with the same number of inputs.)

Boolean formulae: Similar to DNF, but arbitrary structure using AND, OR, and NOT. For example

$$(BD \vee A)(\overline{B} \vee C \vee (\overline{DB})).$$

The interpretations for figure A.6 are as follows:

1. A-heavy arrow-$B \Rightarrow A \gg B$.
2. A-solid arrow-$B \Rightarrow A \overset{\pi}{>} B$.
3. A-dashed arrow-$B \Rightarrow A \overset{\lambda}{>} B$.

4. Every directed path that contains at least one solid or heavy line gives a π-stronger relationship (e.g., $DL \overset{\pi}{>} ENUM$).

5. Every directed path along heavy or dashed lines yields a λ-stronger relationship; if the path contains at least one heavy line then it gives an awesomely stronger relationship (e.g., $LDN \gg DNF$).

The last two rules are easily derived from the definitions.

Relations implied by the above 5 rules (such as $LDN \gg DNF$) have been removed from the diagram so that it is as simple as possible. Also, no

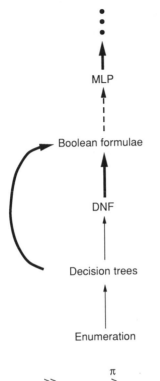

Figure A.6
π-λ diagram for space comparisons of various representations. Corresponding equation numbers are shown on links.

stronger relation exists than those given in figure A.6. For example it is not true that $DNF \gg DT$. Proofs are omitted.

A.4   Symmetric Functions and Depth Complexity

Neural network models provide a wonderful meadow in which a complexity theorist can romp to his or her heart's content. This section gives but a small taste of the possibilities by looking at some recent work by Hajnal et al. [84]. They have studied classes of functions that are linearly or polynomially representable (with respect to the number of inputs p) using strictly k-layered networks for a fixed number of layers (k).

An important class of Boolean functions are *symmetric functions* on p Boolean inputs. Symmetric functions give outputs that are not changed if inputs are permuted. Hence the only important characteristic of the settings for the input cells must be the number of input cells with values of true $(+1)$.

A symmetric function is determined by a subset $C = \{c_1, .., c_r\}$ of the integers between 0 and p. If the total number of input cells that have values of true is in the subset C then the output of the function is true; otherwise the output is false. We have already seen many special cases of symmetric functions:

- AND *function:* $C = \{p\}$
- OR *function:* $C = \{1, 2, \ldots, p\}$
- *parity function:* $C = \left\{0, 2, 4, \ldots, 2\left\lfloor\dfrac{p}{2}\right\rfloor\right\}$
- *k or more out of p function:* $C = \{k, k+1, \ldots, p\}$
- *plurality/majority function:* $\left\lceil\dfrac{p}{2}\right\rceil$ or more out of p function.

PROPOSITION A.8   *A symmetric function with p inputs is linearly representable (with respect to p) by a strictly 2-layer network having nonbias weights that assume values of $+1$ or -1 only.*

Note that for all of the special cases except parity there is actually a single-layer network that does the job.

Proof: Consider an arbitrary symmetric function specified by $C = \{c_1, \ldots, c_r\}$. For each c_j we place 2 cells in layer L_1, one that computes c_j *or more out of p true* and another that computes c_j *or more out of p false* (see figure A.7). Therefore an input to the network with d true cells will produce one output of true and one output of false from every such pair of cells, unless $d = c_j$ in which case the outputs from both cells will be true.

Now in layer L_2 we simply place a single cell that computes $r + 1$ *or more out of 2r true*. The output from this cell will compute the desired symmetric function. It is easy to verify that all nonbias weights are $+1$ or -1 as required.   □

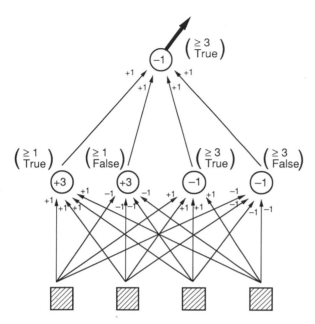

Figure A.7
A network to compute the symmetric function given by $C = \{1, 3\}$.

Another function studied by Hajnal and colleagues is the *split parity function* for p inputs.[3] Here p must be an even number, $p = 2k$. The split parity function is defined to be the parity function applied to k intermediate cells $\{u_{p+1}, u_{p+2}, \ldots, u_{p+k}\}$, where u_{p+j} is true if and only if input cells u_{2j} and u_{2j-1} are both true. Hence this function is formed by taking a parity function and splitting each input into 2 subinputs, both of which must be true to produce a true input to the parity function.

THEOREM A.9 *Split parity for p inputs is linearly representable (with respect to p) by strictly 3-layer networks but is not even polynomially representable by strictly 2-layer networks.*

The first part of the proof is exercise 10, and the proof of the second part is omitted.

3. They call this function *inner product mod 2*.

A.5   Concluding Remarks

In this appendix we have developed a framework for comparing representations.

Multilayer perceptrons have a significant space advantage over disjunctive normal form expressions and decision trees. With respect to speed, decision trees have an advantage over MLP's, but that advantage disappears if we slightly modify the MLP dynamics. DNF expressions are slowest to evaluate.

A.6   Exercises

*1. Compare the space requirements for MLP_{list} and MLP_{matrix} representations (section A.1.2) for n-cell networks as $n \to \infty$ where an average of c cells are connected to each (intermediate and output) cell.

2. Prove formally that MLP using base 16 weights is λ-representable by MLP using base 2 weights over the set of Boolean functions.

3. Prove that if R_2 is λ-representable by R_1 and R_3 is λ-representable by R_2 then R_3 is λ-representable by R_1.

*4. For representations R_1 and R_2:

(a) Show that $R_1 \overset{\pi}{\gtrsim} R_2 \not\Rightarrow R_1 \overset{\lambda}{\gtrsim} R_2$.

(b) Show that $R_1 \overset{\lambda}{\gtrsim} R_2 \not\Rightarrow R_1 \overset{\pi}{\gtrsim} R_2$.

(c) Show that $R_1 \overset{\pi}{\gtrsim} R_2 \Rightarrow R_2 \overset{\lambda}{\not\gtrsim} R_1$.

(d) Show that $R_1 \overset{\lambda}{\gtrsim} R_2 \Rightarrow R_2 \overset{\pi}{\not\gtrsim} R_1$.

5. Prove that $MLP_{matrix} \overset{\pi}{\gtrsim} DNF$ but $MLP_{matrix} \overset{\lambda}{\not\gtrsim} DNF$ (over Boolean functions).

6. Prove that DNF $\gg$ selector cell representation (section 2.1.4).

*7. Show that

(a) DNF representations $\overset{\pi}{\gtrsim}$ decision trees

(b) decision trees are not λ-representable by DNF.

8. Prove that decision trees are π-representable by DNF.

*9. Prove that if R_2 is a representation of an infinite set of objects Q then there exists a representation R_1 of Q such that $R_1 \gg R_2$. This means that there can be no "strongest" (or even maximally strong) representation of an infinite set of objects.

10. Show that the split parity function for p inputs is linearly representable (with respect to p) by strictly 3-layer networks having all nonbias weights of $+1$ or -1.

Bibliography

[1] Ackley, D. H., Hinton, G. E., and Sejnowski, T. J. A Learning Algorithm for Boltzmann Machines. *Cognitive Science* 9, 1985, 147–169.

[2] Amari, S. Learning Patterns and Pattern Sequences by Self-Organizing Nets of Threshold Elements. *IEEE Trans. Computers* C-21, no. 11, November 1972, 1197–1206.

[3] Amari, S. A Method of Statistical Neurodynamics. *Kybernetik* 14, no. 4, April 1974, 201–215.

[4] Amari, S. Mathematical Foundations of Neurocomputing. Report METR89-06, Faculty of Engineering, University of Tokyo, August 1989. (Journal version to appear.)

[5] Amit, D. J. *Modelling Brain Function: The World of Attractor Neural Networks*. Cambridge University Press, 1989.

[6] Anderberg, M. R. *Cluster Analysis for Applications*. Academic Press, New York, 1973.

[7] Anderson, J. A., Silverstein, J. W., Ritz, S. A., and Jones, R. S. Distinctive Features, Categorical Perception, and Probability Learning: Some Applications of a Neural Model. *Psychological Review* 84, 1977, 413–451.

[8] Anderson, J. A., and Rosenfeld, E. (eds.). *Neurocomputing, A Reader*. MIT Press, Cambridge, 1988.

[9] Anderson, J. A., and Mozer, M. Categorization and Selective Neurons. In Hinton, G. E., and Anderson, J. A. (eds.), *Parallel Models of Associative Memory*. Lawrence Erlbaum Assoc., Hillsdale, NJ, 1981, 213–236.

[10] Aspvall, B., and Stone, R. E. Khachiyan's Linear Programming Algorithm. *Journal of Algorithms*, 1, 1980, 1–13.

[11] Bachant, J., and McDermott, J. R1 Revisited: Four Years in the Trenches. *AI Magazine*, Fall 1984, 21–32.

[12] Ball, G. H. A Comparison of Some Cluster-Seeking Techniques. Report RADC-TR-66-514, AD 643287, Stanford Research Institute, Menlo Park, CA, 1966. Also available under the title "Data Analysis in Social Sciences: What About the Details?," *Proc. Fall Joint Computer Conference* 27, pt. I, 533–559. Spartan Books, Washington, DC, 1965.

[13] Ball, G. H. Classification Analysis. Report AD 716482, Stanford Research Institute, Menlo Park, CA, 1970.

[14] Ball, G. H., and Hall, D. J. ISODATA, A Novel Method of Data Analysis and Pattern Classification. Report AD 699616, Stanford Research Institute, Menlo Park, CA, 1965.

[15] Ball, G. H., and Hall, D. J. PROMENADE—An On-Line Pattern Recognition System. Report RADC-TR-67-310, AD 822174, Stanford Research Institute, Menlo Park, CA, 1967.

[16] Barto, A. G. Learning by Statistical Cooperation of Self-Interested Neuron-like Computing Elements. *Human Neurobiology* 4, 1985, 229–256.

[17] Barto, A. G. Neural Network Learning for Control: An Overview. Chapter in Miller, T., Sutton, R. S., and Werbos, P. J. (eds.), *Neural Networks for Control*. MIT Press, Cambridge, 1990.

[18] Barto, A. G., Sutton, R. S., and Anderson, C. W. Neuronlike Adaptive Elements That Can Solve Difficult Learning Control Problems. *IEEE Trans. on Systems, Man, and Cybernetics* SMC-13, no. 5, September-October 1983, 834–846.

[19] Baum, E. B. The Perceptron Algorithm Is Fast for Nonmalicious Distributions. *Neural Computation* 2, 1990, 248–260.

[20] Baum, E. B., and Haussler, D. What Size Net Gives Valid Generalization? *Neural Computation* 1, no. 1, 1989, 151–160.

[21] Baxt, W. G. Use of an Artificial Neural Network for Data Analysis in Clinical Decision-Making: The Diagnosis of Acute Coronary Occlusion. *Neural Computation* 2, 1990, 480–489.

[22] Block, H. D., and Levin, S. A. On the Boundedness of an Iterative Procedure for Solving a System of Linear Inequalities. *Proc. AMS* 26, 1970, 229–235.

[23] Bloom, B. H. Space/Time Trade-offs in Hash Coding with Allowable Errors. *CACM* 13, no. 7, July 1970, 422–426.

[24] Blum, A., and Rivest, R. Training a 3-Node Neural Network Is NP-Complete. In Haussler, D., and Pitt, L. (eds.), *COLT '88, Proceedings of the 1988 Workshop on Computational Learning Theory*, MIT, August 3–5, 1988. Morgan Kaufmann Publishers, San Mateo, CA, 9–18.

[25] Blumer, A., Ehrenfeucht, A., Haussler, D., and Warmuth, M. Occam's Razor. *Information Processing Letters* 24, 1987, 377–380.

[26] Blumer, A., Ehrenfeucht, A., Haussler, D., and Warmuth, M. Learnability and the Vapnik-Chervonenkis Dimension. University of California at Santa Cruz Technical Report UCSC-CRL-87-20, revised October 1988. To appear in *JACM*.

[27] Brachman, R. J. What ISA Is and Isn't. *IEEE Computer* 16, no. 10, October 1983, 30–36. Reprinted in Gupta and Prasad (eds.), *Principles of Expert Systems*. IEEE Press, Piscataway, NJ, 1988.

[28] Brachman, R. J. "I Lied about the Trees" Or, Defaults and Definitions in Knowledge Representation. *AI Magazine*, Fall 1985, 80–93.

[29] Breiman, L., Friedman, J., Olshen, R., and Stone, C. *Classification and Regression Trees.* Wadsworth International Group, Belmont, CA, 1984.

[30] Brownston, L., Farrell, R., Kant, E., and Martin, N. *Programming Expert Systems in OPS5.* Addison-Wesley, Reading, MA, 1985.

[31] Buchanan, B., and Shortliffe, E. Rule-Based Expert Systems. Addison-Wesley, Reading, MA, 1984.

[32] Buntine, W. A Critique of the Valiant Model. AAAI '89. Detroit, MI, 837–842.

[33] Carpenter, G., and Grossberg, S. A Massively Parallel Architecture for a Self-Organizing Neural Pattern Recognition Machine. *Computer Vision, Graphics, and Image Processing* 37, 1987, 54–115.

[34] Carpenter, G., and Grossberg, S. ART 2: Self-Organization of Stable Category Recognition Codes for Analog Input Patterns. *Applied Optics* 26, 1987, 4919–4930.

[35] Carpenter, G., Grossberg, S., and Reynolds, J. ARTMAP: A Self-Organizing Neural Network Architecture for Fast Supervised Learning and Pattern Recognition. International Joint Conference on Neural Networks, Seattle, WA, July 8–12, 1991, I-863 to I-868.

[36] Carpenter, G., Grossberg, S., and Reynolds, J. ARTMAP: Supervised Real-Time Learning and Classification of Nonstationary Data by a Self-Organizing Neural Network. *IEEE Expert*, in press.

[37] Carpenter, G. ART 2-A: An Adaptive Resonance Algorithm for Rapid Category Learning and Recognition. *Neural Networks* 4, no. 4, 1991, 493–504.

[38] Cheeseman, P. C., Kelly, J., Self, M., Stutz, J., Taylor, W., and Freeman, D. AutoClass: A Bayesian Classification System. Fifth International Workshop on Machine Learning, University of Michigan, Ann Arbor, MI, June 12–14, 1988, 54–64.

[39] Cohen, M., and Grossberg, S. Absolute Stability of Global Pattern Formation and Parallel Memory Storage by Competitive Neural Networks. *IEEE Transactions on Systems, Man, and Cybernetics* SMC-13, no. 5, September-October 1983, 815–826.

[40] Cottrell, G., Munro, P., and Zipser, D. Image Compression by Back Propagation: An Example of Extensional Programming. In N. Sharkey (ed.), *Advances in Cognitive Science*, vol. 3. Norwood, NJ: Ablex, 1988. See also Proceedings of the Ninth Annual Conference of the Cognitive Science Society, July 1987, Seattle, Washington. Hillsdale, NJ: Lawrence Erlbaum, 462–473.

[41] Cover, T. M. Geometrical and Statistical Properties of Systems of Linear Inequalities with Applications in Pattern Recognition. *IEEE Trans. Electronic Computers* 14, 1965, 326–334.

[42] Devroye, L. Automatic Pattern Recognition, a Study of the Probability of Error. *IEEE Trans. PAMI* 10, no. 4, 1988, 530–543.

[43] Dolan, C. P., and Smolensky, P. Implementing a Neural Network Production System Using Tensor Products. University of Colorado Department of Computer Science Tech Report CU-CS-411-88, September 1988.

[44] Dreyfus, H. L. *What Computers Can't Do.* Harper and Row, New York, 1972.

[45] Dreyfus, H. L., and Dreyfus, S. E. Making a Mind versus Modeling the Brain: Artificial Intelligence Back at a Branchpoint. *Daedalus*, Winter 1988, 15–43.

[46] Dubes, R. C. Information Compression, Structure Analysis and Decision Making with a Correlation Matrix. Report AD 720811, Michigan State University, 1970.

[47] Duda, R. O., and Hart, P. E. *Pattern Classification and Scene Analysis.* John Wiley and Sons, New York, 1973.

[48] Duda, R. O., and Reboh, R. AI and Decision Making: The PROSPECTOR Experience. In Reitman, W. (ed.), *Artificial Intelligence Applications for Business.* Ablex Publishing Co., Norwood, NJ, 1983.

[49] Duda, R. O., and Shortliffe, E. H. Expert Systems Research. *Science* 220, no. 4594, April 15, 1983, 261–268.

[50] Efron, B. The Perceptron Correction Procedure in Nonseparable Situations. Rome Air Development Center Technical Documentary, 1964.

[51] Fahlman, S. E. Faster-Learning Variations on Back-Propagation: An Empirical Study. In Touretsky, D., Hinton, G., and Sejnowski, T. (eds.), *Proceedings of the 1988 Neural Network Model Summer School.* Morgan Kaufmann Publishers, San Mateo, CA, 1988, 38–51.

[52] Fahlman, S. E., and Labiere, C. The Cascade-Correlation Learning Architecture. In Touretzky, D. (ed.), *Advances in Neural Information Processing Systems 2.* Morgan Kaufmann Publishers, San Mateo, CA, 1990, 524–532.

[53] Feldman, J. A., and Ballard, D. H. Connectionist Models and Their Properties. *Cognitive Science* 6, 1982, 205–254.

[54] Firebaugh, M. W. *Artificial Intelligence: A Knowledge-Based Approach.* Boyd and Fraser, Boston, MA, 1988.

[55] Fisher, R. A. The Use of Multiple Measurements in Taxonomic Problems. *Ann. Eugenics* 7, 1936, part II, 179–188. Also in *Contributions to Mathematical Statistics*, John Wiley, New York, 1950.

[56] Forgy, C. L. OPS5 User's Manual. Technical Report CMU-CS-81-135. Department of Computer Science, Carnegie-Mellon University, July 1981.

[57] Frean, M. The Upstart Algorithm: A Method for Constructing and Training Feedforward Neural Networks. *Neural Computation* 2, 1990, 198–209.

[58] Frean, M. Small Nets and Short Paths: Optimising Neural Computation. Ph.D. thesis, University of Edinburgh, Center for Cognitive Science, 1990.

[59] Frydenberg, M., and Gallant, S. I. Fuzziness and Expert System Generation. International Conference on Information Processing and Management of Uncertainty in Knowledge-Based Systems, Paris, France, June 30–July 4, 1986. Extended paper reprinted in Bouchon, B., and Yager, R. (eds.), *Uncertainty in Knowledge-Based Systems.* Springer-Verlag, Berlin, 1987.

[60] Fukushima, K. Cognitron: A Self-Organizing Multilayered Neural Network. *Biological Cybernetics* 20, November 1975, 121–136.

[61] Fukushima, K., Miyake, S., and Ito, T. Neocognitron: A Neural Network Model for a Mechanism of Visual Pattern Recognition. *IEEE Trans. Syst., Man, and Cyber.* SMC-13, no. 5, Sept./Oct. 1983, 826–834.

[62] Fukushima, K. Neocognitron: A Hierarchical Neural Network Capable of Visual Pattern Recognition. *Neural Networks* 1, 1988, 119–130.

[63] Gallant, S. I. Automatic Generation of Expert Systems from Examples. Proceedings of Second International Conference on Artificial Intelligence Applications, sponsored by IEEE Computer Society, Miami Beach, FL, Dec. 11–13, 1985, 313–319.

[64] Gallant, S. I. Three Constructive Algorithms for Network Learning. Proc. Eighth Annual Conference of the Cognitive Science Society, Amherst, MA, Aug. 15–17, 1986, 652–660.

[65] Gallant, S. I. Optimal Linear Discriminants. Proc. Eighth International Conference on Pattern Recognition, Paris, France, Oct. 28–31, 1986, 849–852.

[66] Gallant, S. I. Automated Generation of Expert Systems for Problems Involving Noise and Redundancy. AAAI Workshop on Uncertainty in Artificial Intelligence, Seattle, WA, July 10–12, 1987, 212–221.

[67] Gallant, S. I. Connectionist Expert Systems. *Communications of the ACM* 31, no. 2, Feb. 1988, 152–169. (Japanese translation in *Neurocomputer*, published by Nikkei Artificial Intelligence, 114–136, 1988.)

[68] Gallant, S. I. Matrix Controlled Expert System Producible from Examples. United States Patent 4,730,259, March 8, 1988.

[69] Gallant, S. I. Bayesian Assessment of a Connectionist Model for Fault Detection. AAAI Fourth Workshop on Uncertainty in Artificial Intelligence, St. Paul, MN, August 19–21, 1988, 127–135.

[70] Gallant, S. I. Example-Based Knowledge Engineering with Connectionist Expert Systems. *Proc. IEEE MIDCON*, Dallas, Texas, August 30–September 1, 1988, 32–37.

[71] Gallant, S. I. A Connectionist Learning Algorithm with Provable Generalization and Scaling Bounds. *Neural Networks* 3, 1990, 191–201.

[72] Gallant, S. I. Perceptron-Based Learning Algorithms. *IEEE Transactions on Neural Networks* 1, no. 2, June 1990, 179–192.

[73] Gallant, S. I., and Hayashi, Y. A Neural Network Expert System with Confidence Measurements. In Bouchon-Meunier, B., Yager, R. R., and Zadeh, L. A. (eds.), *Uncertainty in Knowledge Bases.* Lecture Notes in Computer Science 521, Springer Verlag, Berlin, Spring 1991, 562–567.

[74] Gallant, S. I., and Smith, D. Random Cells: An Idea Whose Time Has Come and Gone ... and Come Again? IEEE International Conference on Neural Networks, San Diego, CA, vol. II, June 1987, 671–678.

[75] Garey, M. R., and Johnson, D. S. *Computers and Intractability, A Guide to the Theory of NP-Completeness.* Freeman, New York, 1979.

[76] Geman, S., and Geman, D. Stochastic Relaxation, Gibbs Distributions, and the Bayesian Restoration of Images. *IEEE Transactions on Pattern Analysis and Machine Intelligence* PAMI-6, 1984, 721–741.

[77] Geman, S., Bienenstock, E., and Doursat, R. Neural Networks and the Bias/Variance Dilemma. *Neural Computation* 4, 1992, 1–58.

[78] Golea, M., and Marchand, M. A Growth Algorithm for Neural Network Decision Trees. *Europhysics Letters* 12, 1990, 205.

[79] Golub, G. H., and van Loan, C. F. *Matrix Computations.* North Oxford Academic Publishing Co. Ltd., Oxford, 1983.

[80] Grossberg, S. Embedding Fields: A Theory of Learning with Physiological Implications. *Journal of Mathematical Psychology* 6, 1969, 209–239.

[81] Grossberg, S. Classical and Instrumental Learning by Neural Networks. In Rosen, R., and Snell, F. (eds.), *Progress in Theoretical Biology*, vol. 3. Academic Press, New York, 1974, 51–141.

[82] Grossberg, S. How Does a Brain Build a Cognitive Code? *Psychological Review* 87, 1980, 1–51.

[83] Hacijan, L. G. A Polynomial Algorithm in Linear Programming. *Soviet Mathematics Doklady* 20, 1979, 191–194.

[84] Hajnal, A., Maass, W., Pudlák, P., Szegedy, M., and Turán, G. Threshold Circuits of Bounded Depth. 28th Annual Symposium on Foundations of Computer Science, Los Angeles, CA, October 12–14, 1987.

[85] Hall, L. O., and Romaniuk, S. G. A Hybrid Neural Network, Symbolic Learning System. AAAI-90, July 29–August 3, 1990, Boston, MA, 783–788.

[86] Hanson, S. J. Meiosis Networks. In Touretzky, D. (ed.), *Advances in Neural Information Processing Systems 2*. Morgan Kaufmann Publishers, San Mateo, CA, 1990, 533–541.

[87] Haussler, D. Applying Valiant's Learning Framework to AI Concept Learning Problems. Tech Report UCSC-CRL-87-11, Computer Research Laboratory, University of California at Santa Cruz, September 1987.

[88] Haussler, D., and Pitt, L. (eds.). *COLT '88, Proceedings of the 1988 Workshop on Computational Learning Theory*, MIT, August 3–5, 1988. Morgan Kaufmann Publishers, San Mateo, CA.

[89] Hayashi, Y. A Neural Expert System with Automated Extraction of Fuzzy If-Then Rules and Its Application to Medical Diagnosis. In Touretzky, D. S., and Lippman, R. (eds.), *Advances in Neural Information Processing Systems*, vol. 3. Morgan Kaufmann Publishers, San Mateo, CA, 1991, 578–584.

[90] Hayashi, Y., and Nakai, M. Reasoning Methods Using a Fuzzy Production Rule with Linguistic Relative Importance in an Antecedent. (In Japanese.) *Trans. IEE of Japan* 109-C, no. 9, Sept. 1989, 661–668.

[91] Hayashi, Y., Imura, A., and Yoshida, K. A Neural Expert System under Uncertain Environments and Its Evaluation. The Eleventh Knowledge and Intelligence System Symposium, Tokyo, March 12–13, 1990, 13–18.

[92] Hayashi, Y., and Imura, A. Fuzzy Neural Expert System with Automated Extraction of Fuzzy If-Then Rules from a Trained Neural Network. Proceedings of the First Int. Symposium on Uncertainty Modeling and Analysis, Maryland, Dec. 3–5, 1990, 489–494.

[93] Hayashi, Y., Sakata, M., and Gallant, S. I. *Multi-Layer vs. Single-Layer Neural Networks and an Application to Reading Hand-Stamped Characters*. International Neural Network Conference (INNC 90), Paris, France, July 9–13, 1990, 781–784.

[94] Hebb, D. O. *The Organization of Behavior*. Wiley, New York, 1949.

[95] Hecht-Nielsen, R. Nearest Matched Filter Classification of Spatiotemporal Patterns. *Applied Optics* 26, no. 10, 1987, 1892–1899.

[96] Hecht-Nielsen, R. *Neurocomputing*. Addison-Wesley, Reading, MA, 1990.

[97] Hinton, G. E. Distributed Representations. Technical Report CMU-CS-84-157, Carnegie-Mellon University, Department of Computer Science. Revised version in Rumelhart, D. E., and McClelland, J. L. (eds.), *Parallel Distributed Processing: Explorations in the Microstructures of Cognition*, vol. 1. MIT Press, Cambridge, 1986.

[98] Hinton, G. E., and Anderson, J. A. (eds.). *Parallel Models of Associative Memory*. Lawrence Erlbaum Assoc., Hillsdale, NJ, 1981.

[99] Hinton, G. E., Sejnowski, T. J., and Ackley, D. H. Boltzmann Machines: Constraint Satisfaction Networks That Learn. Technical Report CMU-CS-84-119, Carnegie-Mellon University, Department of Computer Science, 1984.

[100] Hoeffding, W. Probability Inequalities for Sums of Bounded Random Variables. *J. Amer. Stat. Assoc.* 58, 1963, 13–30.

[101] Hopfield, J. J. Neural Networks and Physical Systems with Emergent Collective Computational Abilities. Proceedings of the National Academy of Sciences USA, 79, 1982, 2554–2558.

[102] Hopfield, J. J., and Tank, D. W. "Neural" Computation of Decisions in Optimization Problems. *Biological Cybernetics* 52, 1985, 141–152.

[103] Hudak, M. J. RCE Networks: An Experimental Investigation. International Joint Conference on Neural Networks, Seattle, WA, July 8–12, 1991, I-849 to I-854.

[104] Jackson, P. *Introduction to Expert Systems*, 2d ed. Addison-Wesley, Reading, MA, 1990.

[105] Jacobs, R. A. Increased Rates of Convergence through Learning Rate Adaptation. *Neural Networks* 1, 1988, 295–307.

[106] Jordan, M. I. Serial Order: A Parallel Distributed Processing Approach. Institute for Cognitive Science Report 8604, University of California, San Diego, May 1986.

[107] Jordan, M. I. Attractor Dynamics and Parallelism in a Connectionist Sequential Machine. Proceedings of the Eighth Annual Conference of the Cognitive Science Society, Amherst, MA, 1986.

[108] Jordan, M. I. Supervised Learning and Systems with Excess Degrees of Freedom. University of Massachusetts at Amherst, Technical Report COINS TR 88-27, May 1988.

[109] Judd, S. Learning in Networks Is Hard. IEEE International Conference on Neural Networks, San Diego, CA, vol. II, June 1987, 685–692.

[110] Judd, S. Learning in Neural Networks. In Haussler, D., and Pitt, L. (eds.), *COLT '88, Proceedings of the 1988 Workshop on Computational Learning Theory*, MIT, August 3–5, 1988. Morgan Kaufmann Publishers, San Mateo, CA, 2–8.

[111] Kanerva, P. Parallel Structures in Human and Computer Memory. COGNITIVA '85, Paris, France, June 4–7, 1985.

[112] Kanerva, P. *Sparse Distributed Memory*. MIT Press, Cambridge, 1988.

[113] Karmarker, N. A New Polynomial Time Algorithm for Linear Programming. *Combinatorica* 1, 1984, 373–395.

[114] Kearns, M., Li, M., Pitt, L., and Valiant, L. On the Learnability of Boolean Formulae. ACM Press: Proceedings of the Nineteenth Annual ACM Symposium on Theory of Computing, New York City, May 25–27, 1987, 285–295.

[115] Kim, J. H., and Pearl, J. CONVINCE: A Conversational Inference Consolidation Engine. *IEEE Transactions on Systems, Man, and Cybernetics* SMC-17, no. 2, March/April 1987, 120–132.

[116] Kohonen, T. Correlation Matrix Memories. *IEEE Trans.* C-21, 1972, 353–359.

[117] Kohonen, T. *Associative Memory—A System-Theoretic Approach*. Springer, New York, 1977.

[118] Kohonen, T. Clustering, Taxonomy, and Topological Maps of Patterns. IEEE Sixth International Conference on Pattern Recognition, October 1982, 114–128.

[119] Kohonen, T. Self-Organized Formation of Topologically Correct Feature Maps. *Biological Cybernetics* 43, 1982, 59–69.

[120] Kohonen, T. *Self-Organization and Associative Memory*, 2d ed. Springer-Verlag, 1988.

[121] Kohonen, T. The "Neural" Phonetic Typewriter. *IEEE Computer*, March 1988, 11–22.

[122] Kohonen, T., Makisara, K., and Saramaki, T. Phonotopic Maps—Insightful Representation of Phonological Features for Speech Recognition. IEEE Seventh International Conference on Pattern Recognition, Montreal, July 30–August 2, 1984, 182–185.

[123] Kosko, B. *Neural Networks and Fuzzy Systems: A Dynamical Systems Approach to Machine Intelligence*. Prentice-Hall, Englewood Cliffs, NJ, 1991.

[124] Kullback, S. *Information Theory and Statistics*. Wiley, New York, 1959.

[125] Larsen, R. J., and Marx, M. L. *An Introduction to Mathematical Statistics and Its Applications*. Prentice-Hall, Englewood Cliffs, NJ, 1986.

[126] Lauritzen, S. L., and Spiegelhalter, D. J. Local Computations with Probabilities on Graphical Structures and Their Application to Expert Systems. *Journal of the Royal Statistical Society*, Series B, 50, 1988, 157–224.

[127] LeCun, Y. A Theoretical Framework for Back-Propagation. In Touretsky, D., Hinton, G., and Sejnowski, T. (eds.), *Proceedings of the 1988 Neural Network Model Summer School*. Morgan Kaufmann Publishers, San Mateo, CA, 1988. Quoted in Barto [17].

[128] LeCun, Y., Boser, B., Denker, J., Henderson, D., Howard, R., Hubbard, W., and Jackel, L. Backpropagation Applied to Handwritten Zip Code Recognition. *Neural Computation* 1, no. 4, Winter 1989, 541–551.

[129] Lee, Y. Handwritten Digit Recognition Using K Nearest-Neighbor, Radial-Basis Function, and Backpropagation Neural Networks. *Neural Computation* 3, 1991, 440–449.

[130] Lee, Y. C., Doolen, G., Chen, H. H., Sun, G. Z., Maxwell, T., Lee, H. Y., and Giles, C. L. Machine Learning Using a Higher Order Correlational Network. *Physica D*, 22-D, no. 1–3, 1986, 276.

[131] Littlestone, N. Learning Quickly when Irrelevant Attributes Abound: A New Linear-Threshold Algorithm. *Machine Learning* 2, 1988, 285–318.

[132] Lucky, R. W. Automatic Equalization for Digital Communication. *Bell Syst. Tech. J.* 44, April 1965, 547–588.

[133] Mézard, M., and Nadal, J.-P. Learning in Feedforward Layered Networks: The Tiling Algorithm *J. Phys. A: Math. and Gen.* 22, no. 12, 1989, 2191–2203.

[134] MacQueen, J. B. Some Methods for Classification and Analysis of Multivariate Observations. Proc. Symp. Math. Statist. and Probability, 5th, Berkeley, 1, 281–297, 1967, AD 669871. University of California Press, Berkeley.

[135] Mansfield, A. J. Training Perceptrons by Linear Programming. Report DITC 181/91, National Physical Laboratory, Middlesex, England, August 1991.

[136] Mansfield, A. J. Comparison of Perceptron Training by Linear Programming and by the Perceptron Convergence Procedure. International Joint Conference on Neural Networks, Seattle, WA, July 8–12, 1991, II-25 to II-30.

[137] McClelland, J. L., and Rumelhart, D. E. An Interactive Activation Model of Context Effects in Letter Perception: Part 1. An Account of Basic Finding. *Psychological Review* 88, 1981, 375–407.

[138] McClelland, J. L., and Rumelhart, D. E. (eds.). *Parallel Distributed Processing: Explorations in the Microstructures of Cognition*, vol. 2. MIT Press, Cambridge, 1986.

[139] McCulloch, W. S., and Pitts, W. H. A Logical Calculus of the Ideas Immanent in Nervous Activity. *Bulletin of Math. Biophysics* 5, 1943, 115–133.

[140] McDermott, J. R1: The Formative Years. *AI Magazine* 2, no. 2, 1981, 21–29.

[141] Miccheli. Interpolation of Scattered Data: Distance Matrices and Conditionally Positive Definite Functions. *Constructive Approximation* 2, 1986, 11–22.

[142] Michalski, R. S., Carbonell, J. G., and Mitchell, T. M. *Machine Learning*. Tioga Pub. Co., Palo Alto, CA, 1983.

[143] Miller, R. A., Pople, H. E., and Myers, J. D. INTERNIST-I, an Experimental Computer-Based Diagnostic Consultant for General Internal Medicine. *New England Journal of Medicine* 307, August 1982, 468–476.

[144] Minsky, M. Steps toward Artificial Intelligence. Proceedings IRE, 1961, 49, 8–30. Reprinted in Feigenbaum, E. A., and Feldman, J. (eds.), *Computers and Thought*. McGraw-Hill, New York, 1963.

[145] Minsky, M., and Papert, S. *Perceptrons: An Introduction to Computational Geometry*. MIT Press, Cambridge, 1969.

[146] Minsky, M., and Selfridge, O. G. Learning in Random Nets. Fourth Symposium on Information Theory, London, England, 1960. In Cherry, C. (ed.), *Information Theory*. Butterworths, Washington, DC, 1961.

[147] Moore, B. ART1 and Pattern Clustering. In Touretzky, D., Hinton, G., and Sejnowski, T. (eds.), *Proceedings of the 1988 Neural Network Models Summer School*, Carnegie Mellon University, June 17–26, 1988. Morgan Kaufmann Publishers, San Mateo, CA, 174–185.

[148] Nadal, J. P. Study of a Growth Algorithm for Neural Networks. *International Journal of Neural Systems* 1, 1989, 55–59.

[149] Nilsson, N. J. *Learning Machines*. McGraw-Hill, New York, 1965. Reissued as *Mathematical Foundations of Learning Machines*, Morgan Kaufmann Publishers, San Mateo, CA, 1990.

[150] Niranjan, M., and Fallside, F. Neural Networks and Radial Basis Functions in Classifying Static Speech Patterns. Report CUED/FINFENG/TR 22, University Engineering Department, Cambridge University, England, 1988.

[151] Parker, D. B. Learning Logic. Invention Report, S81-64, File 1, Office of Technology Licensing, Stanford University, 1982.

[152] Parker, D. B. Learning Logic. Technical Report TR-47, Center for Computational Research in Economics and Management Science, MIT, April 1985.

[153] Pearl, J. On the Connection between the Complexity and Credibility of Inferred Models. *Int. J. General Systems* 4, 1978, 255–264.

[154] Pearl, J. How to Do with Probabilities What People Say You Can't. Proceedings of Second International Conference on Artificial Intelligence Applications, sponsored by IEEE Computer Society, Miami Beach, FL, Dec. 11–13, 1985, 6–12.

[155] Pearl, J. Fusion, Propagation, and Structuring in Belief Networks. *Artificial Intelligence* 29, no. 3, Sept. 1986, 241–288.

[156] Pearl, J. The Logic of Representing Dependencies by Directed Graphs. AAAI-87, Seattle, WA, 1987, 374–379.

[157] Pearl, J. *Probabilistic Reasoning in Intelligent Systems*. Morgan Kaufmann Publishers, San Mateo, CA, 1988.

[158] Perrone, M. P. A Novel Recursive Partitioning Criterion. Physics Department and Center for Neural Science Technical Report, Brown University, 1991.

[159] Plate, T. Holographic Reduced Representations. University of Toronto, Department of Computer Science Technical Report CRG-TR-91-1, May 1991.

[160] Poggio, T., and Girosi, F. A Theory of Networks for Learning. *Science* 247, 1990, 978–982.

[161] Poggio, T., and Girosi, F. Networks for Approximation and Learning. *Proceedings of the IEEE* 78, September 1990.

[162] Pollack, J. Recursive Auto-Associative Memory: Devising Compositional Distributed Representations. Cognitive Science Society Annual Conference, Montreal, August 17–19, 1988.

[163] Pomerleau, D. A. Efficient Training of Artificial Neural Networks for Autonomous Navigation. *Neural Computation* 3, 1991, 88–97.

[164] Powell, M. J. D. Radial Basis Functions for Multi-variable Interpolation: A Review. IMA Conference on Algorithms for the Approximation of Functions and Data, RMCS, Shrivenham, England. Also Report DAMTP/NA12, Department of Applied Mathematics and Theoretical Physics, University of Cambridge, 1985.

[165] Qian, N., and Sejnowski, T. J. Predicting the Secondary Structure of Globular Proteins Using Neural Network Models. *Journal of Molecular Biology* 202, 1988, 865–884.

[166] Quillian, M. R. Semantic Memory. In Minsky, M. (ed.), *Semantic Information Processing*. MIT Press, Cambridge, 1968.

[167] Quinlan, J. R. Learning Efficient Classification Procedures and Their Application to Chess End Games. In Michalski, R. S., Carbonell, J. G., and Mitchell, T. M. (eds.), *Machine Learning*. Tioga Pub. Co., Palo Alto, CA, 1983.

[168] Reilly, D. L., Scofield, C., Elbaum. C., and Cooper, L. N. Learning System Architectures Composed of Multiple Modules. IEEE International Conference on Neural Networks, San Diego, CA, June 1987.

[169] Renals, S., and Rohwer, R. Phoneme Classification Experiments Using Radial Basis Functions. International Joint Conference on Neural Networks, Washington, DC, June 18–22, 1989, I-461 to I-467.

[170] Rivest, R. L. Learning Decision Lists. *Machine Learning* 2, November 1987, 229–246.

[171] Rosenberg, C. R. Revealing the Structure of NETtalk's Internal Representations. Ninth Cognitive Science Society Conference, Seattle, WA, July 16–18, 1987, 537–554.

[172] Rosenblatt, F. Two Theorems of Statistical Separability in the Perceptron. Proceedings of a Symposium on the Mechanization of Thought Processes, Her Majesty's Stationery Office, London, 1959, 421–456.

[173] Rosenblatt, F. *Principles of Neurodynamics: Perceptrons and the Theory of Brain Mechanisms*. Spartan Press, Washington, DC, 1961.

[174] Rosenfeld, R., and Touretzky, D. S. Four Capacity Models for Coarse-Coded Symbol Memories. Carnegie Mellon Computer Science Department Technical Report CMU-CS-87-182, December 1987.

[175] Ruman, P., and Marchand, M. Learning by Minimizing Resources in Neural Networks. *Complex Systems* 3, 1989, 229.

[176] Rumelhart, D. E., and McClelland, J. L. An Interactive Activation Model of Context Effects in Letter Perception: Part 2: The Contextual Enhancement Effect and Some Tests and Extensions of the Model. *Psychological Review* 89, 1982, 60–94.

[177] Rumelhart, D. E., and McClelland, J. L. (eds.), *Parallel Distributed Processing: Explorations in the Microstructures of Cognition*, vol. 1. MIT Press, Cambridge, 1986.

[178] Rumelhart, D. E., Hinton, G. E., and Williams, R. J. Learning Internal Representations by Error Propagation. In Rumelhart, D. E., and McClelland, J. L. (eds.), *Parallel Distributed Processing: Explorations in the Microstructures of Cognition*, vol. 1. MIT Press, Cambridge, 1986.

[179] SAS User's Guide: Statistics, 1982, 381–396.

[180] *SPSS-X User's Guide*. McGraw-Hill, New York, 1984.

[181] Saito, K., and Nakano, R. Automatic Extraction of Classification Rules. International Neural Network Conference, July 9–13, 1990, Paris, France.

[182] Sammon, Jr., J. W. On-Line Pattern Analysis and Recognition System (OLPARS). Report RADC-TR-68-263, AD 675212, Rome Air Development Center, Griffiss Air Force. Base, New York, 1968.

[183] Samuel, A. L. Some Studies in Machine Learning Using the Game of Checkers. *IBM Journal of Research and Development* 3, no. 3, 1959, 210–223.

[184] Saund, E. Dimensionality-Reduction and Constraint in Later Vision. Proceedings of the Ninth Annual Conference of the Cognitive Science Society, July 1987, Seattle, Washington. Hillsdale, NJ: Lawrence Erlbaum, 908–915.

[185] Scofield, C., Reilly, D. L., Elbaum, C., and Cooper. L. N. Pattern Class Degeneracy in an Unrestricted Storage Density Memory. In Anderson, D. Z. (ed.), *Neural Information Processing Systems*. American Institute of Physics, New York, 1988, 674–682.

[186] Sejnowski, T. J., and Rosenberg, C. R. NETtalk: A Parallel Network That Learns to Read Aloud. Johns Hopkins University Electrical Engineering and Computer Science Technical Report JHU/EECS-86/01, 1986.

[187] Smolensky, P. Information Processing in Dynamical Systems: Foundations of Harmony Theory. In Rumelhart, D. E., and McClelland, J. L. (eds.), *Parallel Distributed Processing: Explorations in the Microstructures of Cognition*, vol. 1, 194–281. MIT Press, Cambridge, 1986.

[188] Smolensky, P. Tensor Product Variable Binding and the Representation of Symbolic Structures in Neural Network Systems. *Artificial Intelligence* 46 (1–2), 1990, 159–216.

[189] Spiegelhalter, D. J. Probabilistic Reasoning in Predictive Expert Systems. In Kanal, L. N., and Lemmer, J. F. (eds.), *Uncertainty in Artificial Intelligence*. Elsevier Science Publishers, North-Holland, 1986.

[190] Stanfill, C., and Waltz, D. Toward Memory Based Reasoning. *CACM* 29, no. 12, December 1986.

[191] Sutton, R. S. Learning to Predict by the Methods of Temporal Differences. *Machine Learning* 3, 1988, 9–44.

[192] Szu, H. Fast Simulated Annealing. In *AIP Conference Proceedings 151: Neural Networks for Computing*, 1986, 420–425.

[193] Utgoff, P. E. *Machine Learning of Inductive Bias*. Kluwer Academic Publishers, Boston, 1986.

[194] Valiant, L. G. A Theory of the Learnable. *Communications of the ACM* 27, 1984, 1134–1142.

[195] Van den Bout, D. E., and Miller, T. K. A Traveling Salesman Objective Function That Works. IEEE Int. Conf. on Neural Networks, San Diego, CA, vol. 2, 1988, 299–304.

[196] Vapnik, V. N. *Estimation of Dependences Based on Empirical Data*. Springer Verlag, New York, 1982.

[197] Vapnik, V. N., and Chervonenkis, A. Y. On the Uniform Convergence of Relative Frequencies of Event to Their Probabilities. In *Theory of Probability and Its Applications* 16, 1971, 264–280.

[198] Wald, J., Farach, M., Tagamets, M., and Reggia, J. Generating Plausible Diagnostic Hypotheses with Self-Processing Causal Networks. *Journal of Experimental & Theoretical Artificial Intelligence* 2, 1989, 91–112.

[199] Wenocur, R. S., and Dudley, R. M. Some Special Vapnik-Chervonenkis Classes. *Discrete Math.* 33, 1981, 313–318.

[200] Werbos, P. J. Beyond Regression: New Tools for Prediction and Analysis in the Behavioral Sciences. Ph.D. thesis, Harvard University, 1974.

[201] Werbos, P. J. Backpropagation through Time: What It Does and How to Do It. *Proceedings of the IEEE* 78, 1990, 1550–1560.

[202] Widrow, B., and Hoff, M. E. Adaptive Switching Circuits. Institute of Radio Engineers, Western Electronic Show and Convention, Convention Record, part 4, 1960, 96–104.

[203] Widrow, B., and Stearns, S. D. *Adaptive Signal Processing.* Prentice Hall, Englewood Cliffs, NJ, 1985.

[204] Widrow, B., and Winter, R. Neural Nets for Adaptive Filtering and Adaptive Pattern Recognition. *IEEE Computer,* March 1988, 25–39.

[205] Williams, R. J. Reinforcement-Learning Connectionist Systems. Technical Report NU-CCS-88-3, Northeastern University College of Computer Science, July 1988.

[206] Williams, R. J., and Zipser, D. A Learning Algorithm for Continually Running Fully Recurrent Neural Networks. *Neural Computation* 1, 1989, 270–280.

[207] Williams, R. J., and Zipser, D. Experimental Analysis of the Real-Time Recurrent Learning Algorithm. *Connection Science* 1, 1989, 87–111.

[208] Williams, R. J., and Zipser, D. Gradient-Based Learning Algorithms for Recurrent Networks. To appear in: Chauvin, Y., and Rumelhart, D. E. (eds.), *Back-propagation: Theory, Architectures and Applications.* Erlbaum, Hillsdale, NJ (in press).

[209] Wilson, G. V., and Pawley, G. S. On the Stability of the Travelling Salesman Problem Algorithm of Hopfield and Tank. *Biological Cybernetics* 58, 1988, 63–70.

[210] Winston, P. H. Learning Structural Descriptions from Examples. In Winston, P. H. (ed.), *The Psychology of Computer Vision.* McGraw-Hill, New York, 1975, 157–209.

[211] Winston, P. *Artificial Intelligence.* Addison-Wesley, Reading, MA, 1984; 2d ed., 1987.

[212] Wishart, D. An Algorithm for Hierarchical Classifications. *Biometrics,* 1969.

[213] Wishart, D. FORTRAN II Programs for 8 Methods of Cluster Analysis (CLUSTAN I). Comput. Contrib. 38, State Geological Survey, Univ. of Kansas, Lawrence, 1969.

[214] Wolf, D. E. PROMENADE: Complete Listing of PROMENADE Programs. RADC-TR-68-572, Appendix 9d, AD 694114, Stanford Research Institute, Menlo Park, CA, 1968.

[215] Xu, X., and Tsai, W. T. Effective Neural Algorithms for the Traveling Salesman Problem. *Neural Networks* 4, 1991, 193–205.

[216] Yoshida, K., Hayashi, Y., and Imura, A. A Neural Network Expert System for Diagnosing Hepatobiliary Disorders. MEDINFO '89: Proceedings of the Sixth Conference on Medical Informatics, Beijing, October 16–20, 1989, and Singapore, December 11–15, 1989, North-Holland Press, 116–120.

[217] Zadeh, L. A. Fuzzy Sets. *Information and Control* 8, 1965, 338–353.

Index